Architecture on my mind

Architecture on my mind:

critical readings in design by Alan Lipman

UNIVERSITY OF SOUTH AFRICA
PRETORIA

© 2003 University of South Africa

First edition, first impression

ISBN 1-86888-241-1

Published by Unisa Press
University of South Africa
P O Box 392, 0003 PRETORIA

Cover design and layout: Thea Bester-Swanepoel
Typeset by Thea Bester-Swanepoel
Editor: Charl Schutte

© All rights reserved. No part of this publication may be reproduced in any form or by any means—mechanical or electronic, including recordings or tape recording and photocopying — without the prior permission of the publisher, excluding fair quotations for purposes of research or review

Contents

Foreword	vii
Autobiographic note	ix
Preface	xi
Acknowledgements	xix
Hope renewed	**1**
Johannesburg – an architectural homecoming	3
Towering indifference – is this my Jo'burg city?	7
Civic spine: the 'primitive hut' comes to town	11
Urban but not, distinctly not, urbane	15
Architecture and sculpture – an interrupted coupling?	19
Desire in the suburbs – desire consumed	23
Gatvol van wat die gat volmaak? ('Sick and tired of what fills the hole?')	27
Downtown South Africa – everywhere, anywhere, nowhere	31
Egoli – city of dislocation?	**35**
Under siege in outer suburbia	37
Civic futures – a telling interlude	41
Continuity of form and substance – the Mai Mai Bazaar, Johannesburg	47
Corporate giant, design gnat?	53
City of clutter – matter out of place	61
Beauty and the beast – northern Johannesburg	65
Constitutional matters	71
Alexandra – an unfulfilled Odyssey	76
Social housing	81
Other-directed Johannesburg	85
All that glitters is Jo'burg	89
Housing – nothing learnt, nothing forgotten?	93
The Hyatt touch – blue-chip Africa in Rosebank	97

Architectures of alienated nostalgia — **101**
- Cornwall on the Highveld — 103
- Office parks – not quite cricket — 107
- Sammy Marks Square, Pretoria – impressions and obsessions — 111
- Taking a step back — 117
- Counterfeit facelift — 125
- Forsaken glory? — 129
- The dreariness of ostentation – Johannesburg's Reserve Bank — 133

Nuggets in the dust — **137**
- Modest enterprise – worthy award — 139
- Almost barefoot on the lowveld — 143
- Architecture as backdrop to life — 147
- Heavenly detail — 151
- Shack settlements – architecture without architects — 155
- Royal Bafokeng sports stadium — 161
- Wayside containers, local shenanigans — 165
- Serenity in clamour – the new Mosque, Johannesburg — 169
- The Hagia Sophia on Wolmarans Street, Johannesburg — 175
- Straightforward and good — 179
- Gropius comes to Midrand? — 183
- Architecture to sing about — 189
- Sometime too hot . . . — 195
- Handsome sheds, elegant dignity — 201
- In the swim — 205
- Highveld offices – doing it in style — 209
- Rosebank relief — 215
- Jo'burg, that is the place for me — 219

Hope sustained? — **223**
- Spatial imagination — 225
- Housing – asking those who matter most — 229
- Alex, the far east bank — 235
- Housing layouts — 239
- Melville story — 243
- On thin ice in Troyeville — 247
- The present in the past – architecture and memory — 251
- Educating desire — 257
- Glittering futures, utopias realised? — 261

Further readings — **265**

Foreword

In the early nineties, *The Sunday Independent* was looking for an architectural critic. The brief was difficult: someone who knew about the subject, whose opinions would not be muted by professional affiliation and who could write succinctly, clearly and frequently.

Alan Lipman was suggested; he easily met all three criteria; and in the years he has been writing for the newspaper has probably done more than anyone I can think of to bring issues of the architectural quality to the attention of a lay readership.

Lipman's professional credentials are impeccable: he practised as an architect in South Africa and taught it in Wales and later in Johannesburg. As an exile and by personality – courageous and independent – he was free of professional cageyness. Good writing by journalists is different from good writing by writers: Lipman's belongs in the latter category while embracing qualities of the former.

His writing is clear and stylish: the cadences and discriminations of his prose are always well judged and have the stamp of his personality: generous, principled and lacking all meanness. It considers the reader and the personality defers to the subject of discussion. He is informed but wears that lightly: learning flavours – but does not burden – his style. (This is unusual: architectural writing is notoriously showy or inchoate.) Nor – which sets his writing apart from most newspaper criticism – does it skirt complexity: Lipman assumes at least equal interest and knowledge in his readers.

Finally, and most importantly, never does he forget that buildings are for people: those who live in or use them and those on whose views they impinge. The humanity of Lipman's writing is impressive and underlying it is an ethic. He praises works that harmonise with physical and spiritual surroundings and deprecates those that gatecrash or jar with the setting. He focuses, rightly, I think, for our times, on buildings that are intended for the body politic, rather than the individual. His eye is always firmly on relationships between buildings, between the past and present, and between this environment and others. For him, the building represents the result of successful negotiations in time, space, economic interest and personality, negotiations that ultimately depend for success on agreement, not overpowering.

This ethical approach is what makes his writing attractive and impressive. And it is this quality that, predictably, has upset those who would warp the public realm for private purpose or commercial gain. (I think, for example, of his controversial review of the Hyatt Hotel in Rosebank, Johannesburg, where he precisely identified what he found objectionable about it: the bombastic arresting of public space and its air of simultaneously, aggressively, turning its back on those whose space it appropriated.)

To be an architect is probably more difficult than to be a stage or film director because it involves commercial, historical and aesthetic sensitivity. Having acknowledged that, which Lipman does, it must be tempting for an architectural writer to let his or her gaze be deflected from the final structure to the negotiations. Lipman does not comment on the make of stove used in cooking, but on the final dish. To achieve such clarity bespeaks rare single mindedness and courage. His readers benefit from both.

Robert Greig
Arts Editor, *The Sunday Independent*

Autobiographic note

A few autobiographical details are probably in order. After serving, during the latter years of World War II, as a navigator in the South African Air Force, I studied architecture at the University of the Witwatersrand. On graduating in 1950, I worked as an architectural assistant in Johannesburg, Durban, Cape Town and for a 12-month period overseas, in the architectural division of the then London County Council. When, back home, throughout the mid- and late-1950s and early 1960s, my wife's and my overt anti-apartheid activities brought ever more harsh police restrictions, we were edged, none too gently, into exile with our two small children.

Once more in London (1963) I worked in the offices of Maxwell Fry and Ove Arup, Associates – two internationally renowned architectural practices. From there, I moved to academic teaching and research at the University of Wales, where I read for a Master's degree and later, for a research-based doctorate. During these years, I was promoted from lecturer, to senior lecturer, to reader and then to an *ad hominem* professorship. I remained at my home college in Cardiff for 27 years but, from that base, travelled as visiting professor to various universities in Europe, north America, India, Australia and New Zealand. I retired in the late 1980s to, gratifyingly, be awarded an emeritus professorship. Then, teaching temporarily at Wits, I was fortunate to win that university's accolade of honorary doctorate. A similar award – honorary doctorate – was also made by the University of Natal in April 2003.

During this past decade in Johannesburg, I have written consistently on design and also worked as a collaborator with and consultant to, among others, a local architectural practice, Henry Paine, Architects. There, in 1996, my immediate colleague and I were granted two awards of merit by the Gauteng Institute of Architecture and an award of excellence by the Institute of South African Architects.

Preface

This is a book of pained protest, a call for resistance to the pervasive banality of contemporary South African architecture. The tone is often angry: in retrospect, an ineffectual antidote to the frustrations born of sustained opposition which, if heard, is unheeded. Yet the mood is by no means bound by gloom, resentment, defeat. Quite the contrary, there are, thankfully, occasions for joy. There are opportunities for celebration in many of the heartening, persistent efforts to over-leap the coarseness that marks the physical settings we inhabit – our city centres, small towns, *dorpe* and especially our design-hungry 'townships'.

Look about you, the evidence is all too patent. It despoils the sub-continent with its brash, makeshift building materials, shoddy workmanship and numbing poverty of architectural imagination.

We are in the thrall of faked-up materials: imitation timber veneers on flabby chipboards, counterfeit 'marble' surfaces complete with mica chips to add so-called sparkle, stock bricks that crumble to the touch, concrete mixed in casually unchecked proportions – particularly *vis-à-vis* its cement content. Shuttering that swells and distorts; to be corrected, smothered by thickly ladled plaster. Much, if not all of this – and more – is like so many of our societal values; shallow, short-lived, seemingly glitzy, tinsel.

Then that old-time respect for craftsmanship – lost in the continuing afterglow of 'job reservation'. Why do a job conscientiously when your – usually white – overseer habitually looks on while you labour without prospect of advancement? Why exercise your skills while he outstrips your poor earnings by virtue of his race? And, not least, our misnamed design professionals; folk who, lacking roots in their own societies, turn facilely to superficial borrowings from other cultures – now ye olde England, now Tuscan, now Roman – always elsewhere, not at home.

The bleatings of a fuddy-duddy relic, a contemporary Luddite filled with nostalgic longings for lost pasts? Probably. Yet the nagging realities remain. Gone are the robust and handsome building materials that one knew as a boy, just sixty years ago. Gone the proud satisfactions of fine workmanship, of a 'job well done'. Gone or going those unpretentious pre-industrial buildings – the bee-hive huts of KwaZulu, the tough simplicities of *trekboer* homes, the gracefully *stoeped* ('verandahed') colonial houses of, say, Grahamstown or Pietermaritzburg. Gone for what? Quick-fix, unreliable and – above all else – cheap building materials, uncaring craftsmanship and inevitably, the blundering, aesthetically impoverished built surroundings which we all suffer.

These and similar crude insults offend one's sensibilities. And I suspect many, many others feel the same – as their phlegmatic disinterest might well suggest. Our buildings are indifferent to us, small surprise then that we should become indifferent to them. So why bother? Why have I taken monthly to my PC in a now decade-long series of exasperated newspaper articles?

Well . . . the most direct answer is that I love the discipline, have done so since enrolling some 55 years ago – after a brief spell of war service – in the Department of Architecture at the University of the Witwatersrand (Wits). For me, building design is compulsively engaging: it is rooted in the ever-demanding pragmatics of construction, in the less tangible realm of social symbolism and simultaneously, in the exacting limits so implacably set by socio-political/economic power. Each is as testing as it is challenging; each is a potential and actual domain of struggle for designers. Together, they call repeatedly on one's energies, abilities, desires.

As student architects, my colleagues and I were schooled in the precepts and practices of modernism; principles and procedures with which I have concurred throughout my subsequent career, whether an architectural practitioner, an academic, a research worker or public commentator. A quarter of a century later, in about the mid-1970s, modernist architecture, as was the case in other fields of academic and professional activity, came under severe pressure. We were subjected to fierce, unswerving attack by postmodern theorists. Having, as an academic must, attended to their critical charges, I and others rejected them. Ironically – doubly so since irony is a major weapon in the postmodern armoury – that searching re-examination led, with minor amendments, to a committed reaffirmation. Rather than obsolete, I found my modernist principles to be increasingly relevant. They had been strengthened, reinforced, re-invigorated. This will doubtless become evident as readers dip deeper into the texts that follow

A word of warning on that count: I am and have long been an unreconstructed polemicist. I punch in earnest, do not seek to spare those with whom I disagree and expect the same from them. Indeed, invective is, for me, ever close at hand. An eventual turn in the fate of architecture in southern Africa is far too urgent a matter for genteel, drawing-room chatter. In this context, it seems advisable to highlight some of the key premises on which the often belligerent writings in this volume are founded.

First, this is not an architectural treatise, a discourse on 'high theory' in the discipline. My years of research and academic reportage were wholly absorbing. I was engrossed for almost four decades and – as attested by continuing publication in this area – remain a devotee. I have, though, since formal retirement, come to feel that to be insufficient. Exchanging research findings and interpretations with fellow academics is gratifying but no longer fully satisfying. I now wish also to engage with a wider, a predominately lay audience; to participate in informed public debate on the urban and architectural issues which so mark, so distort our emerging, newly democratic society. That has been the purpose of the newspaper pieces on which this collection draws. It remains the thrust of my work: to stimulate, to provoke and desirably, to help inform.

Accordingly, the arguments presented here centre on attempts to forge architectures that are urgently appropriate to the new South Africa. They are rooted in a long-held, overtly modernist commitment to architectures – as practices and products – that do not simply reflect the societies in which they are produced. Buildings are, I insist, not merely images of what is, of how we live presently. Quite the contrary, through its material presence as embodied human action, architecture can and does speak of what might be, of how we might live. Appropriate architectures for the newly established South Africa must, then, help to shape, to educate people's desires; to enable them to 'read' what might be in what is.

This, of course, is far from being solely a matter of form, of style. In the nineteenth century, engineers and architects were called on to accommodate new social relationships in the new building types they designed: factories, railway stations, hospitals, public libraries and the like. So, since the 1990s, South African designers have been summonsed to apply their knowledge and skills to the new spatial demands of their burgeoning democratic society.

In confronting these expectations, architects are pressed to work closely with the potential users of the buildings they design; with, that is, the people, the communities whose needs their work is intended to serve. In short, the new spatial forms which professionals propose are to embrace and to represent the participatory processes by which they must be produced. Democratic architecture is pre-eminently a public, a social activity; one whose products are but rarely confined to single individuals or even small groups.

From that somewhat abstract, but decidedly firm commitment, I pass to what are, surely, the bases of design practice. Architecture is, I believe, about order and relationship rather than surface appearance. It certainly need not invoke that hoary chestnut, 'good taste'. It is about space, light and organisation, not style, charm or whimsy. A work of architecture springs from the nature of its materials, the quality of its site, the methods of its production. The most exacting questions about a building that is recognisably architecture are 'how is it made?' 'what gives it order?' 'how does it respond to its context?' 'what is the idea (or set of ideas) that lies behind its form, its image?' and 'what, in short, are its human purposes?'

Architectural design, I was told early in my formal and unquestioningly male-dominated education, is 'the imaginative manipulation of space for the convenience of man'. Amended to embrace all humanity, that maxim has stuck with me through the vicissitudes and abrupt dislocations of life. Architectural designs, I have long come deeply to appreciate, are conceived, erected and used purposefully. Sound architecture is socially responsible and responsive.

In this context, my reference to modernism needs elaboration. There are, patently, at least two modern architectures. The first appears in scholarly books as works of inspiration, the outstanding buildings of modernism which few see, let alone live or work in. These are the *avant-garde* buildings of the early twentieth century – mainly in Europe – when for the first time architects grappled with the issues surrounding mass populations, industrial production, technological innovation. This is an architecture of change, a time of revolution, crumbling empires, social hope . . . of futures. This is the architecture of the founders of the Modern Movement, the dreams made concrete of a cultural elite. These are the buildings through which designers strained to express humane ideals.

What happened? In the 'socialist' East – rejection, expulsion, exile; social content ripped from form, deformed. In the 'free' West – incorporation: an architecture of defeat, of aesthetic form torn from social content, misformed. This, of course, is the second modern architecture, the all too familiar one in which many live and work. This is the segregated township, the suburb of individual, of social isolation – neighbourhood without community. This is rampant urban growth, unbridled speculative development; banks, office towers, finance houses . . . shopping malls. This is the new factory, a fine-tooled envelope around a stripped, cheap interior – packaged exploitation in a landscaped industrial park.

This is Speculator–Modern, the architecture of the international market: inflated opulence for the few, pinched spaces, shoddy materials, botched work for the rest. It is a rotten architecture. But then, for most, it has been a pretty rotten society. And the postmodern response? Well . . . architecture is about making the mess acceptable, popular. It is also about sharing in the profits – the treason of the clerics.

Then there is what some have termed the 'star system' a phenomenon that particularly impinges on student architects, but also affects public perceptions of architects and their work. This is a frame of reference – confidently presented as 'learning from excellence' – in which architectural students are regularly, if not constantly, required to attend on 'star' designers; on especially selected, meritorious exemplars.

The notion is often associated with an appealing myth to which practitioners, like architectural teaching staff, tend to subscribe: their comforting belief that architects lead 'the building team'. Since about the end of World War II, the professional status of designers has shifted decisively; especially of those who work in urban centres. Where formerly, as a hangover from gentlemanly Victorian custom, practitioners were regarded – or regarded themselves – as team leaders, they are now firmly known – and know themselves – to be members *inter pares*. Or, as those commissioned by corporate agglomerates frequently complain, as something less than equals. The aura of primacy is no longer apposite.

The fable is nurtured in the role image presented to students; one that centres on membership of an occupational elite, of being favoured neophytes who must aspire to design genius. Not surprisingly, many view themselves as creatively exceptional participants in an otherwise mundane construction industry. This indulgence is consistent with yet another illusion: the disabling mystique of architectural stardom – each student a future le Corbusier, Aldo Rossi, Rem Koolhaas. Students' actual, their latent abilities are bypassed, undermined or frustrated in debilitating strivings for unique artistic superiority. That is not lessened by a rapid turnover of heroes as successions of stars are made obsolete by newly anointed idols. It is a rough, tough game. Who is in favour, who out? Who knows whether or why she/he is now 'in' or has been summarily thrust into limbo? Being in the know brings social kudos; a state with little if any bearing on acquiring or exercising design knowledge or architectural experience.

This cluster of commitments has been highlighted here, that is, before one undertakes the readings that follow – because they underpin most of the comment in the essays reproduced below. They are, as it were, ubiquitous to this volume.

The collection comprises some 50 previously published newspaper and occasional journal articles. They have been selected, edited and grouped for fresh appearance in book form. The chosen pieces are loosely – rather than chronologically – arranged under five headings, each of which is editorially linked to its predecessor and/or successor by deliberately summary explanatory comment on, principally, their pragmatic but also their theoretical thrust.

Hope renewed

This is a particularly splenetic, acerbic chapter; one which briefly presents the nature of the project and as briefly, illustrates its overall content. It records my initial and changing views of Johannesburg and its environs since returning to the city in 1990. It alludes to the impact on building construction of the sociol-political and economic circumstances to which I returned, to my impressions of the architectural profession at work and most emphatically, to the state of local building design then and during the ensuing decade.

Egoli: City of dislocation?

Another testy, choleric collection; one that offers architectural readings on Johannesburg in order critically to assess the city as an assembly of companionable buildings, a venue for civic or social gatherings as a congenial urban layout . It contains particular comment on the absence of public open space in the city centre; on the persistent competitiveness of its buildings, the aesthetic incompatibility of its building stock. And, in enlivening contrast, the chapter carries observations on Egoli as an increasingly pulsating, throbbing African city. Attention is then draw to the divergent, but related, conditions in the suburbs: to the ever-present phenomena of 'gated' communities, office parks, shopping malls and 'closed' streets and by way of more contrast, to the bustling street life of Africa in such unexpected settings as Sandton and Rosebank. This is 'fortress Johannesburg'.

Architectures of alienated nostalgia

More spleen. Here the focus is the recent and continuing, preference among local developers and designers for recycled neo-classicisms; all of which are filched, invariably somewhat clumsily, from abroad – from anywhere but southern Africa. Of course, borrowed neo-classical building styles are not unknown to the city: the usually dignified structures of the late nineteenth century are witness to that. What is new however is the wholesale, the crass, the unstudied application of surface effects that are presumed to carry the cachet of established historical or, on occasion, of 'high' contemporary styles. This yearning for imported status, this regrettable off-shoot of supposedly postmodern design, now disfigures swathes of the city and its suburbs, including its new office enclaves, cluster or town houses and other emphatically commercial enterprises. They will surely remain *in situ* for many years.

Nuggets in the dust

Here, happily, the material is more positive, cheerful. This, probably the most lengthy section of the book, calls on my celebratory newspaper articles. The basis of these is an abiding interest in 'critical regionalism', a viewpoint that stands in opposition to the seemingly unchallenged goal of a seamless, world-wide sameness – each city a near-replica of all other cities, each downtown a model of all other central business areas, each suburb a . . . well, an enclave of wealth or poverty. Regional designers, of whom there is a substantial minority in South Africa, seek to interpret and give expressive form to local identities; to distinctively local ways of living, of constructing and of using buildings. This group of articles records some of the many faces of this simple, but decidedly not simplistic commitment. It springs from and runs parallel to the practices of community participation in architectural work. It is antipathetic to the reigning consumerist doctrine.

Hope sustained?

More positive, encouraging architectural reportage? Well . . . mostly. This chapter contains articles that highlight the work of a minority of southern African architects; the few who seek consistently, boldly to reach for, to forge local and regional architectures. Here one attempts analytically to explore their efforts in the often courageous building designs for which they are responsible. Theirs are open architectures; architectures in search of deliberately meaningful identities. They give rise to hope; hope that the currently arrant consumerism can be, if not superceded, at least bridled.

Johannesburg architecture: if you have tears to shed, prepare to shed them, but remember that, unlike Caesar, the city lives, it is not interred.

Alan Lipman
August 2003

Acknowledgements

My debts of gratitude are wide; they include people with whom I have engaged in casual conversation, with those who have alerted me to interesting buildings or design events, as well as those who have berated me for my disagreeable pronouncements. Not least, they include Max du Preez and Robert Greig who invited me to write 'on architecture' for their respective pages in *Vrye Weekblad* and *The Sunday Independent.* Their encouragement, patience and continued support are not amenable to bald statements of written appreciation. That, though, does not prohibit me from writing 'Thank you Max, thank you Robert; heartfelt thanks'.

It has become customary in statements of this nature to acknowledge the contribution made by one's spouse. In my case, this reaches beyond compliance with custom. I doubt whether there is a single passage in these texts that has not gained from her questioning, her critical appraisal and her refusal to be impressed by architectural pretensions. Further, by insisting that I attempt to apply to my writing what I believe are the best standards of her onetime profession – journalism – she has helped me to reduce the otherwise overwhelming tendencies toward pomposity and obscurity in my written style.

My thanks go especially to those of my fellow architects who have generously, unstintingly provided me with illustrative images that I was otherwise unable to obtain. They include Clive Chipkin, Rod Lloyd, Italo Lupini, Jo Noero, Peter Rich, Colin Savage, Paul Wygers, and members of the Waterson Weyer Roon partnership in Pretoria. They have all helped to supplement my own less than brilliant photography. My apologies to any omissions, they are regrettably consequent on a faulty memory.

Beyond and above these, my deep gratitude goes to John Hogg and Siphiwe Sibeko of *The Sunday Independent*. Their work features among the best of the shots published here. John, an award-winning professional photographer, has given his artistry, skill and time unsparingly – how but in grossly inadequate words does one effectively thank such selflessness?

Hope renewed

The material in this opening section of the book illustrates the nature and content of the entire project. It is, quite simply, a selected collection of newspaper articles on matters architectural which were written over a ten-year period, 1992 to 2002. The pieces are personal observations about a subject which is, surprisingly, seldom broached in the South African media, a marked departure from what prevails in other countries. Yet we who live here – especially those in urban settings – cannot but be exposed to the products of architectural labour: we live and/or work in buildings designed or, however marginally, influenced by members of the profession.

Their ideas about how we live and might live impinge with immediacy on us. If we are to attend to the other public arts that are regularly covered in our press, for example, painting, sculpture or theatrical, dance and musical performances, we must, surely, focus as forcefully on this hugely important facet of our everyday environs. But we do not. Why? While these essays do not attempt an answer to this deeply perplexing question, they do at least raise the matter.

In so doing, the articles cover my impressions – uplifting as well as depressing of Johannesburg architecture shortly after returning to the city from many years' absence. They also attest to the enduring sentiments that were awakened after my wife and I had settled once more into our long-interrupted Egoli lives. Given my views of architecture and the social world in which it is wrought, not unexpectedly, these pieces also bear on the prevailing socio-political and economic circumstances in the country and on the state of the local design professions.

The inner city – Johannesburg's office block canyons, looking east down Commissioner Street.

Johannesburg — an architectural homecoming

Home after some three decades. Flying into a Johannesburg (Jo'burg) summer from a quarter of a century abroad. Across the Limpopo, over that vast northern Transvaal bush, that unforgettable, beloved, highveld. Then the metropolis, the Rand. The once gaudily yellow dumps now tricked out in patches of green; carpets of leafy suburban order, the mandatory swimming pools flashing blindingly; Egoli, its corporate towers shimmering vertical, air conditioned pools. And, inescapable, the townships; dusty, scrambled smudges marked, as of old, by drifts of low smoke. Are they still known as 'locations', no place, every place blurs seen by the privileged from speeding freeways?

Glimpses of apartheid, more than three hundred bloody years of it, through the stained porthole of an airliner. Home to the daily realities of spatial, racial dominance. Home to the politics of space, South African style.

Into Jan Smuts Airport, the bland, anaesthetic architecture of airway terminals anywhere, everywhere. Through customs and immigration – entangled in the anxieties of old time, listed, banned dissidents – and out to the mid day sunlight, stunning in its crisp precision. Off to central Jo'burg in the oven hot car of ever-thoughtful friends. No 'locations' to be seen from this well engineered, multi lane highway, but we pass much else. Blowzy hotels built and named in internationally recognisable styles; factories, warehouses and office buildings wearing the tired trappings of architectural fashions now past. Others in familiar transplants of currently trendy architecture anywhere, everywhere. Passing glances at spacious houses and gardens behind walls . . . ubiquitous walls and fences, spikes, bars, razor wire, electronic gates, closed circuit tv, even moats; security guards, 'beware vicious dogs', 'immediate armed response' the paraphernalia of spatial defence. A beleaguered city. Who are inside, who outside? Who defend, who threaten?

Top to bottom: The ubiquitous, shimmering swimming pools of home; the glistening, inhospitable towers of downtown Johannesburg; back at home, relaxation after a taxing day in the city.

Here as elsewhere (especially through the moneyed suburbs to the north) the smooth freeway is often embellished with road side landscaping of what must, surely, be unmatched splendour. Parks of the highway – manicured lawns, cropped trees, tended flower beds, groomed shrubbery, water falls, pools – rivalling many private gardens, those still visible behind their solid walls. A profligate use of cheap labour, of folk who live somewhere other, in no place, every place; in the, above all, distant townships.

All the while the profiled city ahead, towering on its sublime series of rocky ridges, the Witwatersrand. Citadel of gold – white owned. Stronghold of corporate enterprise – white. Powerhouse of mining, banking, investment, commerce, industry ... and more, and more and more – all white. Seat of social power, of snow white economic, political, ideological power. The buildings express this in their content, their imagery. As does the crassly utilitarian, mining camp layout; an unrelentingly banal street grid with scarcely a civic place (a square, plaza), a communal focus, an urban vista, a punctuated view, a nod to that singular highveld beyond.

Once in these dreary, unimaginative streets, the change is overwhelming. Central Jo'burg – staid, respectable – was not like this 30 years ago. Faraway no place/every place has penetrated, occupied the ramparts. The city is alive with kaleidoscopic life: ambling residents, curious as well as studiously indifferent; street hawkers, the insistent calls of hucksters, the urgings of bargaining sellers, buyers; intent shoppers, scurrying business folk; youthful street dwellers, gossiping bystanders, sad eyed beggars, eager eyed tricksters ever on the make; noisily impatient traffic; colour, enticing and not so enticing smells; above all, music – from radios carried by pedestrians, from cars and taxis, from trumpeting shops, fast food joints. Township jazz has come to town. And the polite, established world has vacated the centre for sanitised business parks and shopping malls in the suburbs.

Corporate power however, the big stuff, remains intact, unmoved in its downtown enclaves. Here the social symbolism of the buildings, reinforced at guarded entrances, is all too clear: *Restricted, Keep Out*. Niceties of architectural style are irrelevant. Hulks of columned, pedimented, Edwardian Classic (exported from imperial Britain, begat of endlessly recycled neo-classicisms) say it haughtily: *No Trespassers, By Order*. Bland slabs of inter and post war Speculator Modern say it dismissively: *No Entry*. Priapic towers, sheathed in mirrored glass, say it with macho egotism: reflect/deflect all, admit none but fellow big fellows.

Who are inside, who outside? Who defend, who threaten?

Meanwhile, beyond the city and its cosseted suburbs, there are demanding spatial issues; land, homes, schools, hospitals, nearby work . . . a chance to live a life of dignity. A politically charged world as yet untouched by architectural imagination, by design skills, by humane intervention.

Political exchanges are, of course, about power; about access, mostly privileged access, to resources; about who is to realise, to deploy, to manage physical and social resources. Space, patently, is such a resource, its use an exercise of social power. And architectural design is centrally about enclosing, manipulating, space. Architects, then, like their occupational predecessors, align and must align themselves with those who exert or, more rarely, who seek to exert power. Indeed, since the initial stirrings of building design as a distinct occupation (in the *bottegas*, the craft workshops of renaissance Florence) designers have, with notable exceptions, worked for the wealthy, the mighty. Architecture – privilege of the privileged.

What is to be done? Architects are pressed to choose. Do they embrace corporate power, grab the main chance, go for the big sell, hit the headlines – become *STARS*? Do they, like the majority, persist with Speculator Modern – the pared down, mean architecture of speculative development? Or do they . . . what? Most pressing, do they – like a minority, a handful – struggle to forge a socially committed, a humane architecture?

Home, architecturally at home in this, the 'new' South Africa?

Mirrored glass reflections on Sauer Street – the pseudo old twisted in the brash new.

Towering indifference — is this my Jo'burg city?

Johannesburg, central Jo'burg, needs a new architectural protest group; one, like so many, whose initials describe the cause. Something off-putting... SLUB (Stop Lousy Ugly Buildings). Or maybe a pained cry – AUU! (Anti-Uglies Unite). I would initiate the launch, although there must be many, many who are as eager. Not least among them, the now ageing Egoli fans who spent much of their recent, enforced, 25 or so years away recalling this never lovely but often endearing city.

It is a shock to be back. It is exciting, endlessly so: the life, the peopled streets, the vibrancy. Those repetitive city blocks – boringly alike – are now alive: hawkers, shoppers, peddlers, sharp-eyed hustlers, weary-faced beggars, local residents walking their pavements – action; smells, the coaxing trails to braai-vendors. And always, the music – from shops, hand-held radios, passing taxis, from the singing talk, the rocking laughter of hurrying, shifting crowds.

All new: quite unlike those ever-so-respectable 30 years ago when people from the suburbs came 'to town' for smart shopping. They have fled the city, gone to polite, protected worlds – the outlying shopping malls, business parks. Leaving, of course, much public neglect. Downtown Jo'burg is becoming an open, an African city, more and more.

It is indeed a shock to be back. Much has changed, a great deal remains. The buildings which tower anew over that now vital street-life: different looks, the same ownership, management, control. The same privileged access. Not many of those bustling pavement folk occupy the plush executive roof gardens, the corporate suites, the hushed conference rooms, the potted plant, open-plan offices. It is hard enough getting past the armoured-glass entrances, the security uniforms. Secured chunks of high-rise territory.

Top to bottom: vertiginous verticality on Commissioner Street; a graph paper slab in Main Street – transported from New York; massive reinforced concrete balanced, precariously, on sheet glass – Commissioner Street again.

What is new? Well... the looks, the parade of chic architectural fashions, fads. Surfaces lifted from central city everywhere, downtown nowhere. New York, Toronto, Kansas City, Denver, San Francisco, Wellington, Melbourne, Bangkok, even New Delhi; modish bits and pieces snatched like copybook images from contemporary Paris, Rotterdam, London to be plonked here, at the edge of our dying and dead mine dumps.

Boycotted, sanctioned, culturally isolated. No. Here, at the pulse of industrial southern Africa, we have got our own proud, anonymous elsewhere – just like all the other no-places in that greedily imitated, supposedly magic, very-special-tone-of-voice 'overseas'.

Perhaps worse. This lot lacks what little unity, cohesion might be claimed for the others. We're locked in competitive disorder, in ever-busy architectural individuality. Each new import has to outdo, to kill the previous one; each new image must differ from, be more unusual than the most recent. From graph paper slabs (124 Main Street) to alternating bands of concrete and glass (70 Fox St.). From rows of vertical fins (141 Commissioner) to mirrored glass sheathes (corner Jeppe and von Welligh streets). From the single, applied Postmodern pediment (Commissioner facing Fraser) to the current rage, Art Deco galore (28 Harrison). And, as ever, a determined ferreting out of the perverse (4 Pritchard and 100 Main streets).

It is go, go, go for novelty. Every new building a full-scale monument to a large-scale ego; the owner's, the designer's, some macho corporative self. Rugged, tough, swaggering display. All, presumably, in the name of go-getting drive, of aggressive promotion. Business is business, shove or go under. The bigger the enterprise, the more seemingly assured the building, the advertisement. Maybe. Perhaps the more desperate the clutching at gimmickry.

Odd, distinctly odd. The colonising planters, the merchant adventurers of eighteenth century, Georgian England were no slouches on commercial belligerence, on knock-about, robust wheeler-dealing; yet they left whole regions of urbane, confident architectural unity. Still further back: the penetrative traders of late-medieval Venice were not, for sure, business softies, commercial push-overs; but even now their city sings with a diverse harmony. More: seventeenth-century Amsterdam, or the Hanseatic towns of Hamburg and Lubeck; no architectural mish-mashes here and certainly no snug havens for coy merchant jobbers.

What is it that each new Jo'burg show piece must outdo? To what is all this competitive energy being turned? Let us get specific, let us focus briefly on some examples.

Trust Bank, 128 Fox Street: a towering slab modelled on similar grey, black, bronze, green, blue shafts and blocks the world over; especially the elegantly sterile originals in New York and Chicago.

The architecture of corporate indifference: coldly aloof, disengaged from local climate, location, history, culture and above all else, people. At one time the shock of another new; displacing the previous, less bland, horizontally and/or vertically ribbed façades. Uncaring, frigid but, of course, different, novel.

Then the mirror-glass envelope, like Nedfin Bank, 66 Sauer Street: taken from all those who, earlier, grabbed it from Silicon Valley, California. An even more bland, cool 'advance' on the soulless packaging it replaced. No less indifferent to the constantly reflected, deflected people and city about it. For a while very smart, different.

And the latest? Volkskas at 41 Kruis Sreet: full-throttle Art Deco on all sides, out and in. Definitely different. Also borrowed from the United States of America (US) and many, too many, other borrowers. Anything you can do, we can do better (worse?). Oh yes, very different: tired 1920s decor puffed-up and ladled over storey upon storey of conventional accommodation, standard construction – the same icy indifference to its tightly packed surroundings.

Contemporary architecture in central Johannesburg, the really big stuff. Each newly arrived model having a different look from the previous one. Tediously the cycle starts again: more uncaring, more frantic novelty; plucked again from elsewhere.

It need not be like this. There are areas of the city, such as Fordsburg, that still, after heavy abuse, show how a style – here Victorian/Edwardian colonial – can flourish in diversity. There are buildings, many of them, that do not relentlessly outsmart their fellows: Cuthberts Building (Eloff Street) – Arts and Crafts adapted to local conditions – stands serenely and in spirited tension, with even its present clutter of neighbours; the old Union Club (corner Bree and Joubert streets), bruised as it now is, pushes its surroundings to urban dignity. And the Jo'burg–Modern pair at 233 and 235 Bree Street hint at how, licked into local shape, that approach might yet fulfil its early promise.

The latter would be a shock of joy. A socially responsible and responsive architecture for a newly forged democracy; one that needs no borrowed crutches.

Formerly a peaceful garden of remembrance – now an urban blunder nestling among monsters.

Civic spine: the 'primitive hut' comes to town

The highveld 1991, a decidedly long way from Tuscany *circa* 500 BC. How did a clutch of sub-sub-Etruscan temples get here? Etruscan? – pre-cast concrete, rolled steel I-beams, striated beige brickwork! Temples? – bus stops, kiosks, restaurants! What brought this lot to Johannesburg's new Civic Spine, right between the Library and City Hall?

Someone, with 31 March as the desperately sought completion date, has suggested a laboured hoax for the day after. And a more exalted authority, Jo'burg's town planning chief, is reported to have offered a similarly convincing account. The project is, we learn, a 'proactive innovation'. Well . . . neither novelty nor 'proactivity' (new-speak for something other than mundane, everyday, activity?), come readily to mind for a geographically dislocated, 2 000-year resurrection.

Another explanation? While we are with the bizarre, how about a lesson from that ennobling Latin inscription on the Library façade, *Libri Thesaurus Animi*. Perhaps the whole thing is an ingeniously erudite message for the citizens of greater Johannesburg. A subtle reminder of their architectural heritage – *via* ancient Rome to fondly recalled Etruscan precedent?

No? Let us try another interpretation; one drawing on what currently passes for architectural theory, history, criticism. Like many such exercises, this starts with a tale, a mythic origin.

We are in eighteenth-century France, Age of Reason, of Enlightenment; since the late 1960s, *the* stamping ground for many architectural theorists. The abbé and man of letters Marc-Antoine Laugier is, like his and our contemporaries, seeking scientifically to deduce the fundamental principles, the fixed and essential beauties, the infallible and immutable laws of architecture. He turns to

Top to bottom: an inner city open space reduced to bleak, unattended commerce by the fiat of our city fathers; Tuscan temples come to central Johannesburg – with neither rhyme nor reason; the west end of the City Hall – a touch of civic grandeur amongst the dross.

imagined origins, to given sources of truth; those irreducible verities that are, apparently, independent of custom, convention. He invokes 'man in his prime origin' (Laugier, with his fellow *philosophes*, is nothing if not gender-specific), maker of 'the small rustic hut... model upon which all the wonders of Architecture have been conceived... [by which] true perfection is attained'.

Man (the abbé insists on this limiting designation), having sheltered without success under trees in a forest and then in a cave, selects four stout branches which he stands upright to mark the corners of a square. This done, he spans horizontal branches from upright to upright. Now, 'man (sic!)... with no help or guide other than the natural instinct of his needs', arranges sloping branches from two opposite horizontals to meet at a ridge and so form a skeletal roof. He covers this, instinctively we gather, with leaves. Voila! Man, now one assumes joined by a mate, has a dwelling. Architecture has begun; its essentials embodied in 'the primitive hut': supporting columns and/or walls, horizontal entablatures, roof pediments. 'There will be,' we are told, 'nothing to add to make the work perfect.'

Laugier's arcadian reverie, his somewhat cloying romance has, in recent years, become a cultic myth. Ritually exhumed, commended, embroidered by architectural theorists and historians, the primal hut is now daily currency in academic comment. And more. Designers have embraced the notion, made it concrete; especially the Stars, those whose works are attended upon in the chic, exquisitely illustrated, internationally available design journals. Yet more. Not to be eclipsed, lesser stars, and many without such claims, have taken up the image; zealously, untiringly.

Primitive huts, like broken pediments, fallen keystones, obese columns and other 'classical' features, are all the rage: from Aldo Rossi on the Lombardy plain, to Demetri Porphyrios at Highgate, London; from Paul Keogh in Dublin to Leon Krier's Belvedere House, Florida; from Rafael Moneo in Merida, Spain to Jones and Kirkland in Toronto; from Melbourne, to Auckland, New Delhi, Berlin, Paris, New York, San Francisco... Now central, municipal, Johannesburg. We have arrived, we are on circuit... officially.

Supporters of early 'modern movement' architecture have been censured for, among other misdeeds, their commitment to utopian futures, to anticipatory symbolism in buildings. That, we've been assured, is naive. Those who make this charge are, they tell us, rationalists. They seek quintessential forms, atavistic symbols; mythic models from which to derive enduring principles, laws, of architectural design that transcend time, place and above all culture.

All this has come to town, to our very own library. For once, that suspect rebuke 'eurocentrism' may have some, passing, utility.

Turn now from Highveld–Etruscan to stroll eastward, to the revamped space in front of the City Hall. We are on an arid plane the starkness of which is marked, underscored by two ineptly sited trees, each encircled by a homely garden bench, no doubt discarded by the Parks Department. We are facing the old Post Office across what must, surely, be an exemplar for banal civic symbolism. Those thrusting watery plumes, that cascade of white water: presumably our driving, our dynamic Witwatersrand. Those phallic shafts bound by ascending bronze collars – gold painfully won from minehead pylons? Both, fountain and flanking obelisks, marooned on a rushed street that slices through the space – inadvertent emblem of an often traffic-locked city?

There are, there must be, symbolic issues for this central focus that are of social moment. A programme of consultation among all sections of the people would, assuredly, have revealed many. These might include, after that moving Washington memorial to the US dead of Vietnam, a homage to those here who toiled and died underground to wrest wealth for others. They might comprise a celebration of known human settlement in the area; starting, probably, with the Stone Age presence on these splendid ridges. They may incorporate a tribute to those who have resisted racial domination in the city, concluding with the return of released prisoners and exiles during the very year in which the spine was being built.

And, changing emphasis, to initiate an image of concerned municipal administration, they may also include amenities for citizens from distant townships – crèches, advice centres, wall newspapers, rest rooms and the like.

Proactive innovation. What? Where? This weary project does though offer something to be welcomed, far as it is from being innovatory. The City Hall forecourt has been restored to its former standing as a potential public forum.

A passing moment of urbane sociability in the midst of Johannesburg's stolid mining houses – helped by summer's pressing blooms.

Urban but not, distinctly not, urbane

Droll thing, memory. Especially after 30 years. Now back in South Africa, more and more frequently I experience intense recalls; play backs, that occur only on returning physically to places. There, with startling immediacy, fragments, quirky remnants of lost recollections, surface. Time-locked but vivid snapshots – on occasion whole movie clips – bump, shove, crowd into consciousness; into, to be sure, strictly South African, black and white, awareness.

Nowhere more than in the plush, lush suburbs of long ago youth; of Johannesburg, Cape Town, Durban . . . even Vrede, Free State. Nothing more abruptly reminiscent of South Africa than looking transposed, jolted again to callow greenness at 'intruders' on the gardened streets of comfy suburbs. Seeing once more the black, brown, olive (how to escape this colour besotted storehouse of the mind?), the ever present 'outsiders': aliens.

Droll thing, memory. Especially when today echoes the past so fixedly. Now as then, 'off time' appears to be spent in left over suburban spaces: watching from beside 'the madam's' gate; walking verdant streets that serve other people's homes; sitting, chatting, playing cards, feeding infants at uncomfortable kerb sides; relaxing on sidewalk lawns to which access is usually work-bound planting, mowing, trimming, tending. Now as then, fracturing the genteel quiet with spirited, convivial talk, with rocking, head back laughter, with rhythm, song. Now as then, bringing vibrancy to the rarefied, privatised world of suburban privilege; a world throbbing, one imagines, with the discreet charm of the bourgeoisie. Now as then, necessary and ingenious appropriations of space, blurring of public/private conventions – the make shift social clubs of the street, *ad hoc* conversions of residual spaces to sociable, lived in places. Everyday refusals of no place, anyplace. Daily reachings, in grossly limiting conditions, for space to be, for urbanity.

Top to bottom: that relaxed moment re-captured against the backdrop of stripped 'classicism', ostentatious wealth and power; always those grim towers – unsmiling bulwarks of bureaucratic commerce; Fox Street, a brave attempt to humanise the impressive (oppressive?) mansions of mined wealth.

Urbanity. What am I getting at? Urban spaces, physical places, are, patently, not urbane in and of themselves. They are made so by the people who have used and now use them; by the ways in which, characteristically, they are used, by the qualities which their users give them. So, in trying to identify this facet of urbanity in a town or city, one seeks out places in which people regularly come together, usually but not necessarily informally. Places – often interstitial gaps, nooks, recesses as well as small squares, plazas – where folk gather with others, to be with them, to be seen, to see, to watch that ceaselessly fascinating spectacle, other people. Places where singly or in groups they stand about, stroll, sit, eat, drink, talk, play dice, chess... where they can be participants in the public world about them and/or spectators of that world where they can engage with civil society, contribute to and share in urban life. Of course, features of and objects in the physical world may well become associated with, facilitate such social activities, such public events. Suntraps seem particularly helpful, so do trees and water and food and – most of all – seats.

Downtown South Africa offered precious little of this three decades ago. Folk in, say, central Cape Town enjoyed not too distant access to The Gardens with that singular, that majestic backdrop. Those in Johannesburg might wander, across railway tracks, into the peripheral (now brutally truncated) Joubert Park. There was then, at the edge of the commercial centre in Durban, a bedraggled Medwood Gardens; now an urban delight with its gentle pool, meandering path, outdoor snack bar, discrete spaces, seating in shaded corners, giant chessboard... people. But, then as now, little to speak of at the cores of these cities; not, for sure, Cape Town's inhospitable Parade, the bleak forecourt to Jo'burg's Public Library, or Durban's rail blighted Victoria Embankment.

So in city areas, as in suburbia, my correspondences of memory and present experience have been discouragingly direct. Downtown remains as innocent of urbane settings as in years past. Now, however, at least two other factors are at work.

As elsewhere, the practices and ethos, the pragmatics and ideology – the power – of consumer capitalism prevail, seldom more crassly, more crudely. It's rapid turnover: 'Grab the quick buck, go for the big sell', 'Get 'em in, get 'em out, fast', 'Move the merchandise'. Downtown has become a mechanism for processing consumers. Time and space are money; chatting, strolling, watching other 'punters' are not. Urbanity is, quite simply, not a money spinner. And of course, the racial composition (an unlovable, colour fixated notion) of central city and adjacent areas has changed. 'Black' traders, shoppers, residents and others have arrived and, coincidentally (?), 'whites' have departed for outlying business parks, shopping malls, town houses. Commonly, indeed regularly in such circumstances, resources have been redirected; leaving the changed, changing centres in relative neglect, and worse. Environmental props for everyday street theatre have, quite simply, not been on the agenda. Consumerism and spatial apartheid conjoined.

The signs of this are clear. Take Johannesburg, putative dynamo of urban South Africa. Pedestrian precincts, like Eloff Street, unencumbered by trees under which one might comfortably stand, by building ledges on which briefly to sit, by facilities for hawkers, by kiosks, open air cafes, drinking fountains, racks for parked bicycles . . . by seats other than 'shove off quick' back benders at bus stops. Unspoilt by distractions from serious shopping. Find, if you can, nooks for buskers, street bands, entertainers. Wander through the city: patches of lawn protected by walls and railings that defy human backsides, promising damage most dread; pools and fountains at which few but gymnasts sit restfully; polished, sloped, marble parapets exacting muscular dexterity from hardy sitters . . . fierce cacti warning off the footsore. The goal – maximum discomfort?

There are, though, also hints at what might be. Consider, as one of the two or three examples, the amenity filled area at the foot of that glitzy Johannesburg Sun: trees, pools, a cascade, stepped paths, bushes and ground cover, shaded benches grouped in off pavement alcoves, discrete spaces by the water, parapets of width and height suitable for sitting, a food kiosk, a newspaper and magazine vendor, street artists, hawkers, photographers, hucksters . . . people.

Urbanity: for the politically tough minded probably a trivial, a piddling loss of spatial apartheid. Maybe. Apparently, South African democracy does not call for places of everyday, informal contact. Seemingly, there is no need to come out from the exclusive clubs, shebeens and other segregated lairs into civil, open, public, life. Maybe.

Unintended baroque irony? – muscular, semi-clad males straining to support far-seeing females, the customarily gender-determined symbols of knowledge and craft.

Architecture and sculpture
— an interrupted coupling?

Carving and building have, historically and across the continents, been inseparable. Buildings, especially those heavy with communal, public symbolism, have been graced with sculpted figures in, on and about them. Surfaces of timber, stone, brick, adobe, stucco have been incised, moulded, inside and out, on niches, arches, ceilings and in domes. Spires and finials have been decorated with chiselled foliage and small animals; the cathedral of Notre-Dame at Amiens (begun in 1220) being a singularly flamboyant and glorious, instance.

There is much else, from, say, the deeply undercut carvings of the Galilee Porch at Ely Cathedral (1198) to the complex panels of Meso-American buildings (around 500 BC). From the elaborated *dougung* brackets under the roofs of Chinese buildings, around AD 800, to the stunning *muqarnas* ('stalactite') vaulting of Islamic architecture, as in the fourteenth-century Hall of Two Sisters at the Alhambra, Granada.

So it has been. Making and shaping, building and carving, architecture and applied sculpture. An aged, venerable marriage: on the sculpted fronts of Maori ceremonial halls; in relief-cut figures at the open-air sanctuaries of bronze-age cities; on the moulded, puddled earth dwellings of Upper Volta; in the rock-cut Buddhist temples of India; in the geometric figures and feathered serpents of the stone-clad, 2 000-year-old pyramids of Mexico; in baroque churches, like S Luis of Seville, where structure and carved embellishment merge fervidly. Through to modern work by architects such as Frank Lloyd Wright in the US, Antoni Gaudi in Catalonia and Hassan Fathy in Egypt.

All this seems to have been lost to the pared-down economics of much current architecture; especially to the public faces of con-

Top to bottom: lionesses of power, Fox Street – what's next for a jungle meal among the passing crowd or timorous visitors to the magistrate's courts opposite? De Villiers Street – the old Johannesburg railway station – Ndlovu and the rush of progress in transport above; a fountain on our often parched highveld – Jacob Epstein come to Johanneburg's financial district?

19

temporary cities. At most there's an occasional addition (afterthought?) cut into or fixed on an otherwise bald, soaring wall. More frequently, architectural sculpture is reduced to an isolated piece near a parent building which rises, dominant, into the sky. In either case, one often feels that a client or an architect is self-consciously, perhaps apologetically, exhibiting his or her cultivated dedication to 'the plastic arts'.

Central Johannesburg is no exception. Far from it. Ours must be close to bottom on a rating of cities that celebrate the crafts of sculpture on buildings: carving, cutting, casting, moulding and assembling – a casual, offhand neglect. Even when one thinks of civic statuary; like those mawkish buck leaping behind the old Post Office building or the kitsch pair at the top of Jan Smuts Avenue. Like that stuffy worthy on his ponderous pedestal by the Supreme Court or the banal, stilted 'homage' to mine workers at the Civic Centre in Braamfontein. Like all those disjointed pieces placed on forlorn plazas at the entrances to the priapic towers of CBD-land.

There are, though, relics of another way; one that calls for attention. One passing beyond the pedantically, the flaccidly carved: the quite simply, poorly crafted entablatures, swags and other worn-out baggage with which our local, borrowed, neo-classicisms are decked.

Take a look at a few examples. Most sit on the distinctly up-market, costly façades of our entrenched financial establishment – the mining houses, banks, building societies. Some are on the fronts of our embedded public bureaucracies – as at the central railway station and the municipal library.

Start, I suggest, with that bulky duo immediately west of the Magistrates' Courts. The upper storeys of 45 Main Street (and through to 40 Fox Street): two relief-cut bases for flag-poles and a series of protruding, sculpture-encrusted panels. All unimaginatively disposed on ill-proportioned, bland, even brutal façades. But the carving, that's something else; transcending those awkward, squeezed-in window spandrels. Sensitively observed and fluidly stylised plants and animals of southern Africa; crisply incised, sharp in our glowing highveld light. Abundant but still. Re-interpreting what may well be commonly known to all who stop to look.

Then 44 Main Street: its elegantly carved panels on the parapet walls that flank the entrance to an otherwise coarse building. Again the wildlife, here formalised in a low-cut relief which readily catches the movements of impala, elephants . . . hadedahs. Again a perceptive response to the vivid local light. Again active and also serene. These qualities are not, one notes, also evident in the dreary, hackneyed scene high over the entry. Decidedly not in that triumphant male figure flourishing darts of lightning above the heads of four maidens – passive, awe-struck, admiring nymphs. Abstracted, stereotyped icons.

Walk eastward along Main Street. Past the embossed aluminium spandrels on the Chamber of Mines building, dull images of mining equipment. Turn south into the pedestrian area that was upper Hollard Street. There, on the General Mining Building, is a deeply incised frieze – depictions from a selected history. More static, lifeless stereotypes: black people who labour, sing and die while whites discover, create, think, declaim . . . shoot. Not unlike – now strolling northward – the shallow relief in granite at the Volkskas, 74 Market St. Crudely carved scenes from a mythic South African past in which blacks toil at menial work whilst whites watch, instruct, administer . . . make history.

Also not unlike, in their implicit assumptions, the more veiled signals from the Public Library diagonally opposite. Carved symbols of learning drawn from a distant, distinctively European tradition; incised heads of Socrates, Virgil, Dante, Darwin, Einstein . . . No Mahatma Gandhi, no Sol Plaatjie, no Eugene Marais. But pious homilies via idealised, feebly executed figures: an unclad scholar languidly pointing to an open book, another strumming at a lyre, a third – just thinking.

While in this area look also at a contemporary alternate to the now rare practice of craft-carving: the abstract, moulded pre-cast panels on the First National Bank at the south-east corner of Simmonds and Market streets. This technique need not be expensive and is open to a variety of treatments, figurative as well as abstract.

A last, brisk walk; north-east to the de Villiers Street entrance to Park Station. Three doorways, each with a carved elephant head above. Flattened, squashed – unimposing representations of an animal which is anything but unimposing. And above that sad trio there's a long prosaic frieze in bronze: another reconstructed past, another tale of progress brought to those whom Kipling dismissively described as 'the lesser breeds without the law'. A torpid progression; from African bearers to an ox-wagon, a horse-drawn carriage and then a railway engine plus coaches. From simple innocence to technological complexity! Courtesy of white enterprise no doubt.

Downtown Johannesburg: not, to date, a joyful milieu for architectural sculpture. What about the future, expressly for figurative work? Something, surely, other than the taken for granted, partisan notions of human relations which suffuse the examples we have just seen.

Sandton City in a wholly uncharacteristic setting – bested, for once, by nature in the surrounding suburbs.

Desire in the suburbs – desire consumed

'Hop in, we'll go for a spin, have a coffee. I'll take you to something that's totally changed since you left SA.' . . . 'Here's parking! It's usually choked but you can find a place. Let's go in, have a look around. See what you think'.

We are in buy, buy, buy land. Shopping time, bliss time. Its always happy hour here. Consume your desires . . . spend, spend, spend.

Where else but the shopping malls of Jo'burg; especially, but not only, in the northern suburbs. Also beyond Egoli, elsewhere. Ubiquitous islands of consumption rising none too ethereally, downright clumsily, from shifting seas of parking lot. Fed by tentacles of interweaving roadway. Motor traffic, that obsession of town planners (and others), is paramount. Not surprisingly, it is *the* means of getting shoppers, that is, spenders, to and from.

We are at the civic cores, the community pulses, the cathedrals of suburbia. We are at the fulcrum of commodity exchange, the endpoint of productive endeavour. We are not, clearly not, in public debating arenas, communal fora; in, say, the dissenting coffee houses of earlier, more politically robust times – of Pringle's Cape Town, Samuel Johnson's London, eighteenth-century Amsterdam.

These isles of plenty, I was told shortly after arrival, are what I've expressly returned to from those years abroad. These cornucopias are a promise of our about-to-arrive, *net oorkant die bult* ('just on the other side of the hill') 'new' South Africa. We really need them. After all, your spender is your essential patriot: he, she keeps the economy moving, the deals of commerce wheeling, the pistons of production copulating. It is well . . . un-South African not to buy, buy, buy.

Top to bottom: three 'celebrations' of the internal glories of up-market shopping in the northern suburbs of Johannesburg – why, we can out-strip Dallas effortlessly – we recognise what is gross, crass, crude without trying.

Shopping, in the suburbs, is the focus of public activity. The nucleus of entertainment (cinemas), medical services (consulting rooms), legal advice (lawyers' suites), posting, banking, eating out. And much, much more of the clobber of contemporary life. All packaged in those unlovable buildings astride the malls. Get it profitably under one roof; hotels, conference centres, keep-fit-get-slim gymnasiums, whatever. But remember, at bottom it's the retail trade that fetches them in, keeps the show going.

And it works, at least for some. The haves are in, the have-nots rarely get here even to gawp at what is on offer. There lies the rub. Apartheid, we keep on and on being assured, is going. Segregation, it is whispered, is to remain. To now be wrapped in euphemisms such as 'inequable spending potential' or antiseptic business lunch phrases like 'disassociation by income'. But then, self-righteous and plaintive, 'It's the same the world over, you get rich and poor everywhere you know.' Very likely. Here though the cleavage is overwhelmingly founded, perpetuated and still justified on grounds of so-called race, colour.

No wonder I was whisked to the malls, introduced to the future in preparation. 'Whites' are there, their well-publicised, unique standards of civilised behaviour fluttering, fitfully, above security-checked entrances. 'Blacks' are, as ever, on the margins, their labour conveniently — and inexpensively — at hand. Plus, of course, the few who enjoy incomes that permit them to spend with appropriate, cultivated, sensitivity. More pointedly, to do so with acceptable sufficiency; that is, heavily.

Like their neighbouring and similarly gross business parks, suburban malls differ from many shopping and commercial areas in and around our city centres — now left behind, neglected. The malls, encased, unthreatening (well . . . sort of), are used by and geared to use by the privileged — largely whites. They are serviced by those at the further end of disassociation by income. They consist, in essence, of encapsulated, artificially lit and ventilated walkways that connect retail outlets to escalators, lifts, and judiciously concealed (segregated?) service zones. Whether restrained or daring, conventionally 'tasteful' or bold (*alias* postmodern), the architecture and decor remain comforting, reassuring. We are in the right place, where right-thinking — right-spending — folk ought to be, be seen to be. Protected, sanitised, unchallenging, dispassionate: vacuous. Aloof, self-conscious withdrawal from the risks of public being.

Back in the city centres it is quite otherwise. Vibrant, open, always chancy, potentially dangerous; shopping here tends to be shunned by the privileged. Some, indeed, boast of 'never really going into town nowadays'. Here the screeched adverts of militant consumerism are being matched if not surpassed by the electric vigour of public, street, life. Spirited: threatening, untidy, dissenting, dynamic. Celebrations of the force of social being.

No. This neat, seemingly fixed division will not do. We are back with that world-weary sigh, the poor are always with us. Now a a bitter-sweet, patronising afterthought – they are so alive, so resilient, so colourful.

We are enmeshed in a specifically South African gloss on that trumpeted Third/First World rupture – this, some claim, is the one place in which the two occur side by side. They do, but everywhere. They must, each entails the other. The riches of some are the deprivations of many. To look back, for instance, at the glistening towers of Jo'burg as one travels to Soweto is to experience interdependent phenomena. The one exists because of the other; poverty sustains affluence, conspicuous wealth calls for and on penury. Abundance in suburban malls is predicated on central city and much other, squalor.

A spin in the car, a coffee, a look around; appeals to buy, to spend. But other matters obtrude. Especially the often suppressed desire to desire better, to desire in a different way, to desire a more abundant life.

We had better get a move on. New kitsch looks to outkitsch current models. In Ronald Reagan's moving words, 'You ain't seen nothin' yet'.

California, his base, luxuriates in novel mall games. Beverly Hills, on Rodeo Drive: access via elegantly, expensively, surfaced ramps with antique sculpture (made while you wait) in walled recesses; a rushing fountain in an opulent open-air, sunken courtyard. An exotic atoll of consumerism, surrounded by a moat of traffic. And something newer, also on Rodeo: vast façades of costly marble, glazed terracotta; an hotel-like lobby with receptionist, attendants and rare, sumptuous, potted plants; each shop behind its own Art Deco or similar front; clad, lavishly, in balconies, entablatures, columns. The Wheel, in Durban is only more so, far more so. Then the latest: 'European-style', pedestrian streets; Xeroxed copies of Florence, Paris, Vienna, London. Shopping in costly, competing Disneylands.

The technological excitement of Norman Foster, of Richard Rogers come to our own Tyrwhitt Avenue, Rosebank, Johannesburg – all steel, glass and, surely by error, a touch of humanity.

Gatvol van wat die gat vol maak?
('Sick and tired of what fills the hole?')

'Ek is gatvol vir Alan Lipman se ewig-klaende beskrywings en aanvalle teen die "establishment" ... ' So skryf N Botes van Nieuw Muckleneuk in die Vrye Weekblad, *1 Augustus.* A polite translation: (I have had a belly-full of Alan Lipman's ever-complaining descriptions of and attacks on the "establishment", writes N Botes of New Muckleneuk in the [now defunct] Free Weekly, 1 August.)

I am with you N Botes. I am also fed-up, *gatvol*. Especially with the clumsy, pretentious, borrowed 'new' architecture of what you call our 'large apartheid cities', our towns and middle-sized cities; (*'Groot apartheidstede'. Ook van ons dorpe en middelslag stede*. These no-places where most South Africans find themselves most of the time. Where the pressing issues of decent accommodation for the population are by-passed, are negated day by day; all too often in the cause of *finansiële realiteite* (financial realities).

To fill *weekblad* columns, as you urge, with the work of our few socially alert designers like Rodney Harber or Dennis Claude at the School of Architecture in Durban would be comforting. A pleasing way to avoid the mean mess which others, the majority, have dumped us in and are still unloading on us. An enticing distraction rather than the presently necessary confrontation.

Difficult, however, wholly to shake off that disturbing, that telling observation from Nieuw Muckleneuk: I am forever, you say, complaining, moaning. So let us focus on something worthy, on a finely crafted building. Let us look at the recently opened Cradock Heights, standing coolly in one of the ever so smart real estate circuses of Johannesburg's northern suburbs. Take a trip to Rosebank's expanding shopping complex, exemplar of local design crassness.

Top to bottom: three glimpses of technical purity – trim, white-finished metal, polished glass under complex sun-shading and a modicum of carefully positioned greenery, it works but at considerable monetary and environmental cost.

There it is, corner Cradock and Tyrwhitt avenues, a pair of jacaranda-lined suburban streets. A 'hi-tech' interpretation of early modern, inspirational architecture; currently the whipping-boy of every glib, frequently shallow critic and often, amazingly, from an academic address. The building embraces and illustrates among the best, the most life-enhancing visions of that now maligned, that specifically twentieth-century thrust in architecture.

Some instances. The lucid, precise relationships between parts of the building: between, say the muscular, concrete columns and the airy, perforated aluminium fins that support and provide wind-bracing for the windows; between those severely proportioned vertical windows and the horizontal sun-screens on the north-facing façades; between the two long, low wings of the building and the tall, over-sailing 'atrium' which links them.

Then the attempt to convey directly, with clarity, how it is assembled: by, say, extending, by 'flying' beams and columns to indicate how the upper floors are carried on the reinforced concrete frame; by highlighting how those beams are attached, are 'strapped' to the columns; by demonstrating, exhibiting how the light tubular steel structure of the atrium and of the bridges across it, are braced with adjustable 'outriggers'; by revealing how the glass lift rises through the building in its neat, glazed shaft.

This is a technologically crafted artefact; a celebration of the punctilious accuracy, the pristine precision which is claimed to be characteristic of contemporary, industrial manufacture. This is a machined aesthetic. Decoration and function are tooled simultaneously, they are integral to production and use. Like, say, the complementary patterns of the perforated aluminium fins and the slatted horizontal sun-screening – plus the associated shadows which these components cast.

This is, above all perhaps, a legible building. How and for what purposes its elements have been formed, shaped and put together are purposefully, clear. Each part can be 'read', its manufacture, functions and connections to other parts are intended to be manifest.

It is also meant to be transparent, literally so – a visually permeable structure. Glass, modernist architects argue, has helped to 'free the building-box', has opened interiors and exteriors to each other, has connected life inside to that outside. Walls need no longer be load-bearing (that is for steel or concrete supports), they can now be screens, partitions, light membranes. They can be glass; a metaphor for accessibility, openness, even, some have said, an invitation to democratic, public involvement . . . participation.

All this and more in Rosebank; among those heavy, pompous banks and building societies, those shut-off shopping malls – citadels of commercialism. It is impressive, a moment of skilled design, meticulously executed. A patently technological building on an humane scale.

But more complaining, *nog meer klaery*. There are problems. Handsome is not necessarily as handsome does.

Take, as a case in point, the subtly disposed, elegantly proportioned windows and sun-screens. The former are, quite simply, insufficiently served by the latter. There is no screening to the east-facing windows on the two upper floors, none to those on the west or to the extensive north-facing fenestration of the two ground floor wings. So a considerable chunk of the building is exposed to the powerful Gauteng sun.

Tenants have, consequently, installed air-conditioning units (hardly a boost for energy conservation) and/or extensive internal louvre blinds. A central quality of that urbanely detailed glass, its transparency, remains a potential rather than a fulfilled promise.

Further, all that glazing, like the unsullied white finish to the building, calls for repeated, costly, attention. Within months of completion, the external paintwork was given a 'major wash-down'. Of course the continuous, generous runs of windows are cleaned more frequently and also expensively. Then the soaring atrium: a periodic job for agile members of the nearby university mountaineering club.

Perhaps, though, the most worrying aspect of this crisp, aloof building lies in its probable symbolic, social connotations.

Cradock Heights constitutes an unmistakably establishment, a patently cosmopolitan aesthetic. As such, it is unlikely to contribute effectively to searches for culturally rooted – contextual, local, regional – architectural identities. Quite the contrary. This is a – probably *the* – impassive corporate image, world-wide. A mid- and late-twentieth-century version of emaciated modernism, the so-called International Style.

This is the expertly packaged insignia of transnational enterprise, of global groupings that are as obsessed with 'technological fixes' as they are with abstract, macho administration. This is the symbolic home of bureaucratic, remote management. Little scope here for the democratic impulse that might now come to mark architecture in South Africa.

The diamond on Diagonal Street – Helmut Jahn brings Chicago to Newtown, Johannesburg *via* a strikingly inappropriate, a shimmering, glass-clad, reflecting hot spot in the sun.

Downtown South Africa
— everywhere, anywhere, nowhere

The corporate office blocks of urban South Africa are not showpieces of local design. They are all too frequently, as unsuited to our exacting climates as they are, stylistic borrowings from 'overseas' – the nebulous and distant anywhere that seems so to befuddle the creative vision of our designers. More and more they clutter our city landscapes: priapic towers soaring unnecessarily; mirror-glass palaces aggressively reflecting all and anything about them; masonry-clad giants bearing heavily on all below ... and increasingly, recycled neo-classical oddities that announce the supposed origins and participation in European history of our minority population. In this, as in many other architectural spheres, we filch assiduously.

On occasion, modish guest designers have left bulky imports; like the New York firm Skidmore, Owings and Merrill's Carlton Centre on Commissioner Street in Johannesburg, the Chicago architect Helmut Jahn's over-glazed deposits at the corner Diagonal and President or, in Durban, Field and Pine Streets. Mostly, though, we struggle with home-grown echoes of elsewhere; like Johannesburg's massive Bank City and, also from the hands of Revel Fox and his colleagues, the incongruous BP Centre in Cape Town. Nor are the ubiquitous office units that litter the many crass outlying areas similar to Rosebank and Sandton any less worrying.

All this prompts a brief sociological excursion, an attempt to place these and similar design derelictions in a social context.

> Our revels now are ended ... are melted into air ... the cloud-capp'd towers, the gorgeous palaces, the solemn temples ... shall dissolve. ... We are such stuff as dreams are made on ...
> (*The tempest*)

Globalisation, the geo-politics of finance capital now transcends local boundaries. Wherever they may be, most people experience

Top to bottom: three views of aloof, arrogant indifference – but who cares, after all, we're top dog.

a world that is dominated by international capital. Since the mid-1970s in particular, this pervasive penetration has wrought far-reaching restructuring processes. Different localities, however, have been affected differently – at global, regional, national and local levels. Change alone is constant, 'the great globe itself, yea all which it inherit, shall dissolve'.

This, the second wave of modernisation following World War II, has occurred with heightened emphasis in cities; in urban and architectural design. Previously neglected, socially segregated and shunned neighbourhoods have become desirable localities for upwardly aspiring groups. Remnants of the redundant, decayed centres of the first machine age – mainly industrial heartlands, the mines, the docks – are now suitable cases for urban regeneration.

Few, if any of us, can be certain about who or where we are. Our identities, like the very ground beneath us, are in threatened or continuous upheaval. This sense of dislocation, of alienation, is probably most keenly felt in the metropolitan centres of capitalist enterprise. Here, as a case in point, new terms have gained currency - terms that depict the present as being distinctive only in that it is not the past. Apparently, we now live in a world of post-industrial, postmodern, post-feminist and post-enlightenment reality. We live in, we are post-history. The relevance of overarching, grand narratives, that is, of history, has been rejected in the name of that hoary myth, the 'golden age' of repeatedly recycled classicism. Superficiality pervades.

The idea of revivalist heritage has been used to package this world-wide anomie. Heritage has become a balm for soothing, quietening, the dispossessed as well as the *nouveau riche* who aspire to social leadership. The former are told they must be 'realistic'; they must give way to a post-Darwinian, a survival-of-the-fittest modernisation. For the latter the past is up for sale, as is all else they touch. They buy status - and thus legitimacy - in the recurring façades of social power, of historic and mock-historic fronts behind which interiors are stuffed with 'all mod cons'.

This, the revivalist industry, is coupled with widespread cultural stagnation. A society whose spokesmen and women, whose intelligentsia, are obsessed with representing the present as a sanitised, an asocial, ahistorical, version of the past is one whose purported leaders are incapable of confronting their social futures. They, the 'opinion makers', fear what is likely to come. Their revivals are focused on lifting 'themes' from the past, on treating heritages as warehouses for readily re-captured meanings – the past as scenography. History, on the contrary, is an analytic, a critical activity. Its practitioners interrogate and interpret rather than appropriate the past. They grasp the force of George Orwell's chilling observation, 'who controls the past controls the future; who controls the present controls the past'.

Of course, the past is not unproblematic. History is more than a collation of facts waiting to be parcelled and consumed. By drawing selectively on elements of the past, the entrepreneurs of revivalism compound our difficulties in seeking to make sense of the alienated, alienating world about us. By treating history as a means of bolstering consumerism – of hurrying museum turnstiles, of pushing tourism at fragile sites, of selling period-costume buildings – the proponents of heritage–revivalism as a business enterprise confuse rather than help to clarify contemporary dislocations.

For them, anywhere is now everywhere . . . and nowhere. Rather than being challenged, change is made palatable. Pressing sociol-architectural demands are disguised by dressing buildings in historical drag. Pillaged 'histories' are cleansed, portrayed in seductive panasonic colour rather than in revealing black and white. Lifting from the past is a means of acquiring historical legitimacy.

In this revivalist lexicon, local identities are represented as being rooted in selected aspects of European culture and history; particular emphasis is placed on *beaux arts* readings of favoured instances; from, say, ancient Greece, the Renaissance and subsequent neo-classicisms. These and like examples are borrowed, purchased, from the past to be hung on contemporary structures with their contemporary facilities, equipment, patterns of use. Whose memories do such building stir, whose nostalgias do they gratify, whose cultural roots are being acknowledged?

Visit the instance of new Johannesburg office blocks illustrated here. Examine the façades, venture into the vapid transcontinental interiors. Inside and out, they are symbols of not-belonging; those who identify with them are not from here, from southern Africa. They are from elsewhere. They have impounded this land, they have re-made it into their far-off recollected pasts. Their revivalist embellishments embody a need to erase local senses of place.

These are borrowed architectures, they are filched from not-Africa. They are architectures that abolish local memories in the name of selected, far-off histories.

There is an additional facet of revivalist corporate design: it is also an attempt to demonstrate that its publics are part of the cutting edge of an advanced industrial world. It centres on symbolic forms that bring a sense of familiarity and well-being to those whose lives are bound up with tracking the global circuits of finance capital. It is the nostalgia made concrete of corporate executives and their ilk; a soothing lotion for those caught up in the disorientating maelstrom of current modernisation. It is an architecture of fantasy, of fantastic forms.

Such indulgent reveries are, patently, far removed from the everyday realities of the society to which its practitioners claim to give expression. Can this be otherwise when the overwhelming majority of people in our region are no strangers to being forcibly uprooted, to being culturally repressed? Can one seriously claim that their experiences are adequately, or partially, embraced by drawing on the nostalgia of a minority; of those who, ever so respectably, supported 'separate development' as a means of entombing cultural differences?

> Too many white South Africans have never really lived in Africa in their own minds . . . that they were able to live such pleasant lives only at terrible cost to their fellow black citizens did not appear to dilute their level of comfort.
> (Justice Richard Goldstone).

Egoli _ city of dislocation?

The items in this second set of critical pieces explore in further depth a number of issues hinted at in the previous selection. These deal principally with the marked absence of public gathering spaces throughout the city and its suburbs, the crude competitiveness of its buildings and its rigidly rectangular street grids. The city turns its back on its spectacular setting among ruggedly beautiful *kopjes* as casually, as mindlessly as it does on the civic, the public lives of its citizens. 'Fortress Johannesburg': a place of segregated enclaves, of insecurity, fear, retreat. Who are the cowering defenders, who the constantly threatening attackers?

Swanky mansions, lush gardens set in green sward – always gated, guarded, guarded, guarded.

Under siege in outer suburbia

> Them that's got shall get, them that's not shall lose. So the Bible says and it still is news. Yes, the strong get more while the weak ones fade. Empty pockets don't ever make the grade. (Billie Holiday singing 'God bless the child')

They are to be found in contemporary cities the world over; the smart suburbs in which the well-off, them-that's-got, make their homes. Spacious, select, the best that money will buy. Like other South African cities, Johannesburg offers a spicy extra, especially in its northern, most lush stretches of shruburbia – a marriage of luxury and anxiety, of conspicuous consumption and beleaguered insecurity. A fascinating cocktail.

Conspicuous consumption: a now commonplace term first used by that biting social commentator the late Thorstein Veblen. His phrase for ostentatious exhibitions of buying power, for patterns of consumption that emphasise abundance. His summary description of showy life-styles, lavish use of costly goods and services in order to demonstrate wealth and status. A continual call for 'consumer durables', items that need frequent maintenance and/or periodic replacement.

As Veblen noted, efforts to fulfil such demands often distort national economies. They lead to circumstances in which large portions of a country's resources are directed toward providing facilities that only a minority can and does indulge. A not unfamiliar view of much in our home-grown economy.

Beleaguered insecurity made manifest in street upon street of outsized, sumptuous houses and gardens – entrenched behind barricaded fastnesses: those ubiquitous walls and spikes, electrified fences, bars, razor-wire, electronic gates, closed-circuit televi-

Top to bottom: accumulated money, lots of it, on show – walls and constantly manicured bushes of coarse ostentation; innocent cherubs that smile grimly on passers-by; classical toppings on massive, fear-induced boundary walls. Sunny Sandton.

sion, alarm systems and even moats. Also security guards, beware vicious dogs, immediate armed response: the paraphernalia of spatial defence.

A growing protection industry: building contractors who erect rampart-like defences, guard-dog breeders, experts in subtly contrived electronic installations, suppliers of ornamented gates, burglar bars and the like. They're listed in a hefty section of the recent *Yellow pages* for Johannesburg: armed patrols, trained dogs, panic buttons, ambulance and medical back-up, a 24-hour laser watch, automated technology, 'a young, dynamic, efficient guard force' . . . 'infallible security systems'.

Anxieties about safety – security of self, family, home and possessions – have shifted decisively. They have passed from being the personal troubles of a well-heeled minority to become a major public issue, a threat to whole strata of society. However, those few are still able, privately, to command the resources that might shield them. So the heavy, heady admix of flashy display and fear.

Let us take a brief look at some instances; casually selected from Sandton, that stamping ground of flamboyantly guarded social pretension.

First a solid, stolid wall that stands in Saxon Road as an apt symbol of the phenomenon. A massive bulwark (probably costing more than a dozen Soweto homes) which is certainly no charmed setting for a *Midsummer Night's Dream* – no place for the rustic wall frolics of Pyramus and Thisby. No occasion for levity here. Protection, serious defence is the name of this game.

Dwarfed, we outsiders are offered an unseen, implied interior; one solely accessible to holders of the appropriate key and to visitors identified via an intercom system. Motorists only, it seems. Where do pedestrians apply? Not, surely, at those costly, mammoth, hardwood doors; they're scarcely invitations to friendly callers. Quite the contrary. Like the impassive masonry, they announce curtly, unambiguously 'No entry. Keep out'. What is behind? – 'too much house' I was told by a passer-by, one of Billie Holiday's them-that's-not. An idle, a potentially mischievous question? Not our business: move along there, move along.

Then, in Daisy Street, a row of town-houses secluded behind a huge, hydraulically operated gate and a symbolic lodge in the currently modish architectural style – an up-to-date, modern 'primitive hut'. Individual houses are protected by decorous wrought-iron gates plus the customary warning of swift armed response to intrusion. Now the tall boundary wall is being capped by an electrified fence.

On entry, one is faced by blank wall surfaces, except for glazed double-garage doors that give appropriate precedence to those other emblems of status, the Porsche, Mercedes or similar. All this is framed, in each case, by a ponderous false façade which has been planted on the front; a weighty, conspicuously purposeless structure that adds nothing but pomp – an appearance of greater size.

We return to Saxon Road, at the junction with William Nicol Drive. Here we find inflated ostentation in the making. An all too-much-house that embraces a selection of the noisy fashions from yesterday's glossy architectural journals; grossly fat columns, grandiose outgrowths of 'flying' beams, modernistic curved walls, plastic domes . . . a monumentally heavy entrance porch. And of course an extra-heavy boundary wall that, in the spirit of a medieval castle, forms an outer bailey to the already massive structure. So, another of the many instances of gilded unease in affluent suburbia. Another series of ornate flourishes behind defensive outworks.

A final example: drawn from that curious preoccupation with the north American, Gone-With-the-Wind, colonial style which seems to grip householders in northern Jo'burg. Hardly a street without its lofty colonnaded portico and pediment glimpsed over high garden walls, or between the bars of brocaded metal gates. For some, the plantation image – presumably with obedient, happy 'darkies' in attendance – seems irresistible.

Here, on 3rd Road, Hyde Park, there is a more distinctive case. One that reaches further than Hollywood mythology to grasp at ancient Greek, or Etruscan, or Roman . . . or some wholly imagined architecture. A concrete, off-the-mould classical order of indeterminate origin which fronts what appears to have been a lumpish, puffed-up Cotswold cottage. Yet another enormous portico – elongated 'classical' columns and statuary in the triangular pediment above. As though this were not enough, a smaller, temple-like version of the main house is being built beyond the fountain, statuesque nymphs and gladiators at the entrance. All, of course, behind the customary wall, railings, gates and intercom system.

These are but a smattering of what's on view and they're not necessarily the most bizarre examples. It's a poignant scene – flashy excrescences immured from the massive social deprivation in which they are rooted. Take a look for yourself. But not, I suggest, on foot; the distances are disabling and the snarling dogs, though usually shut in, are frightening.

The revamped MuseumAfrica, on Mary Fitzgerald Square, Newtown, Johannesburg – a permanent exhibition of South African life with a difference, frequented by massed school children.

Civic futures – a telling interlude

Urban Futures 2000, Johannesburg's international conference of beguiling contrasts: lofty academic theory and volcanic street theatre, contemplative art exhibitions and the hottest jazz in town, visits to the city's populous townships and then to secluded lecture halls. Exhausted, one now strains to re-compose in one's mind the sustained excitement of these past five days, from 10 to 14 June.

Only, I imagine, the joint resources of Wits university and the city's Metropolitan Council could so readily have managed the logistics. Some 320 learned papers covering a daunting array of topics were presented by visiting and local academics. The former came from more than 50 countries. There were fifteen key speakers; most of whom, had I been able to attend their talks, would assuredly have held me as much as did the some-time structuralist philosopher-planner Manuel Castells. And that applied to many other of the scholarly addresses which were presented, among which there were studiously formulated ideas about civic life in a variety of projected futures.

Not all of these were benign, many were as distinctly scary as Doris Lessing's forbidding futurist novels. There was, in these analytic offerings, at least as much to be chary of as to hearten. Those among the audiences who may already have been timorous about contemporary urban living could scarcely have been assuaged by the anticipated discomfort, menace, dislocation to which they were introduced.

There were community and business fora, round-table discussions, 26 local tours, theatrical and other performances, musical events and video screenings. There was sufficient exhibition material to occupy one's attention throughout the week. That included the challenging sociol-historical *blank – Architecture, apartheid and after* which opened so dramatically in Rotterdam on our Day of Reconciliation in December 1998. Among the other fine exhibitions,

Top to bottom: the museum in action – an iterative pleasure, a success story?

blank – is notable as a revealing study of the shameful roles urbanists, for example, planners, architects, engineers, played in the racial oppression that disfigured the years before and during apartheid. At Museum Africa, Newtown, this showing unequivocally warrants the repeated return visits which many will wish to make before it closes in January 2001.

For five jam-packed days, sleep seemed a wasteful indulgence. But pause for a moment, as I did early into the second day of this wide-ranging gathering. On what basis – focusing on the academic core alone – was one to choose which of the 50 and upward lectures and seminars of the day to attend? How to grapple with the often opposing ideas, methods, approaches and less frequently, their occasional complementarity?

Feast or deluge? How, in this rush of learned presentations, most of which were allotted less than a half-hour, to engage in thoroughgoing, searching debate? Where might one confer formally with others at the conference? Where to fulfil the participatory promise glimpsed at in the pre-arranged *lekgotlas* and discussion panels? Where to be other than an onlooker? These and like questions were probably but distant echoes of the analogous queries posed at the contemporaneous and far, far larger AIDS gathering in Durban.

I found no way through the frustrations. Perhaps I was on the wrong track. At its scholarly heart, the week came increasingly to resemble an exercise in purportedly encyclopaedic coverage. It was not, could not be a sustained effort – through in-depth, closely focused debate – collectively to confront the pressing issues of humanity's smash into its likely urban futures.

Nonetheless there was absorbing interest, excited stimulation, aplenty. Constraints of time, energy and contending attractions meant that one had to choose sparingly. Not without qualms, I opted briefly to sample the predominantly academic programme and less urgently, the generous range of cultural events; excepting, that is, the 26 inviting group tours.

These merit a separate report: one dealing substantively with venues such as the highveld venue from which, so many years gone, Mahatma Ghandi launched his campaigns of *satyagraha*. Such a report ought, I suggest, especially to highlight the 'sites of struggle' destinations that were visited; places which might in future include Kliptown where the much-debated Freedom Charter was hastily adopted at the People's Congress in 1955. These and like sites are, and will surely remain, as instructive for readers as they have proved to be for visitors from abroad.

I and others with whom I spoke did not find the one-and-a-half hour sessions customarily allocated to three or four academic presentations congenial. An abstract of each paper was made available to participants at registration, to then be read or hastily spoken to by its author/authors. Full texts were rarely to hand, a factor that made overall or detailed comprehension elusive. That severely limited the abilities of those attending to comment adequately. Debate, contrary to one's prior expectations, was confined to general observations and all too often, vague clichés.

There were, though, manifestly informative statements; discussions that are likely to remain lodged in one's memory long into the future. As a case in point, Professor Castells' distinctly dystopian view – from Berkeley, California – of rapid, world-wide urban growth and concomitantly, of ever-increasing reliance on information technology. This was aptly matched by the marginally less ominous overview of managing this staggering growth that was offered by his fellow urban theorist Professor Saskia Sasson of the University of Chicago.

Then a salient contribution from Argentina: Professor Miguel Angel Roca's keynote lecture in which he vividly demonstrated the vigour and utility of socially integrated design for public buildings as well as for open urban spaces. His talk lifted what, in Anglophone countries, is termed *urban design* well above its practitioners' persistent pre-occupation with cosy city squares and folksy public structures.

Specifically African perspectives were provided by, among others, Akinlawon Mabogunje of Nigeria and Xolela Mangcu who is based here in Johannesburg. They, of course, are able to call directly on a wealth of current and historical urban knowledge; on experience that reaches historically from the magnificence of Great Zimbabwe to the turbulent modernity of Lagos and the wondrous Muslim-Arabic cities of northern Nigeria. The richness of the latter tradition – stretching, say, from the splendid medieval city of Fez back to ancient Alexandria – was particularly brought to bear by the renowned Turkish scholar/architect Professor Gulsum Nalbantoglu.

Beyond these and other individual 'stars', whom designers tend to revere and then abandon in disconcertingly speedy succession, there were the many less selectively publicised speakers. For example, the quartet who spoke so crisply and convincingly on a viewpoint under the banner, 'Community, Development and Power', which proved to be firmly antithetical to the Castells–Sasson orthodoxy. Where the latter had focused on forecasting massive, global shifts of power, each of the four papers presented in this session held to the pressing here and now of local intervention by socio-political activists.

So, the audience was told of a survey-based analysis of the perceived decline in the power of mass urban movements in African townships – primarily the civics – since we South Africans achieved representative democracy in 1994. Briefly, we learnt that, contrary to customarily expressed belief, 'there continue to be high levels of popular engagement with self-governing civic structures at the local level'. At present, however, civil and political society cannot readily be separated – 'they form a tangled web in the minds of civic activists'.

Then Daniel Chavez Minos of Uruguay provided a deeply questioning, if not outright sceptical view of how, since 1989, the Broad Front of leftist parties in Montevideo has sought to 'deconcentrate city services and decentralise power to the citizens'. His depiction of a new, ideologically inclusive Latin American Left figured high among the possible lessons for local activists which he emphasised.

Returning to our sub-continent, we were treated to an instance of Gallic intellectual, analytical flair. This constituted a sophisticated argument that centred on the twin notions of urban segregation and fragmentation: 'a geography of public action and territorial re-composition'.

The session concluded with a challenging view from 'below', from the purportedly passive recipients of urban architecture and planning. What, the authors asked, are the salient links between community participation, local empowerment and sustained use of the facilities resulting from such attempts? As in the case of the report mentioned first, here too, rather than being offered packaged answers, we were confronted with provocative questions. Then the ebullient cultural programme of exhibitions, dance, musical and theatrical performances . . . and more.

I stepped from the burnished sophistication of the *blank – Architecture, apartheid and after* show into the less polished environs of the student architects' exhibition, *At Home and Away*, which had been assembled in the foyer of their faculty building. From smooth expertise to burning commitment. Working in unison, undergraduate groups drawn from each year of study had assembled the results of three weeks research into topics such as migration, displacement and the notion of home. I found much of their work to be gripping, imaginative, even explosive.

There was the exhibit, *A Home for Domestic Workers*, which examined the potential of revamping large houses for single families, mostly white, as accommodation for domestic workers. From tucked-away, humiliating back-yard 'boys' and girls' rooms' to dignified communal housing. Then the group whose members studied the distinctive culture of and the presently appalling conditions under which Ethiopian refugees live in this city of gold. The students compiled a moving written and pictorial report of their harrowing and simultaneously, inspiriting experiences.

Then the . . . A Place Between . . . project, principally an inquiry into homelessness. Here the young researchers presented verbatim reports from their respondents. An example: 'Hope flowed into my heart, expectation flowed into my spirit. After eating from the bins, sleeping in the cold street of Gauteng, being a wanderer for so long, this place sounds like heaven . . . '

No less compelling, *Voices, amazwi, mantswe, mantsoe,* a dramatic/musical performance, I attended in the tiny arena theatre at Museum Africa. This was presented by adults and children from the Alexandra/Tara Child Psychiatric Clinic. As individuals each spoke, sang and enacted her/his life's story; tales that centred on diverse forms of abuse and neglect. As an ensemble, they captivated their attentive audience with lovely choral singing, harmonious counter-point, rhythmic swaying, group dances and poetry. In the telling words of their pamphlet, 'These are presented as a reflection of their young hearts yearning to speak, to tell us that they too are here.'

Finally to one of the two imported presentations sponsored by the French Institute of South Africa, the entrancing *Tragic flute, a street opera.* The mature Mozart's robust eighteenth-century opera brought to the Market Theatre precinct in Johannesburg by the *Les Grooms* (the Bellboys) company – a fine soprano, a baritone and eight brass instrumentalists. What more could one have desired in the warm highveld winter's sun?

This was an unexpected banquet: gifted improvisation by accomplished musicians who are, at the same time, adroit comedians; a group that performs with talented, intelligent, humour-packed wit. Caught up in this impromptu musical event, the usually taut street faces of the city relaxed into easy smiles and at especially intense comic moments, spontaneous laughter. *Très charmante.*

There was of course more, a great deal more: movies, musical theatre, orchestral performances, a fire dance, ballet, *kwela,* art installations, public lectures, panel discussions and . . . yet more, including a parallel conference for and with young people, 'Children in the Landscape'.

Insofar as my dip into the ocean of scholarly matter which was on offer is an indication of its overall calibre, one can but look eagerly to the conference organisers' collected volume of all the papers they received. That promises to be an engrossing amalgam of excitingly disparate texts. And if the cultural events which one witnessed exemplify what can be made available in Johannesburg then, while assuredly not Edinburgh's or Buenos Aires's, an annual arts festival as engaging as those elsewhere in southern Africa could well be held in this, our otherwise crass city.

Mai Mai bazaar – an occupant at work in a handsome shed made fresh, an architecth-designed place where the users and visitors prevail.

Continuity of form and substance
— the Mai Mai Bazaar, Johannesburg

Travel south-east through the central business district in Johannesburg to the unkempt City and Suburban area. Take Albert Street to the knot of on- and off-ramps that, at Berea Street, marks the very edge of the inner city. Stop where, from under the screaming M31 traffic, you can almost touch those eroding symbols of Egoli, the yellow mine dumps.

Here, in what has long been a decidedly un-salubrious, for some a menacing corner, you will find an intensely active cultural enclave, the Mai Mai Bazaar. This is a, if not *the* social and economic centre, *the* meeting ground on the Witwatersrand of Zulu life, of newly arrived rural folk and established urbanites. It is a place of transition.

Mai Mai, initially stables for the municipal mule trains that cleared the city's night soil and a walled compound for migrant workers, is now — almost a century on — a busy commercial market. Here, many of the traders live *in situ*, squeezed above their tiny stalls, workshops and storerooms. Here, unaware that all about was built on a waste tip, one can wander among arrays of herbal medicines, *sangomas'* displays and crowded retail stores; almost anything is on sale, from kitchen soap to arcane love elixirs. One can shop for live goats and chickens, for a myriad of everyday domestic appliances, for specialist ceremonial and other cultural artefacts.

There is a beer-hall, there are barbers, cobblers, carpenters, snake skins, sjamboks, tree-bark *mutis*, zinc baths, extensive motor service and panel-beating shops, a long-range taxi terminus. There is a novel industry, pillow-packing using multi-coloured foam rubber pellets. There is a southern African speciality, richly decorated bridal *kists* (chests) crafted from discarded timber palettes. During the evenings and over weekends, the site accommodates activities such as dancing, singing, card-playing, social gatherings, open-air meetings and church services.

Top to bottom: glimpses of the active, thronging spaces that architect Rod Lloyd made of the once broken-down Mai Mai Bazaar, where the yellow mine dumps press on Egoli city.

The place is agog with talk, laughter, singing, children at play, gaily and soberly clothed people. Snacks are bought at food stalls to be shared and eaten on the move. Groups debate intently, stall-holders shout their wares, shoppers insistently – deliberately and often painstakingly – negotiate their purchases. Music pulsates everywhere while, simultaneously, full-volume radio announcers assault one's ears. The throbbing beat of visual and aural colour is accompanied by smells that entice and on occasion, do not.

There is no place at this centre for the languid, genteel, politely cool exchanges of the malls that serve shoppers in the more manicured parts of Johannesburg. On the contrary. These are energetically public, vibrantly sociable assemblies of customers who engage with potential sellers assertively, examine the merchandise pointedly, spend their money cautiously, slowly. All the while, Mai Mai pounds with life; much, I imagine, as medieval markets did, as do the *souks* of north Africa and the similar market places across the continent. This is a distinctively African bazaar.

The robustly detailed mule stables, like the few remnants of the workers' hostel, are characteristic of the sturdy imported workmanship that made so many of the official South African buildings of those times. Well-baked deeply coloured brickwork, finely crafted bullnose brick window-sills and jamb linings were carefully selected and matched, neatly bonded and finished with crisply struck mortar joints. The stable doors that are still in place, like the rain-water down pipes and other ancillary fitments, are of solid materials which, in turn, are firmly fixed to the adjoining surfaces. One is, clearly, in the presence of confident craftsmanship and appropriate design.

These tough, squat, enduring structures are, in the main, arranged in lengthy terraces. They crouch in rows that face similar ranks of accommodation across open walkways. The powerful focused vistas that result are closed-off by further rows set at right-angles. It is an orderly, blunt, encampment-like layout; one that is consistent with the unpretentious, workaday ethos of the buildings. There is nothing contrived, showy or cute: it is what it is, primarily a series of over 100 adapted mule stables.

Much of the building stock on the site, including parts of the bazaar but, thankfully, not a handsome group of incinerator buildings on the western edge, has been damaged over the years. According to an official site plan, this was variously caused by demolition, fire and – cryptically – 'destruction'. After ages of the customary municipal prevarication, in 1989 the city's Town Planning Committee resolved that the premises, particularly the bazaar, be retained and upgraded.

Work has proceeded since then, often sporadically. Electrical and plumbing installations were improved, roofs, doors, windows and other fittings have been repaired. Unpaved areas, scoured by un-channelled stormwater, have been graded and covered with brick paviours. Some 15 shops gutted by fire were re-built, sheltered eating space was added to the beer-hall and the scrapyard was removed to allow for extensions, especially to the motor repair and panel beating premises.

All this has been carried out in an appropriately vigorous, an unshowy architectural idiom – quite the match of what has for so long existed, been used and occupied, been adapted or converted.

Rod Lloyd, designer of the project, has paid fitting tribute to the ensemble which he found. He has bypassed simple-minded reproduction, arrogant dismissal, feeble pastiche and the other seductive, easily executed architectural formulae presently on offer. He has spurned the 'isms' that currently pose as design novelty. The existing buildings – their construction, layout, the functions and needs they fulfil – have been analysed in an effort to grasp the ideas and practices which underpin them and of like import, there have been attempts to understand how they have been used, re-used, changed over time.

On these bases, he has applied his well-honed design skills to the task of re-interpreting, not replicating the old Mai Mai. What we now have is as respectful of the present as the original complex was of the time when it was built and of those periods during which it was altered. We are able now to 'read' the past and present of the bazaar, to sense its possible futures. We are able to grasp its history as a series of related, interdependent events, not as disconnected episodes or as an emaciated, seemingly seamless continuum.

A rapid verbal journey through the complex might convey something of this.

One's first view is of a massive, arched brickwork gateway set into a similarly powerful and lofty wall – the rear of the most westerly row of shops. The wall, which conceals the bazaar beyond, is punctuated by high, rhythmically positioned ventilation openings, each with a canted corrugated iron sun-cowl. It is pierced by the entry gate, which projects onto the large paved forecourt. There is, about this rugged prospect, a pervasive air of expectation, an enigmatic sense of hidden space waiting to be entered.

Then one passes – one is propelled – into that space, into those jostling walkways between the stables/shops. Here, as on the forecourt, there are interlinked motifs of brick paving; all in restrained circular and rectilineal patterns that mark the pathways between the rows of stalls. The old, the existing, takes precedence; new paving is subtly inserted to reinforce that prerogative and simultaneously, to underscore the compelling vistas which characterise the layout. The architect's touch seems minimal, his intervention muted.

What of the extended beer-hall, those burnt-out shops now rebuilt, the new carpenters' sheds, the as yet unfinished central meeting place, the courtyards, stalls, workshops and other accommodation on the cleared scrapyard? These constitute new incursions into the site: happily, they also constitute architecture.

Lloyd has caught the ambience of old Mai Mai – the emphatic horizontal proportions, the tough textures, the reserved colours, the humane scale – to transpose that complex of attributes to what he has designed. He has added to, enriched and transformed these qualities *via* contemporary processes of construction, by current ways of accommodating spatial usages. He has imbued the new brickwork, timber, corrugated and sheet iron, those quintessentially colonial materials, with timely purpose; using them in a contemporaneous manner; one that is at once commonplace and sensitively inventive.

In his hands, the enlarged bazaar area has been made as receptive to the constantly intriguing activities of repairing, manufacturing, trading, shopping, bargaining, living and enjoying as were, and are, the earlier stalls and walkways.

Long, long ago, in 1624, Henry Wotton coined the aphorism, 'Well building hath three Conditions. Commoditie, Firmenes and Delight.' Mai Mai is well built.

Mai-Mai: cosy, homely, comfy, snug.

Outer, northern Johannesburg – built in the year 2002 to ape the appearances of the so-called British Renaissance (sic), south German pastiche and whatever else takes your fancy.

Corporate giant, design gnat?

Among my assorted architectural adages, the pithy 'architecture is the privilege of the privileged' is probably the preferred. The evidence lies all about us: from cloistered business parks to suave office complexes, smooth shopping malls, elaborate conference centres; from luxurious hotels, marinas, cluster houses and game-park lodges to urbane museums and art galleries, showy suburban villas, smart restaurants. Most or all of which we, the privileged, keep under careful security surveillance.

The wealthy are accommodated ever more affluently, the poor multiply in their ever more makeshift structures. The philosophical mutter reassuringly, 'It was ever thus'.

What, for instance, does the avidly IT, up-to-the-very-minute, decidedly CompuLingo, international accountancy eminence PriceWaterhouseCoopers (PWC) do when its corporate chiefs call for a new headquarters building? This is no passing, no flip matter. We are dealing here with a world-wide consultant to the global mighty: an organisation that offers guidance through the shrouded quandaries of corporate taxation, of massive financial transactions, multi-national mergers, cross-national take-overs – of moneyed manoeuvres beyond my ken. PWC is confidant to the latter-day Riccardi, Strozzi, Grimani, Medici and similarly powerful renaissance conglomerates. Personnel in its upper echelons are the necessary intimates of our present corporate merchant princes.

Although not especially comprehensive, Diane Ghirardo's handbook *Architecture after Modernism* (1996) provides a convenient guide to recent corporate design. She takes one along a trail of familiar acquaintances: Ricardo Bofill's mock-masonry Abraxas Theater, Marne-la-Vallee, 1978 to1982, Michael Graves' contrived Swan Hotel, Disney World, 1987, Arata Isozaki's sleek Team Disney build-

Top to bottom: all sham, all history purloined, all poverty of imagination – the doorways, stairways and courtyard garden 'things' of the PriceWaterhouseCoopers building, a name that, surely, reeks of Elizabethan Britain?

ing in Florida, 1991 and the hi-tech celebrations of Norman Foster's Century Tower, Tokyo, 1991, or Richard Rogers' Lloyd's Building, London, 1978 to 1986.

Then there are those acclaimed foci of corporate urbanity, Canary Wharf, London, 1991, and the largest construction site in Europe, the Potsdamer Platz, Berlin, 1991 onward. In this show-case of competitive pomp, Ghirardo includes such older exemplars as Herman Hertzberger's socially conscious Centraal Beheer building, the Netherlands, 1972. Her admirably illustrated coverage is impressive; it exudes the wealth, power, the design privilege of the topic.

That applies in a different way to her incisive text. Here she all too frequently highlights the part that architects have played in adding force to my terse adage. As well as doing so implicitly, she makes the point explicit in statements such as: 'architects as a rule focus on large, expensive projects, often megaprojects, rather than on the diversity and multiplicity of the experiences of individuals and groups in the social and public spaces of cities and even rural areas.'

More specifically, apropos the two-fold – 'Neubau' and 'Altbau' – building exhibition held in Berlin during the mid-1980s, she wryly notes that, 'Although international architectural magazines published the new buildings, they largely ignored such Altbau projects as garages, nursery schools . . . the reconfiguration of unused factories into youth centers, sports facilities, trade school, recreation and education facilities . . . cultural centers, and old age homes . . . the restructuring of streets, blocks and parks'.

Having drawn attention to that facet of myopic design privilege, Ghirardo broadens her perspective. She argues that, like their architects, 'politicians, developers and real estate moguls [have] dedicated . . . energy to speculating on buildings rather than addressing the plight of the under- and unemployed, to the ever freer movement of capital rather than to the needs of populations in turmoil'.

Whether discussing central Berlin, London's Isle of Dogs, downtown Hong Kong or developments in Orange County, California, she alerts her readers to the profound, seemingly irreconcilable, conflict between what she describes as 'the architects' will to produce a radical urban intervention' and the desires of local community members to retain links to their home city's history, its living past.

Her sustained critique is nothing if not pointed, devastating, always challenging. I am not aware of a similarly measured response, a studied, analytical defence – of the indefensible? – by a member of the design professions, whether a practitioner or, like Ghirardo, an academic.

How, in this ideologically charged context, has the PWC group handled its now completed flagship building (2000)? Apart, that is, from situating it on Eglin Road in Sunninghill, one of Johannesburg's outlying, northern business areas – at what might, in advertising hype, be depicted as the pulse of Africa's entrepreneurial spirit? How, specifically, have their architects approached the overall design?

Not, in my view, especially propitiously.

This, I learnt during a lengthy meeting with the designer, Anton de Jongh of ARC Architects, is probably not unconnected to a conundrum that I pieced together from his responses to my queries. At one point, these centred on the mannered exterior of the building and separately, its internal spaces, decor and furnishings. He described both – the façades and the interiors – as 'British Renaissance', a designation with which I am unfamiliar. Further questions elicited depictions such as 'sort of between Jacobean and Elizabethan' and expressly of the interiors, 'Mackintosh, moving into Arts and Crafts'.

He seemed loth to settle on less vague portrayals, happy to employ a melange of formal terms that range over roughly four centuries of British architectural history.

Subsequent discussion revealed that de Jongh and his colleagues had been schooled in and continued to concur enthusiastically with modern and late modern principles of design. These, though, are firmly at variance with his clients' determined stipulation of a 'period aesthetic'. What, in such potentially fraught circumstances, are architects to do: comply, seek to alter their clients' insistent views, abandon a lucrative, enticing project or . . . what?

This dilemma lies, I suggest, at the core of his enigmatic, consistently evasive responses to my questions. It epitomises, I also suggest, a not uncommon phenomenon; one that appears to have escaped attention in learned architectural publications – whether they deal primarily with historical, aesthetic, social or technical considerations. It is a real but politely ignored issue, not to be raised in genteel discourse.

The building sits on the southern, the convex side of a quarter-circle sweep of road. There is, to the north-east, a transverse roadway that is intended eventually to extend from the undeveloped veld behind the PWC premises to an existing traffic-circle across Eglin Road, at the centre of yet another mock-classical ensemble. This oddly named 'Crescent Axis' is, I was told, evocative of Bath; of, presumably, the Royal Crescent and Brock Street leading to The Circus in that magnificent eighteenth-century city.

Well ... I lived close to and regularly visited Bath over some three decades: the analogy is, if not risible, wholly misplaced. There is no discernible relationship between the urban layout at Sunninghill and the planning of the John Woods, father and son. They, for instance, employed concave crescents to embrace spectacular open spaces, not to ward off heavy traffic by inserted parking lots, strips of supposed 'English formal garden' and obtrusive security fencing. Also neo-classical, the buildings which they erected still remain in mutually resonating harmony; they are not situated in the raucous stylistic miscellany of a burgeoning Johannesburg business suburb, among its visually incompatible office parks.

Neo-classical: at PWC that too is a suspect designation. Using the designer's vast frame of reference – from Elizabethan through to Arts and Crafts – one is struck by many anomalies. Where, as a case in point, the façades of the exemplars he cites are usually, bold, vigorous, innovative, often subtle evocations of preceding classical forms, those of this building are meagre, flaccid to the point of coarseness. That is made explicit by reference to even poorly reproduced photographs of the Bath crescents. Where those façades were intimately linked to the then prevailing methods of construction, of land usage, of rigidly hierarchical lifestyles, the local are limp, mock-relics of long-gone building methods, superseded social orders, ways of living.

Where pilasters rising through two and more storeys were topped by expressive capitals, here they dissolve unmarked. Where the pavilions that closed off lengthy façades protruded confidently, positively, here they do so brusquely, brashly. Where the proportions of window and external door openings were of human scale and order, here they are nondescript, arbitrary. Where stonework was tangible, solid, here one finds 'a simulated rough ... saw-cut sandstone texture'. Where building elements such as string-courses, cornices, pediments and gables were attentively detailed, here they are vestigial, crudely crafted, insipid. And so on, and on: 'The architectural theme of the precinct', members of ARC report, 'has been set as a stylised/modernistic interpretation of the "British Renaissance" period.' It certainly has.

Imperial obeisance lives on, we do as our one-time colonial masters did. But, as witnessed by this building, we do so with far, far less attention to detail, craftsmanship, subtlety – with, incontrovertibly, less panache.

That same tradition lingers internally. The double-volume main entrance lobby is accoutred with a marble-inlay floor, satin-smooth hardwood panelling, plant-boxes, reception desks and full length, moulded timber cladding to its wall-brackets and columns. It is grandly furnished, stylish, self-consciously classy, as are the other lobbies, stairways, reception and conference rooms, circulation areas. People seem to hover, on sound-dampening carpeting, ever so aloofly, discreetly, silently. Struggling to pin-point a likely model, I recalled the hushed, consciously expensive, pretentious, ever so snobbish county 'hostelries' which my wife and I occasionally indulged when travelling in Britain.

Internal space is, unsurprisingly, graded hierarchically; principally by accommodating so-called lower ranks of personnel in open-plan settings and others – of managerial status – in personal, cellular offices. This culminates, on the uppermost level, in spacious private offices to which access is gained through poised personal secretaries. The PWC corporate establishment at work.

That exclusive, privileged occupancy is bolstered by the prestigious main boardroom, a capacious Tudorbethan volume in which the princely furniture and accessories are outshone by a series of timber hammerbeam trusses – echoes of far off medieval castle-halls. Less auspicious, but similarly haughty boardrooms, all seemingly with attached bars, are readily available. In these and like respects – for instance, the four liberally, if conventionally landscaped unroofed atria – the standard of impression management is of a high order. Money talks – clamorously.

Perhaps, though, my most weighty reservation about this and similar corporate structures, whether they are re-cycled classicisms or otherwise, does not lie solely in the matters I have raised here. It springs also from their studied exclusion of public space, of the long cherished architectural tradition of civic responsibility. I recall seeing, and using, seating in sheltered loggias off the streets of old Siena, Warsaw, Bruges ... in Elizabethan cities and county towns across Britain; indeed, throughout medieval and Renaissance Europe. Yet, here at home, even at that elementary level, this and like amenities, such as public drinking fountains, are rare, if at all evident.

The PWC complex is a 'stand alone' structure in a dispersed suburban setting; one that comprises little but similar clones. Most are cut off from the others and the larger world outside, by, it is claimed repeatedly, necessarily conspicuous security fences, boundary walls, electronic devices, awesome warning notices and less frequently, armed patrols. We are all, whether occupants, intruders or security personnel, imprisoned in our fears, barred from planned or spontaneous public activities.

And the ethos of neo-liberal corporatism is anything but civic-minded. To paraphrase Margaret Thatcher's infamous, thoroughly erroneous announcement, 'there is no society, the individual is all'. Urban squares, *piazzas* and similar open spaces are now being or have recently been denuded of their long-established social and political functions. The once politically infused Tudor coffee-houses and their descendants have been swept into privately managed shopping malls or onto the bleak spaces that nestle so awkwardly at the feet of multi-storey blocks. They are protected by closely guarded gates and graffiti-proof surfaces; 'barricaded', as Ghirardo writes, 'against possible urban unrest in deference to middle-class paranoia'. Forbiddingly closed exteriors open – *via* omni-present security checkpoints – onto lavishly appointed interiors.

Our corporate masters – with their overwhelming dedication to white capital – have fled or are fleeing our increasingly African cities. The fear-talk of exclusive bar-counters, club lounges and expense account restaurants is bearing a strange fruit: the shrivelled plums of futile white flight from pulsating black vibrancy; also constant traffic fumes, penetrating noise, follow the rush to sleek business-parks-in-suburbia, as does the hyper-nervous dread of poverty-driven criminal attack – the bogey of genteel cocktail bar, dinner party, cricket pavilion chat.

As this exercise in mutually endorsed fear suggests, electrically charged fences, electronic gates, armed guards in block-houses have not bought peace of mind. Our outer and inner suburbs are fast becoming replicas of central Johannesburg, Durban, Cape Town . . . of downtown everywhere, anywhere. What next on the escape route?

Privatisation is taking command. Public places, where diverse classes and individuals mingle freely, without overt restraint, are becoming rare. Enclosed buildings of the type I have described here are usually governed by elite institutions; organisations whose senior personnel can and do restrict access in accordance with their perceptions of acceptability, desirability, conformity. Architects, clearly, are not initially responsible for this intrusive control; many are, however, ensnared in it. They give it form, shape, substance.

PriceWaterhouseCoopers: at home in the previously unheard of 'British Renaissance'.

Rampant advertising and road signs – try making sense of this from a traffic-bound, moving car: better, perhaps, to be illiterate.

City of clutter – matter out of place

Some areas of Johannesburg, especially the inner city, are distinctly out of favour. There are two commonly accepted bases for the jaundiced repudiations one encounters. The most weighty is fear of seemingly random, often violent crime. The other is, in modish rhyme-talk, grime. This second is usually offered in the teeth of anthropological observations that dirt is best understood as 'matter out of place', that definitions of grime are culture-bound. In mixed cultures like ours, agreement on such descriptions is rare.

When, as occurs frequently, these depictions are yoked – crime and grime – analyses resting on socio-cultural interpretations tend to be ignored. Indignant letters to the press from signatories like 'Apoplectic, Outer-suburbia' are likely to increase rather than dwindle. Forewarned, I shall by-pass that limited, and limiting, view to focus here on a related but less publicised facet of urban clutter.

My gripe lies with what, in the 1940s and 1950s, was described as 'street furniture'. That was when architects attended to such mundane matters as 'street-scape', when, unburdened by postmodern fetishisms, they were concerned with the detailed coherence of their urban surroundings. A glancing revisit may be rewarding.

One can designate two major types of street furniture: municipal litter-bins, bus shelters and similar official objects and, on the other hand, private thingummies like advertising towers, bill-boards or the newly erected timber sentry-boxes at the gates of walled houses. In their inept design, the former make for simmering resentment, while the visually noisy latter are cause for dismay.

Why, if not rooted in bureaucratic indifference, are our public ways so cluttered with unrelated, ill-designed 'things'?. Walk along

Top to bottom: the signs of our times – littering our roads, byways, suburbs, countryside . . . and whatnots.

most streets in central Johannesburg, where they are unmistakable and plentiful. There are obtrusive as well as lurking signals such as the peremptory one-way signs that can confound the most attentive of drivers, the peevish no-parking notices that impel motorists into dank parking garages. There are stern tow-away warnings, rows of coin-hungry parking meters. There is the mushrooming array of traffic lights, known in southern Africa and nowhere else, as robots. Robotic they certainly are, with their mechanically contrived denial of clear runs through successive green lights and for all but the most agile, their alarmingly brief acknowledgement of pedestrians.

What puzzles me is how we make sense of the unruly shambles, especially where it is augmented by screeching advertisements. Over-burdened with information – at once essential, trivial, unwanted and nonsensical – we probably become skilled at selective inattention. In this way, we learn, perhaps, to cope with the incoherence of the city's poorly designed, mostly undesigned street fandangles.

They are everywhere. One may seek a way through pressing pavement crowds from behind the stockades of posts that support miscellaneous traffic notices; one may stumble over unyielding metal boxes that house transformers, telephone or electricity distribution boards. Then there is the melange of litter-bins: squat concrete tubs, stainless steel cones, variously shaped metal canisters and diversely fashioned receptacles on lamp-posts.

All this is, some claim, part of the kaleidoscopic excitement of urban life. Well, there are bustling settings in which these amenities have been ordered differently – in cities like Copenhagen and Barcelona, at the *arts nouveaux* metro-railway entrances of Paris or Vienna. The handsome and co-ordinated – the designed – street furniture of these patently euro-centric examples could well suggest home-grown approaches. They might also re-channel the present pre-occupation with street hawking by furnishing a less inflamed glimpse into what, more pervasively, clutters our city.

Then that chattering admix, advertising. On a late evening visit to the roof-gallery of the Empire State Building, Frank Lloyd Wright is reported to have said, 'It would be magnificent if one couldn't read.' Literacy has become a handicap! How might one escape the pressing commands to spend on this or that? How, in the face of constant commercial injunctions, to relish the gripping pyrotechnics of colour in motion? We are locked in an ethos of spend, spend, spend which has spread from the inner city to suburbia, the outlying townships and beyond.

The strip developments that blight urban US and elsewhere, have taken root, they flourish. That growth is not solely territorial. It is also a matter of size. In advertising lore, bigger is supposedly better – 'Look at me, I'm huge, effective; I'll make somebody special of you'. The next advert must then be larger, more demanding... better. This is a recipe for giantism one for which those swaying, fatuously grinning, jumbo-balloon cartoon figures have become ingredients. What next, what over-sized, raucous banalities are yet to come?

We are frequently reminded that the shopping malls and other now familiar suburban enterprises grew as escapes from inner Johannesburg. Urban cluttet, like the traffic, petrol fumes and jockeying for parking, soon joined the flight. Indeed, the level has intensified. This is especially noticeable on main arterial roadways. Jan Smuts Avenue, particularly the motley strip from Bompas Road to the Randburg border, is a prime instance. Here, designed co-ordination is an alien concept. There is the customary mishmash of bigger, brighter, more electricity-guzzling, multi-coloured lights; of bill-boards signalling over-scaled delights; of bus-shelters that offer little by way of shelter and no seats; of scrambled litter-bins. There is the hodgepodge of placards tied to and fallen from lamp-posts, post-boxes, bollards, trees and other roadside thingamabobs.

See this mess of entangled information for yourself. I find it as incommunicable as it is incommunicative.

Hollywood/Bollywood glamour on Jan Smuts Avenue, Johannesburg – the flashiness of Grosvenor Corner, light fittings by courtesy of Metro Goldwyn Meyer.

Beauty and the beast
— northern Johannesburg

Though battered by loutish Johannesburg architecture, I remain an optimistic dreamer; one who imagines that each new construction site is being prepared for a fresh gem. I pass those dull hoardings and mud-splotched roads in constant expectation: this, I tell myself, calls for attention. So I watch; starting with an ever-hopeful focus on foundation trenches, where I seek hints as to what might emerge.

It is usually a let-down. Take, for instance, Grosvenor Corner at the junction of Jan Smuts and 7th avenues, Parktown North. Initially there was the excitement of bull-dozers razing a large site, of massive machines gorging on walls, concrete slabs, roofs and — alas — trees. Then the pavement hoardings were raised. I studied the notice board to identify the designer of this newly anticipated delight. The names were unfamiliar. But hope lived on as, behind the scaffolding, the structure was given form.

Now there is distress. The building is, to be blunt, gormless. Would that it were like its neighbours, merely mediocre. As the works continued, the numbness intensified. Now that the structure is clad, the design has become patent. It is, in a word, anti-design: an idiosyncratic, discordant curve; yet another pointless display of gimmicky flying beams; glitzy panels to conceal a dreary, irresolute form; contrived, banal roof shapes. At roof level, a make-believe plastic dome is symmetrically flanked by a pair of temporarily moored flying-saucers. It is bereft of vision — intellectual, spatial and aesthetic. No pretensions here of a local, an African architecture.

See this witless assemblage for yourself, if you must. You will weep or laugh and laugh . . . in pain. No need to rush, there are others: opposite the graffiti wall on Jan Smuts Ave.; on the north-west corner of Jan Smuts and Republic; at the south-west corner of Grayston Drive and that boulevard of the bogus, Rivonia Road.

Top to bottom: borrowed glamour writ large, very large — from the dome to the entry announcement, to the presumably whimsical indoor 'objects'.

Inept whimsy is *en vogue*. We are on a roller-coaster to architectural oafishness. If that does not bother you, all right. Enjoy the ride. If you do care, you will need to search out buildings which are not part of this grotesque trip.

For a rewarding start, try the stodgily named new Headquarters for the Pharmaceutical Society of Southern Africa, Southern Gauteng Branch. The building is not stodge. It graces a suburban setting in upmarket Melrose at 52 Glenhove Road. This is a home-grown effort; the architect, Alfio Torrisi, is a Wits graduate who speaks and writes earnestly about discovering 'a South African architecture'. More of that later.

The building, apart from a parking basement for 100 cars, comprises three parts: a glazed atrium or internal street which connects a brick-clad east block and a similar unit to the west. The latter contains the Society's facilities for continuing education – chiefly a 200-person lecture hall – and the other a pharmaceutical museum. Each also accommodates administrative and reception areas.

The link is marked by a soaring, wing-shaped roof that hovers above the anchoring solidity of the two blocks. Its length is emphasised by exposed, rhythmically repetitive steel roof members that end in a startling view: a sweep of blue sky over Killarney golf course to the south, rolling green fairways and close-up, statuesque eucalyptus trees with blackened bark hanging on their grey-white trunks.

Each of the main blocks is carefully proportioned, lovingly detailed and imaginatively set back from busy, narrow Glenhove Road. The façades are handled confidently. Opportunities for distinctively framed views from naturally lit interiors are provided for without the regimented repetition of standard windows that has come to disfigure contemporary, purportedly modern architecture. All elevations, including the largely unseen ones on the east and west boundaries, are lively and varied without affecting the restraint that befits the contained, cubic forms and sturdy construction of the two blocks. This applies also to the façades that line the concourse-like atrium; here too the diverse 'window' openings are ordered by an unobtrusive proportional system.

On detailing, Torrisi and his colleagues have exercised, probably extended their grasp of the craft of architecture. They have done this in a direct, straight-forward manner; such as the way in which they deploy brick patterning around the square 'Hyatt Hotel' openings onto the internal street. There are also more subtle instances. These include the ingenious geometry on the soffit of the bridge over the atrium and the adept details which flow from the directional, the splayed entry ramp that passes across a covered court, through to a terrace facing the golf course. In all this, the designers' skills are matched by those of the building contractors – a congruence which cannot be said of the clients' choice of clumsily inappropriate fixtures in the museum and the bar.

This is a handsome building, a pleasure to walk through, to experience. There are though worries, nagging concerns about practicalities as well as about abstract symbolisms. For example, most of the spaces (those facing north, west and east) are inadequately protected from sustained sun penetration. We found a north-facing office to be unrelentingly sticky on a sunny afternoon in early August. A dismissive reference to faulty air-conditioning compounded the matter. Air-conditioning? Precious resources, expensive installations, pollution; is this how one 'discovers a South African architecture'? And the unsettling, oppressive floor-to-ceiling height of the Society's larger spaces: the museum, two reception areas, the board and committee rooms; is this the locally rooted, humane rationalism to which the architect lays persistent claim?

Comely as it is, the design seems indifferent to, in Torrisi's words, 'contemporary regional South African architecture'. Indeed it might not sit uncomfortably with the far-off work of, amongst other self-declared rationalist architects, the well-known Swiss–Italian Mario Botta.

The issues surrounding contemporary regional architectures are complex. Consensus on even appropriate bases for debate is rare. Torrisi's homily-strewn, his unduly confident references to these often equivocal, certainly unfinished polemics are less than helpful. The comments he made to me, like his writings on the subject, were reductive to the point of being slogans, catch phrases. I recall that throughout our conversation, this multi-faceted topic centred on two unanalysed matters: building materials and climate.

As he wrote in June 1997, for him a regional architecture 'is built out of materials easily available within the place of origin and with the skills available at hand by its builder. It . . . responds to its immediate climatic conditions'. He and his colleagues had, he told me, sought these buzz word objectives by using a reddish face-brick; one that epitomises what he described as 'our dusty South African highveld'. That, presumably, makes for what he had previously depicted as 'a minimalist and pure architectural language which is more understood by our wide spectrum of diverse cultures of our country'.

A final quote: Torrisi calls for 'an archetype that would be homogeneous to our country, culture and landscape . . . as successful as any of the European counterparts we are so mindlessly copying in the absence of an architecture that belongs to us'.

As exemplified by 52 Glenhove Road, his call is, at best, confused. The building is thoroughly, it is fixedly European in derivation, appearance and operation. Good-looking or not, it is far removed from the regional architectures which analytic designers seek. For my part, I am sure that where design of this nature is taken to constitute 'a fresh approach to . . . a South African architecture', there is a long, misdirected haul ahead.

A walk from, in and to trees and bushes – the Pharmaceutical Society, Glenhove Road.

A corner of the competition model – judges' library and northerly tower, a taste of what was then to come and is now (late 2003) nearing completion.

Constitutional matters

South African architects, or a goodly number of them, and competitors from elsewhere have now learnt who is to design the country's Constitutional Court. They, especially the five who were short-listed for the second stage of the recent international competition, have been agog. As have many others. This is the first major building of our newly constituted democracy; it will be an arena for honing the citizenry's rights and obligations.

The choice of site is as propitious as it is imaginative: the Old Fort area in Johannesburg. There, at the disused Awaiting Trial Block, plus spaces to its immediate north and east, the building will sit on the brow of what has become known as Constitution Hill. Later, premises for the Gender and the Human Rights Commissions, the Office of the Public Protector and in the refurbished Old Fort, a Museum of the Constitution will augment this legally entrenched and symbolic home of the freedoms we have won and shall need constantly to defend.

The site and its buildings are packed with historic associations. Built 105 years ago as a military centre (more, some say, to fend off *uitlanders* (foreigners) than to secure Johannesburg), the fort soon became a prison; one which has accommodated upwards of a million people, from political dissenters to pass-law offenders, rapists, murderers and contemporary legislators. Like the adjoining Section 4 cells and the Women's Gaol, it has been a site of abuse, torture, brutality. There is much to recall, much to understand.

It is now to be a place of dignity, of covenanted justice for all: for the poor black people of the city and its outlying townships, for the mixed, forcibly dispersed communities of old Sophiatown, for the white peoples of the comfy suburbs. The court will stand at the very centre of Johannesburg, that populous, industrial, commercial, corporate, political and now constitutional heart of the country.

Top to bottom: three computer-generated perspective views produced for the international competition – two external and an indoor glimpse of the main entry.

The competition has been a two-stage affair. First competitors, international and local, were asked to present conceptual proposals for the building and for developing the entire site. From them, the nine jurors nominated what they considered the most promising five. Their authors were invited to proceed to the second stage, to prepare detailed sketches of their earlier suggestions. That had now occurred. The winner was to proceed with the remaining design work. Construction was to start in 1998 for anticipated completion by late-1999.

Entries to the competition highlighted a range of issues: from the precise location of the new building on this topographically potent site, from its impact on the nearby historic precincts to the many pragmatic factors that attend matters such as parking, accessibility and security, horizontal and vertical circulation, climate control, choice of materials, general services and costs. But the key issues for a building of this public nature are the social meanings likely to be ascribed to it; it's probably contested, seldom static symbolic connotations.

These were alluded to in the competitors' brief. They were asked for 'balance, rationality, security, tranquillity and humanity', for a building of 'distinctive presence . . . dignified and serious'. It should be 'rooted in the South African landscape, both physically and culturally, it should not overemphasise the symbols or vernacular expressions of any section of the South African population, nor be a pastiche of them all'. No easy or readily agreed upon task.

Given the ingrained uncertainty about such matters, one is not surprised to find that, the winner excepted, none of the entries escapes the contemporary dilemmas of universal versus local cultures.

The trumpeted consequences of 'globalisation' are exacting their dues. Local, national or regional, cultures are being brushed aside or have been overwhelmed by the world-wide dominance of bland, corporate, purportedly Western internationalism. Sandwich-spread homogeneity is taking command. Nowhere is this more evident than in urban architecture: our city centres and suburban everywheres become more and more like downtown and outlying anywheres. Both are nowhere. Which built forms, if any, are universal? Which, in our culturally diverse and dynamic local context, is *the* regional or national culture? What are our shared architectural values?

Three of the five finalists address these issues with apparent indifference, especially the Pierce Partnership's submission. This swirling set of quasi-vernacular pavilions has been spread across the site to elbow aside its historic neighbours. Regardless of orientation, heavily colonnaded porticos encircle the pavilions and the sprawling accommodation which links them. That, seemingly, is the designer's attempt to signify the perimeter verandahs of traditional African building. The project is marked by clumsily borrowed symbols of this nature; not least by the roof, a grossly overblown Sotho hat that dominates the court chamber . . . and much else.

This is a further instance of the fake-indigenous structures that threaten to blight the country; of the 'pseudo-authentic game-lodge aesthetic' which the assessors attribute to Pierce's design. Why, one must ask, a specifically Sotho emblem? Where are the evocations of Tswana or Zulu beehive dwellings, of Ndebele or Pedi bilobial homesteads? Why this specific pillaged specimen of our richly pluralist heritage?

Though less facile, that symbolic cop-out is echoed in Justin Snell's entry. Here we venture into current, mostly European efforts to re-instate the architectural forms favoured by the less than democratic, the culturally overbearing elites of ancient Rome. This fashionable dogma arrives in South Africa two and more decades after its noisy advocacy – and decidedly few built instances – by 'rationalist' designers such as Leon Krier or of Robert Delevoy and other doctrinal design theorists. We are in the domain of rigid central and transverse axes, of unbending symmetry, aloof de Chirico-like façades.

We are, Snell announces, at the 'new symbolic heart of the city' where abstraction dominates, the existing buildings, the sloping site, geography and climate. These and more give way to long-gone Olympian frigidity.

Then the like-minded project from Dieter Holm and his associates; a platonically pure spherical court chamber lodged deep in an enveloping, forbidding fortress. This distinctly absolutist symbol is probably as distant as one can get from open, publicly accessible justice.

The remaining unselected entry, from Planning and Design Consultants, epitomises thorough, diligent design without the elusive ingredient of imaginative insight. Despite its emblematic promise – expressly the notion of recessing part of the building into the ramparts of the old fort – the project remains symbolically impoverished: two undistinctive east-west wings with a glazed court chamber projecting northward, disconcertingly like a hilltop surveillance centre. The intended openness of constitutional debate is denied, made banal.

We have been spared all these by a joint project from the OMM Design Workshop of Durban and in Johannesburg, the Urban Solutions group. This, the winning design, is architecture of a high order: subtle symbolism; sensitive planning for local conditions; an empathetic response to a site of unique historic value; a quiet, assured, mature aesthetic. It has, in the assessors' words, 'the potential to express a new architecture which is rooted in the South African landscape, both physically and culturally'.

This clearly is neither local pastiche nor a bland, ill-assimilated import. Quite the contrary, it holds the promise of a fresh, confident southern African architecture. Such design warrants detailed discussion – something which I hope to offer when shortly, the entire competition goes on exhibition.

The Constitutional Court in the making.

No shacks, no squalid make-shift shelters for the unremittingly indigent – new, astonishingly repetitive homes for the poor that overlook and are overlooked by another, middle-class jumble.

Alexandra — an unfulfilled Odyssey

Alexandra Township is quite unlike the other northern suburbs of Johannesburg. Where they are comfy if not wealthy, 'Alex' is uncomfortable, discomforting, impoverished. Its location, services, buildings, the amenities, the very troubled air people breathe, the river that often floods but usually dribbles through their town... all are glaringly suspect if not downright hazardous. Alex is a disgrace; not exactly a show-place for the industrial revolution to which its inhabitants have been exposed for seventy decades and more. Or is it?

My first visits were in the late 1940s when, as a student, I was mesmerised by the township jazz that flourished there, by the men and women who stamped their vigorous idioms on my previously genteel literary consciousness, by the forceful public leaders, like Moses Kotane and J B Marks, who stiffened my vaguely humanist musings. Not least, I was inspired by the everyday life which, as a bystander, I observed: the taut shebeen sociability; the fear and courage induced by wayward police raids; the enduring humour; the fortitude of those boycotting thousands who, twice daily, marched miles to and from work rather than pay peremptorily increased bus-fares.

Since, after 27 years abroad, returning to northerly Johannesburg, I have visited often; most memorably, as a polling assistant during those wondrous days in 1994 when its citizens voted in their first general election. My early impressions remain, at times more intensely. This struck me again when, recently, personnel at the local authority — an architect and a medical officer — invited a colleague and me to join them on a brief tour of the newer buildings in the township.

We entered from the north, via Marlboro Gardens and the industrial estate. It was not a heartening arrival: past regimented sequences of identical match-box houses, each on its tiny, identically bleak plot,

Top to bottom: Alexandra Township, the settled, everyday business of life – from a shopping cubicle to vegetables on sale at a public telephone point and, bottom, an intent youth cycling past an ever-present, loaded washing line.

each as drearily like the drearily similar housing of former administrations. Here and there, we noted small, brave efforts to transform repetitive public housing into individual homes.

We stopped at the new Marlboro clinic, an unpretentious building protected by razor-wire and an almost completed block house, the gate-keeper's lodge. The clinic is simple and straight-forward; an unassuming structure whose architects appear, however, to have been locked in unexamined design decisions: lengthy corridors with rooms on either side, fire-escape doors with steel gates that bar exit or entry, a full-length stoep that relegates the waiting hall to permanent darkness. We, though, were most puzzled by the block house: far removed from the entrance, it seems, perversely, to have been located for surveillance of the heavily inhabited valley to the south. That, of course, is Alex proper; as of old, a weighty blanket of smoke hanging over the people beneath.

Then we drove through Marlboro and its flimsy factory/warehouses, across Vasco da Gama Road with its concrete road barriers and ripped fencing, past more little boxes, mostly old and none too sturdy. We confronted that intractable Alex problem, shack development: shacks at the backs, sides and front yards of houses and shacks on supposedly reserved spaces. Shacks here, there, anywhere; most without open space, water supply, electricity, drainage, garbage disposal. All relying on sewage and storm-water systems installed to accommodate about one-fifth of the present population! Not quite the manicured, greened, sweet smelling northern suburbs.

We crossed Selborne and Rooseveld roads to the hostel zone bordering on that war-torn area of sinister repute, Beirut. Impromptu visits to either of the two huge hostels for males are, we were told, inadvisable. We chose the seemingly less threatening women's accommodation.

At the entrance, a community clinic is being completed. It is a striking building; formally inventive, structurally exciting, innovative. What do local people make of it, what is its symbolism for them? Is that gleaming metal apposite for this setting, or yet another instance of a cultural chasm between building designers and users?.

Across the unmade road, there is an astonishing ensemble of hill-side shacks; almost on top of one another, jostling for light, air, minute patches of open space. The dusty roadway is filled with motor traffic, congested with bustling humanity, with children joyfully at play. People stand, sit, walk, talk animatedly. I am transported to 1946.

We ask for and are given permission to go into the hostel. The architecture is oppressive, hostile, the mark of bureaucratic administration the world over: a ranked series of impassive, barracks-tidy quadrangles surrounded by massive, multi-storey blocks. The fenestration is repetitive, the finishes, materials, stairways and fire-escapes are grim. Women and children watch washing hung to dry on makeshift lines, adolescent boys beg to be photographed, the girls smile shyly, their elders greet and talk to us. The stench of blocked sewers is pervasive, even at a notice recording that this monstrous warehouse 'for surplus' people was opened in 1970 by a ministerial spouse, Mrs Koornhof. She, the architects and contractors share this plaque of shame.

Back in the car, we drive to what, with patent sarcasm, one of our party describes as, 'a sensitive insertion into the fabric of Alex', the new community centre on 8th Avenue. This is another monster; a spread-eagled, almost completed relic of administrative indifference, a crass monument to architectural insensitivity. The building could well be in affluent Sandton: its appearance and facilities are over-lavish, unnecessary; it is far, far too large – without sufficient staff to fill it. Official personnel are searching for possible occupants of whole floors. The aesthetic – if that is the appropriate term – is light-years from Alex.

Thoroughly dispirited, we cross the Jukskei River to a new housing development: more little boxes on minute plots, more inadequate space, more shoddy workmanship, cheap plastic fittings. Alas, more aloof indifference; here relieved, presumably, by the purportedly subtle choice of alternately coloured façades. Precisely what the shack-dwellers and homeless of Alex yearn for.

Later, driving home through suburbia, I realised what, unawares, I had missed earlier: trees, grass and shrubbery. These too have long been denied the people of Alex. Doctors, I am told, bury their mistakes; architects grow creepers. Not in Alexandra.

Shared, social, housing at the eastern edge of central Johannesburg – a quiet hour in the courtyard that, after school hours, throbs with bustling children. The outdoor spaciousness belies the cramped interiors.

Social housing

The notion of social housing has re-surfaced recently. See, as a case in point, the *Reconstruct* supplement of *The Sunday Independent* for 8 November 1998. The concept was especially current immediately prior to the national election of '94, when excited debate on low-cost housing drew public attention to this among other forms of tenure. Now, almost more than a decade later, one might well ask 'what is social housing?' Primarily, it is a matter of tenure.

Four general types of occupancy attract the depiction: tenant-owned companies, co-operative ownership, occupancy through housing associations and rental paid to governmental agencies.

In broad outline, the first type embraces companies, usually Section 21 (non-profit) bodies, under whose aegis prospective occupants build or purchase their homes. Conventionally, householders occupy the dwellings in terms of contracts with these participatory organisations. The latter stipulate and often manage the owner/tenants' tenure. Occupants may own their individual dwellings; access and similar facilities are shared. The second type of tenure, co-operative ownership, differs from this pattern in that the participants own their living accommodation jointly. This may comprise whole high-rise buildings (blocks of flats, converted office buildings) low-rise segments of orthodox townships, grouped dwellings in town-house or cluster home arrangements. Whilst ownership is, by agreement, more or less communal, management is, also more or less, co-operative.

Housing associations follow long-established and far from uniform precedents that were pioneered in Britain, Scandinavia and other, mostly north-European countries. In the main, ownership is vested in separate companies, non-profit and otherwise, that customarily offer accommodation for rental and less often, for purchase. In Sweden, for example, many associations promote joint

Top to bottom: glimpses of an upgraded block – now an unobtrusive haven for its near desperate tenants and, simultaneously, respectful of its dishevelled shebeen and bordello past.

self-build ventures. Generally, householders are tenants, some of whom may become quasi-owners by being appointed to managerial boards.

The fourth general form of tenure, rental from government agencies, has dominated what, in Europe, has been referred to as economic housing since at least the late 1920s. Here, tenants who, less than two decades ago, were offered rights of purchase under Thatcherist governance, occupy housing owned, maintained and administered by government bodies, central or local. This is the well-known for some, the dismissed council housing of 'soft' government.

I was recently shown two social housing projects in Johannesburg, each a hybrid variation of tenure compacts that incorporate elements of the company-owned and the housing association categories. Each is an example of high density, subsidised accommodation; supplemented in this instance, by generous funding from the Flemish Regional Government and the European Union. Financial institutions in South Africa cannot be said to enthuse about, far less to help fund such projects. For them, empathetic investment in a public service of this order remains rhetoric.

Both schemes have the potential of assisting to regenerate the run-down urban areas in which they are located; of revitalising the derelict, often racially undifferentiated central-city sites they occupy. I soon learnt that, while not accommodating the so-called 'poorest of the poor', they do present housing opportunities to people of decidedly modest income. Those two factors alone, namely providing for low-income occupancy and contributing to urban rehabilitation, plus, however chancy and perhaps distant, the possibility of enhancing racial understanding warrant the fitting description, social housing.

We went first to The Oval in Jeppestown, at 27 Browning Street. There, once through a forbidding security gate, past a squat guard box, one is in a series of evocative, delightfully inter-linked closes. People stroll about the site; couples chat, walk hand-in-hand; children play, run, skip across parking areas and driveways; washing flaps on carefully located drying lines; elderly folk sit reading, dozing on intimate patches of lawn. A pair of friends laugh together at an outdoor telephone point, deliveries are made by foot and motor-van. The spaces are animated by people at rest, at work, at play. One is thrust immediately into *Gemütlichkeit* imagery; into the imagined community liveliness, the close-knit companionability of village, *dorp*, small town life. I was guided through domestically scaled, closed-off and open vistas that lead gently from one populated outdoor space to a neighbouring, similarly engaging close. This, assuredly, is humane urban planning – a basis for architecture.

Regrettably, that promise is but barely realised. The scheme comprises 15 three-storey blocks of compactly planned single and two-bedroom flats. Their plaster-finished façades are painted in pastel colours that do little to enhance their po-faced blandness. This, plus the unsubtle fenestration, the machine-pressed and too precisely cut roof tiles, the ungainly external stairways, does not make for uplifting design. Indeed, it is distinctly humdrum. That, unsurprisingly, is not helped by the doubtless welcome but weighty fencing, the stolid entrance gate and gaunt guard-house. It is, though, partially relieved by occasional mature trees and the heartening new planting which already softens the bleak stretches of brick paving to the driveways and parking bays.

Then to 6 Wilhelmina Street, Troyeville; to Douglas Rooms which, with The Oval and three similar developments, provides the Johannesburg Housing Company (JHC) with 482 homes for previously despairing householders. Built almost a century ago, this complex must have been a magnet for sensationalist copywriters. The buildings, originally hostel-type boarding accommodation for miners, had been reduced to broken-down rooming quarters; premises that, with their rough, tough tenantry, housed shebeens, brothels and gambling rooms. Not a quiet moment. The double-storey structures of direct, unforced dignity became dilapidated, rejected hulks.

With a great deal of effort and about two years of negotiation, by June 1998 Douglas Rooms had been handsomely restored. The old hostel became the sturdy, sensitively refurbished relic which now occupies the site. Most of the previous occupants left to make way for social housing tenants; folk who, I was assured, cherish the privacy, order and regular maintenance they enjoy in their Spartan bachelor and studio apartments.

One can scarcely exaggerate the demand: accommodation vacated on a morning is, I was told, rarely unoccupied by the evening of the same day. Across its five properties, JHC Limited has experienced few abusive attacks by or on tenants, less than five per cent rental arrears and little by way of serious maintenance costs. The company's target is 2 000 homes within three years.

The appalling, overwhelming anonymity of Johannesburg International Airport – no place for loving hello's and tearful farewells? Comfy, homely, cosy?

Other-directed Johannesburg

Cities are complex intersections of hopes, fears, dilemmas, contradictions. Multi-layered and multi-faceted, they direct attention to futures and pasts. They are expressions of imaginary geographies, the geography of imagination. They are tapestry-like fragments of past, present and anticipated events. It is in them, in day-to-day metropolitan life, that the mainly unknown desires of anonymous strangers mingle.

Cities though, are not passive, neutral texts; unwitting witnesses to the passage of biographical and historical time. In their physicality they are real, tangible entities. Like other products of social labour, they demand that we humans interpret them, that we excavate beneath their surfaces. Like other cultural phenomena, they are marked by differential access to resources, to the power commanding those resources.

Accordingly, this brief, exploratory foray into Johannesburg is not an attempt to present a realist or comprehensive picture of the city. Such a goal is, surely, as absurd as it is unrealisable. My little story is but one of many possible readings: Johannesburg, a locus of real and imaginary fears, a city as it might be, a city as it never was.

Today the metropolis sits on the edge of unprecedented, far-reaching social transformation, of a revolution in the previously taken for granted facets of its inhabitants' daily lives. It is this, above all else, that colours the perceptions of those who live in it and those who would write about it.

To start at a common beginning for newcomers: a flight into the so-called gateway of Africa from . . . anywhere. Johannesburg Airport fits readily into what the urban anthropologist Marc Auge describes as a non-place. Here, individual identity is confirmed only on entry or exit; each a rite of passage to the anonymity of global

Top to bottom: the whole place oozes humanity, care, fellowship – well, is it not obvious?

transaction and dislocation. Each passage is an implicit licence to enter what Auge refers to as 'world wide consumption space . . . non-place'. There 'alone, but one of many, the user is in contractual relations with the powers that govern it . . . the passenger accedes to his [sic] anonymity only when he has given proof of his identity . . . no individualisation, no right to anonymity, without identity checks'.

Curiously, Auge has little to say about the architecture of such places. Yet the buildings are potent material expressions of an otherwise abstract, de-materialised global market. Auge suggests that 'the traveller's space may . . . be the archetype of *non place*'. Johannesburg International Airport certainly communicates its global affiliations. This occurs externally through a crass incorporation of the US architectural guru Robert Venturi's internationally advocated fake, free-standing fronts to buildings and internally, through replicated, readily recognisable transcontinental spaces which, here, are decorated with bland African 'features'.

This is an architecture that discloses by erasure: history has been abolished, locality expelled. An entire sub-continent has been forgotten, lost in the familiar conventions of international corporate imagery — an architectural equivalent of the everbenign Teletubbies? In compensation, there is a diversionary offering to the safely adventuresome: splashes of applied local scenery, the wilderness, animals, 'natives' in costume. The life of the region has been expunged, in thrall to a monument of consumerism.

Johannesburg International is effectively cleansed of locality, of architectural sense of place. Here only one language is spoken, the global discourse of consumption. Travellers are assured — by the banal exterior, the dutifully familiar assembly of internal lobbies and waiting areas — that they remain in the comforting embrace of worldwide finance. Once that has been established, they may be let loose on the suitably tamed unfamiliar, the exotic, the foreign.

So one is readied for the suave bars, eateries and the 'duty free', where sanitised local baubles are on sale, along with the customary transnational goodies: 'a foreigner lost in a country he [sic] does not know . . . falls with relief on products validated by multinational brand names' (Auge).

In this context, the paradox of Johannesburg, of South Africa, is that for a minority of citizens, chiefly the affluent and white, non-places are where they have come to feel at home, snug. The comfy burghers of Egoli have unsurpassed experience of moving through, of living in non-places. Even a short walk in the central area undermines one's sense of the real, defies one's conception of locality, refuses efforts to sense, to associate with the region, with its peoples.

And when one turns to embrace the majority life on the streets, one turns also from the architecture. One then leaves behind these crass, strained imitations of north European or US modernity. Beyond the plush lobbies and foyers of the citadels of this hastily evacuating corporate centre, one moves into pulsating public realms.

The attractions, for finance capital, of the city's exclusive northern suburbs and newly established municipalities, like, pre-eminently, Sandton, lie in the perceived, the temporary absence of the vibrant street life that now characterises downtown Egoli. That is predominantly black Africa: bustling, open, noisy, good natured, potentially disorderly, mostly beyond white control, not politely genteel, definitely not right.

But that, for these and allied reasons, remains deeply suspect to those who are steeped in or seek entry to the supposedly fastidious culture of corporate capital. The overwhelming white-owned buildings are quite the reverse: aseptic modern, sleek postmodern, ostentatiously draped in recycled neo-neo-classical borrowings, in filched 'historical' drag.

The Canadian urbanist J B Jackson depicted this as 'other-directed architecture'. Developing that telling notion, Edward Relph wrote of 'architecture which is deliberately directed towards outsiders, spectators, passers-by and above all, consumers. The total effect of such an architecture is the creation of other-directed places which suggest almost nothing of the people living and working in them.' In a word, Johannesburg.

Downtown or in the suburbs, there is to be sure social – personal and public – violence. In which contemporary metropolis is this unknown? The especially intense violation, however, lies in the warmly humane conviviality which is denied by these alienated, alienating celebrations of concrete, of steel, glass, plastic; of massive, worldwide, investment. It is all remarkably unremarkable. One has seen it, felt it, experienced it before. Yet one has seen, experienced, nothing.

Showy, smart Sandton, Morningside, Rosebank . . . new 'nodes' like Sunninghill, we are firmly in non-places, we are enveloped by other-directed architectures.

Stolen kerb-sides – attractive but contemptuous of pedestrians, oblivious to blind people, careless of public space.

All that glitters is Jo'burg

Johannesburg, our very own fortress city, is said to be in transition. Its devout body of officials is hard at work, patently for our benefit. Not all citizens are convinced, though. Sensing possible futures is not especially comforting for those whose hopes rest in dreams of an apartheid past, those who long for continuing white supremacy, cleansed now of its more evident atrocities.

In those dystopias there was and is, reason enough to bring on the evident paraphernalia of a fort-like settlement: razor wire fences, electrified and spiked walls, salivating guard-dogs, gun and walkie-talkie bedecked security guards, police sirens, steel gates, hefty burglar-barring . . . . . the ubiquitous Immediate Armed Response signs that decorate the CBD and its suburbs.

Consider first the central area, that paradigm of non-place, the 'colonial capitalist city' which the local architectural historian Clive Chipkin depicts as a 'dustbin of discarded styles'. The shifts in style from, say, the imperial conceits of Herbert Baker (eg, the Supreme Court, Pritchard Street) through the rentier towers of the 1950s and 1960s (eg, Medical Centre, Bree Street) to the brash postmodern isms of the 1980s and 1990s (evenly spread, like anchovy paste) suggest something more than a profession anxiously keeping up with 'overseas'.

On the one hand, here is an up-to-the-moment architecture whose owners and designers attempt consciously to position the city in the vaunted global economy, their abstract, international metropolitan culture. On the other, the glitzy buildings speak to a population which is absent; they speak of an other-directed place which few members of that departing group now inhabit. Except under necessity, most affluent citizens avoid the central city due, perhaps to insufficient policing, security guards and razor wire for comfort. To whom, then, might this architecture speak? Of what does it speak?

Top to bottom: public theft – ubiquitous, supremely arrogant.

Post-modern design is rooted in commercial vernaculars, it comprises purportedly popular façades borrowed, pillaged in the main from western European traditions. Here, in Johannesburg, this shallow appeal to crass populism is unsustainable; there are, after all, few Doric colonnades, Palladian refinements, Baroque palaces in Soweto. As the overwhelmingly black citizens of Johannesburg busy themselves in the metropolis, one is hard-put to imagine them lamenting the lost city of Romulus and Remus. Spartacus, though, might get a look in.

Of course architectural postmodernity in Johannesburg, like its modernist predecessors, is cosily familiar to transnational corporate executives and their ilk. For most others, it is the product of a disordered sensibility; one rooted in an historically and culturally dislocated imagination. The veneered screens of these decorated sky-scrapers correspond to the thin ideology which they embody; the no longer tenable conceits of the 'civilising' lords of the continent.

Here in South Africa we cannot simply dispose of this suspect building stock. These shams are, quite simply, part of our built capital. Designed with small regard to climate or a social realm that is not enveloped in corporate control, they must provide a basis for reconstructing the city. However unpropitious, they constitute a goodly proportion of the concrete foundations for civil society; a society in which civic dignity begins in the streets, in which social respect is not something dispensed from boardrooms or dispersed by CS gas.

'We must kill the street' – this, Le Corbusier's battle cry of the late 1920s, was symptomatic of the master designer's preoccupation with orderly social hygiene. Now, some eighty years later in far-off Johannesburg, it has become the *leitmotiv* of suburban life. Here, in the residential heartlands of the city, a penitentiary, albeit affluent, existence is enacted.

Fear has been transposed to an aesthetic principle. The rich gardens policing housefronts in, for instance, Sandringham, Dunkeld, and Houghton seduce a naive eye; until one realises that pedestrians have been forced into the gutters. Sidewalk pavements have, *sans* apology, been appropriated for carefully tended gardens. Social status is marked by the obtrusively broadcast promise of rapid armed response to those who might trespass on the ubiquitous signs which, with forbidding boundary walls, pass for street furniture.

Behind those walls – their razor-wire and/or electrified copings – some are at home. Here, for fear of real and imagined threats of violence, few openly admit to being home. Their terrors are echoed and amplified in the local evening newspaper, *The Star*, which provides a 'crime count' for troubled citizens. Daily it carries especially unpleasant as well as relatively minor incidents to furnish evidence that life was safer when violence was the prerogative of the apartheid state, when 'respectable' folk could go about their lives unmolested, untroubled. Those on either side of the fortifications perceive and experience themselves as threatened and threatening. Public space has been expunged, overcome by private fear.

Of late, there has been much perturbation about fencing off whole suburbs or, at minimum, entire residential streets. So, one is hardly surprised to encounter road-side signs such as that on Woodside Avenue, Sandton: 'Warning Temporary Security Control Ahead', 'Armed Response', 'A Sandton Precinct Project'. The notice announces a control boom, armed guards and sentry-box. And, on the neighbouring Tweejongegezellen Street, there is a stout metal fence, gate and vehicle crash-barrier, plus high-level television camera and electronic gate for acceptable pedestrians.

Each of these installations restricts public access on a public roadway. Each probably does so in defiance of the constitution: there is little doubt that, were it called on, the constitutional court would rule against private roadblocks that violate free public movement.

The wealthy no longer rely on the state to police and protect their homes; they pay private agencies for these supposedly public, communal services. Privatisation takes command. In a country hungry for employment, we have fallen haplessly on that universally desired goal: we are on the move in one field at least – paid-up security.

And move it seems to be. Some, the suppliers, claim that where installed security measures reduce crime by up to seventy, even eighty per cent. Other, less directly interested parties, argue that such shifts as do occur are mere displacement: criminals turn to less affluent districts, to unprotected neighbourhoods. In each instance the retreat from civic responsibility into vigilante-type institutions accelerates.

Coldly bleak, decidedly unwelcome, minuscule interiors – low-income housing at its very worst, take it or leave it.

Housing – nothing learnt, nothing forgotten?

Thirty or so years ago Pete Seeger turned an evocative ditty into an international hit, 'Little boxes on the hillside, little boxes made of ticky-tacky. Little boxes, little boxes, little boxes all the same'. Could he have envisaged the aesthetics of local low-cost housing? The festering crises of South African housing seem inescapable. We, the comfortably accommodated, are reminded constantly of the deprivations others suffer. Those 'others' need no cues: they live the everyday anguish, the affronts of inadequate shelter, often of outright homelessness.

Thankfully, our legislators and senators are not blind to these tragedies, or are they? In March 1996 members of the relevant committees from each chamber held public hearings on the Housing White Paper, then about a year old. Their report can still be consulted. Its candid appraisals of the lingering problems are as welcome as are its incisive recommendations.

Both – the entangled realities and the proposals – are wide-ranging. They cover matters such as land, housing finance, urban sprawl and much else. All these warrant explicit attention. Most however fall beyond the scope of this comment. I will focus on the issue depicted in the report as 'the kind of product produced and the question of minimum standards'.

Buoyed by the manifest promise of the new document, I gladly accepted a colleague's invitation to visit two projects in that vast housing area south of Johannesburg. We sought to test on the ground what we had read in the report. My euphoria was soon dispelled, replaced by dismay.

We drove first to Devland, off the Golden Highway. There are no nuggets among these sometimes pastel-shaded boxes: 'There's a green one, and a pink one, and a blue one, and a yellow one . . . and they all look just the same.'

Top to bottom: three more views – variations on the theme, take it or leave it.

93

I found this stark development dismal: no schools, churches, shops; no made-up roads, pavements, street lights; no shrubs, trees, parks. Nothing but rock-strewn veld, hard-baked earth, dust (lots of that), clinging blackjacks . . . and ticky-tacky. People, in this wall-to-wall bleakness 'get put in little boxes, all the same!' We circled the site searching for structures that might engage one's social and visual attention. There are none save the street hawkers' familiar plastic-sheeted shelters: splashes of colour, of life.

We stopped to walk, camera-laden, to a group of houses. Most were occupied, others were still under construction. Children eager to be caught by our cameras greeted us, as did the adults in and about the buildings. After explaining our presence as architects, we were invited with grave courtesy into two homes. There are, we learnt, four sizes: an all-purpose space plus 'bathroom' (built-in toilet pan but no bath or wash-basin); two and three-roomed houses also with incomplete bathrooms; then, and the largest, two bedrooms, a lounge, kitchen recess and bathroom. All but the latter are constructed so that they can readily be extended. We were told that, depending on individual circumstances, the occupants had payed from R17 150 (including R15 000 subsidy) for the smallest to about R39 000 for the larger dwelling.

The houses stand on concrete surface beds. Each is built of single-leaf cement blocks; each is roofed with asbestos cement sheeting fixed to rafters that rest on a central tie-beam. The finishings are as elementary as the construction: no flooring materials, skirtings, ceilings or similar finesses. The smaller houses are almost 20 square metres in area, the larger about 63 square metres overall. Both are small. Filled with everyday furniture, the crabbed interiors are difficult to use effectively. We were unable to photograph them adequately, to record their occupants' struggles to transform ticky-tacky into homes. The aesthetic is one of pared-down, reductive functionality. It represents a minimum level of spatial, constructional and finishing standards.

The houses, each on its small plot, are set in tightly packed ranks that spread across the veld on a strictly rectangular pattern; not even a nod toward crescent, serpentine or circus design. Later I noticed a phrase on the sleeve of my battered Pete Seeger record 'endless rows of identical houses . . . if you want it cheap, take it like I make it – rectangular'. In this unbending layout, one is struck by the discordant imagery, by the pervasive aesthetic of regimented domesticity.

Feeling decidedly flat, we left for the south-western edge of Soweto, to our next venue. Compared with what we had come from, this can be said to be up-market. The houses are disposed in conventional suburban blocks; each is on its own plot, the main rooms face the public thoroughfare. Where the other development is a systematised encampment, this is an *ersatz* suburb. Here too we saw none of the amenities – places of worship, community halls, shops, post offices and the like – that characterise suburban life elsewhere. This is yet another dormitory site; far removed from the city, from cultural and social meeting points and – above all – from opportunities for employment. It is, in this sense, yet another apartheid settlement.

The house into which we were invited contains three small, tiny bedrooms (space only for a double-bed and wardrobe in the largest of these), a bathroom, a kitchen recess/entrance and a dining/sitting room. An alcove in the latter extends marginally beyond the rectangular perimeter of the building. The owner told us that of the R85 000 overall payment due for the house, he meets about R1 600 each month. More than half of that is a subsidy from his employer. He is, he added, straining to maintain his contribution: every month he must pay a similar amount for fares to and from work and his eldest child's distant school. The consequences of South African spatial segregation live on.

In sum: we found minimally larger and better finished houses than those at Devland. We found fitted kitchens and bathrooms, floor tiles, ceilings, tile roofs; externally, there are fitfully planted patches of lawn and, we were told, three saplings per plot. Not least, there are those projecting alcoves with their doll-house roofs, banal efforts to relieve the ticky-tacky.

This attempt to make little boxes into something other will, I suspect, be my most lasting memory of the development. It is a scrimpy, inept borrowing in scale, form and purpose from expansive inner-suburban houses; one of their many implanted 'features', themselves often pretentious relics of baronial manor houses.

A few days later I called on friends in Dube, Soweto. They live in a Type NE 51/9 house, a product of the massive official building programmes that occurred during the 1950s and 1960s. Intended for seven or eight people, it comprises two bedrooms, a living/sleeping space, a kitchen/dining area and a bathroom. All this is accommodated in an overall area of 56 square metres. The construction and the finishings are not unlike those at the two contemporary projects which my colleague and I had visited. More significantly, the persistent formula of a single house per plot is also evident here: no cluster, terrace, courtyard or other forms of low-rise-high-density housing; nothing learnt from the inventive *Seidlunge* of central Europe or, in southern Africa, from the traditional models of grouped housing with shared open space.

Excepting the additional seven square metres, little seems to have changed over the past four decades. Are we, like Spike Milligan in his unforgettable Goon Show lament, 'walking backwards to Christmas' – or, unseeingly, into the future?

World-wide Hyatt on Oxford Road, Rosebank, Johannesburg – a great dollop of costly, international urbanity – stately, good-looking but distinctly not African, patently elsewhere.

The Hyatt touch
— blue chip Africa in Rosebank

It is unnerving. The smooth, ever ready charm; the switched on, unstinted smiles that mark visits to the Park Hyatt hotel in Rosebank. 'Have a great day' – repeatedly. Then the rapt tone of unrestrained self-admiration in the official bulletins I was given.

Unused to such dulcet tourist speak, agape at the supposedly ethnic decor, flustered by incessant cordiality, I reached hastily for support. Ah! that cliché of architectural comment, the curate's egg: good in parts, bad in parts.

The tourist-speak is impressive and essential for effective hotel service. The 244 spacious, well furnished, obviously liveable bed rooms and *en suite* bathrooms are equipped with solid, finely crafted, handsome fittings. As, of course, are the larger executive 'guest rooms' and an extensive Presidential Suite. There is a variety of other, also richly finished, admirably crafted facilities: such as the ballroom, a restaurant, a bar room, conference suites, a roof top gymnasium and heated, outdoor swimming pool. All this is accessible from the sumptuously decorated entrance lobby and adjacent atrium, which lead to an indigenously landscaped garden court.

There are three basement levels. They accommodate parking for some 500 cars and a labyrinth of ocean liner like service elements: kitchens, specialist food preparation rooms, staff dining, workshops, housekeeper's stores, refrigeration rooms and plant rooms ... These, I learnt, were planned in the US by appropriately experienced personnel at the Hyatt Technical Services Division. As far as I could gauge from a fleeting tour of this back stage area, the staff use and expect to continue using the hotel and its specialist equipment efficiently and comfortably. They said so, briefly but explicitly.

In designer jargon, the building 'works'. It is decidedly, smoothly functional. This standard of effective day to day operation is evi-

Top to bottom: the Hyatt – an alien citadel from whatever perspective.

denced elsewhere; expressly in the skilful architectural detailing. In that sense too, the building works: the design as well as the for-once-careful workmanship are fitting, crisp. This is a thoroughly conceived and assembled artefact. Regrettably, a rarity in South African architecture. To visit; above all, attentively to experience this corner of Oxford Road and Bierman Avenue is to appreciate the potential of thoughtfully selected building materials, precise detailing, fine construction.

I urge readers to make such a call, not least to see the lively batik work hung on walls throughout the public spaces.

Back to that curate's egg; to the suspect qualities of this, the first Hyatt sortie into southern Africa. We turn now to more subtle, shadowy, but nonetheless central aspects of buildings: the social meanings that are ascribed to them, the symbolic significance with which they are customarily associated.

On one issue, the architect, those puffed up Hyatt notices, and much of the professional comment in the local architectural press seem agreed – this is 'contemporary African design'. The building resonates, one is told, with its geographic and cultural location; from the distinctively 'massive African feeling' of the flush jointed external brickwork, to the manner in which 'African light explodes into and from the entrance area' and to the internal decor, 'gold leaf and gold tiling . . . extensive use of gold is a direct reference to the history of Johannesburg'.

These claims merit attention. Consider first the certainly massive, square windowed façades African? Well . . . hardly. That architectural star, the Italian neo-rationalist Aldo Rossi, appears to have felt his earlier, similar treatment appropriate for northern Italy – as at an apartment building in the Gallaratese Quarter, Milan, 1969 and especially at the Cemetery of San Cataldo, Modena, 1976. Indeed, in an intellectually dense exegesis, Rossi notes that the latter grew from a specific context of time and place: from his thoughts in hospital on recovering from spinal injuries, 'the arrangement of monumental elements and ossuaries . . . can be considered analogous in form to the human spinal column'. In his reflections on 'the architecture of death', he linked the empty, square shaped 'windows' of the cemetery project to anguished recollections of the Holocaust. Rosebank, Johannesburg, Africa? A posh tourist hotel?

Then the protruding drum like form of the restaurant and the similar, glazed, suggestion at that awkward link to the existing Firs shopping mall. Out of Africa? Possibly, but also not far removed from the formal, specifically regional, preoccupations of Mario Botta, a Swiss neo-rationalist architect. That 'African feeling' has, one gathers, thrust deep into Europe, as far as the Alpine foothills.

No doubt, visitors to the building will respond personally to those purportedly explosive bursts of African light at the entrance to Park Hyatt. I appear to lack the distinctive continental sensitivity to grasp this.

And the 'African' decor, gold leafed and otherwise; that 'blend of contemporary ethnic touches and classical style, the overall feel being understated elegance'. All this, including the furniture, fittings, wall coverings, carpets . . . staff uniforms, was designed in Atlanta, Georgia. Clearly, a renowned centre of African studies? Here ethnicity appears to comprise 'unusual beadwork combined with porcupine quills', plastered surfaces that simulate what must, one imagines, be east African wood carving and abstract geometric patterns which could well have been adapted from groupings as diverse as the Maori and the Inuit peoples. While the elegance – understated of course – is not the full blown, the cloying kitsch of our celebrated Lost City, the affinities can scarcely be overlooked.

Quests for local identities in southern African architectures call, I fear, on matters more intractable – more profound – than these formal borrowings, fanciful descriptions and . . . porcupine quills. This is readily exemplified by the tough minded reaching for regional meaning and form in the intellectually committed, the solidly searching work of, among others, Jose Forjaz, Roelof Uytenbogaardt, Rodney Harber, Dennis Claude. That, though, is another discussion.

Why the elevated blather about Africa? Surely not, in this grave, even earnest design, that flip response 'it's fantasy, just fun'. Rather, I suggest, a supposedly necessary admix of titillating exoticism for a much travelled, sophisticated, probably jaded, international clientele. Presumably, Hyatt 'guests' are expected and expect to be comforted by familiar, costly surroundings; by settings with, moreover, a deft touch of the alien, with a muted frisson of the outlandish.

So, this secured citadel-like building – the modelled entrance canopy its symbolic drawbridge? – cossets visitors between their periodic forays into dark Africa. Wrapped in the protective, the hard L shape wings on the two streets, there's the sheltered calm of a serene garden court. Safe, snug familiarity plus a hint of brazen exposure. Intended, in the words of a Hyatt document, 'to attract blue chip business. We are confident that Johannesburg is ready for a "boutique" style hotel, particularly suited to the Continental ambience of the Rosebank area.' Away but not too far from home. Intimate and ever so slightly chancy, daring. Here too the architects have met their brief, they have designed a building that, surely, 'works'.

In the process, Africa has been commercialised; reduced to and packaged as a commodity.

My often dismissive comment apart, Park Hyatt will probably be viewed as a significant step in the developing story of South African architecture. This, after all, is not another post modern hulk of neo classicism, of Tudor bethan, of Neo-Georgian, of revived Victoriana . . . of transposed Etruscan. For which, much thanks. To the north-west, diagonally opposite the hotel, there is just such an instance; one of the more addled, crass, derisible of these ubiquitous 'things'. The Hyatt is something quite other: a meticulously planned, thoughtfully considered and executed modern building. It bears the marks, the love of designing hands. It is, that is to say, a place of architecture.

Yet it shares in, contributes to, even exacerbates the blockage at the core of local design endeavours, forging South African architectural identities. A task which, on the northern rim of the continent, the Egyptian architect Hassan Fathy and his colleagues have confronted brilliantly.

At Park Hyatt, as in the surrounding eclectic pastiche, one's attention is held by the aesthetic of applied appearance. That is where design energy has been focused. In this medley of commandeered surfaces, the questions press. Whose meanings, whose symbols are being invoked? Whose nostalgia is being gratified, whose roots are being honoured? Despite, indeed as a consequence of the fixedly surface evocations of Africa, these are located beyond this continent; in northern, in European cultures. The flaccid African allusions result in an aesthetic of not-Africa.

This is an architecture of alienated experience, a symbolic expression of not belonging. For the majority it is, quite simply, an imposed, an imported aesthetic. To the minority, visitors or not, the building says we are not from here but from elsewhere. Maybe not. Perhaps it says you – that majority, that socially invisible Other – are not from here but from elsewhere: we have wrested this aesthetic from our nostalgic elsewheres. *There* is now *here*, we have made it so.

Such are the losses of place, of identity, that underpin our fantastic architectures, or rather our architectures of displaced fantasy. The debris of apartheid still jangles, commandingly, in our minds – and in our buildings.

Architectures of alienated nostalgia

The picture becomes yet more murky, to now highlight – there is an apt oxymoron – what has become the most abject of architectural phenomena in Johannesburg: recycled neo-classicisms, internal and external façades looted from histories which are located anywhere, everywhere. Bereft of design imagination, lost in shallow, unstudied formalisms, ever ready to filch from abroad, our brave architects reach imprudently, ignorantly for forms that might, they claim, convince. At whom is this directed – a public already floating in fakery?

Architecture becomes abstracted stage design; the sets range from ancient Rome to modish *moderne*. All is up for grabs. In this land the sham is king, queen, prince regent, the whole damn court.

Incongruous incongruity – a baronial home in sunny Cornwall – just a kilometre or two from Irene, north of Johannes

Cornwall on the Highveld

Though tucked away beyond south-west England, the Duchy of Cornwall is seldom far from wider notice. That is ensured by the presence of its eminently newsworthy Duke, the long-in-waiting future monarch Charles Windsor. His county has now, surely unwittingly, garnered additional attention. It has spawned an offspring near our own village of Irene, one-time home to the locally nurtured guru Jan Smuts. The Field Marshall's memorial obelisk on a neighbouring *kopje* overlooks a swanky new residential development-in-the-making, Cornwall Hill Country Estate.

A colleague, an architect who shares my disquiet about the gaucheries that currently pass for much building design, introduced me to the site. He showed me what already exists and is presently under construction. Each is a boorish instance of the coarse, quick-fix architecture that sprawls across Johannesburg's northern suburbs. They are only exceptional in their unfathomable depths of social and aesthetic insensitivity.

Cornwall Hill is, then, but one of many. For me, its specific offence is that it despoils a stretch of veld I have known and loved since my schoolboy hiking and cycling explorations. Its churlishness reaches into cherished memories, there to arouse a dismay which focuses on the all too evident incongruity of the estate layout and relentless profligacy of its pretentious homes. As we passed these overwrought buildings, I tried in vain to rid my mind of dimly recalled lines from D H Lawrence's bitter poem 'How beastly is the bourgeois'. Beastly, Lawrence stressed, is as beastly does.

We drove first past the select private school that abuts the Cornwall Hill site on Nellmapius Drive, Irene. Pupils can, if they manage to breach the overbearing demand for enrollment, start in the lower grades and proceed through to their A-levels; many par-

Top to bottom: scenes of rustic, Celtic grandeur at Cornwall Hill Country Estate, Gauteng – we strain to replicate any nostalgia, from Tuscany to Provence, to Cornwall.

ents, apparently, seek preparation for 'varsity entry' abroad. This is, clearly, not a place for scions of the *hoi polloi*.

The buildings are indeterminate snapshots, faint echoes of vaguely late nineteenth-century British grammar schools: red brick walls, occasional gables, lush gardens, immaculate sports fields. I was inescapably reminded of the self-evidently posh preparatory and upper echelon institutions of the comfy English home counties. Well . . . almost. The local sky is too blue, the veld a dusty late-summer khaki, the parental motor-cars gaudy in their noisy opulence. Cornwall?

Then to more displaced images. We skirted a mock English garden pavilion – the security lodge – to reach an Estate Office of faintly Georgian ilk. There we found a pamphlet carrying the promotional enticement, 'estate living with old values', a set of 'architectural guidelines' and a pictorial display. The latter comprises scenic views of ye olde country homes: flower-bedecked medieval houses; spruce eighteenth-century harbour and river-side row houses; classically clad villas in verdant, expensively tended grounds . . . and more of the imported same. All decidedly elsewhere, not on our shaggy highveld.

The rambling guidelines are no less revealing. They proclaim concocted stylisms from a distant never-never Noddy land. Or, they emphasise images from 'the Irene Village and adjacent farming community'. These we are expected to take at face value; concrete examples are not cited. The guidelines have, one notes 'been developed to protect and maintain the unique environmental and physical attributes of a historical site and river . . . [they] are characterised by simplicity, geometric and non-symmetrical order, harmony and visual continuity . . . set against a . . . landscape of lawns, trees and stables'. A gentrified Cornwall?

That trumpeted 'protection' has ripped history, along with trees and similar 'physical attributes' – tough highveld grasses, shrubbery and rock outcrops – from what was a magnificent site. This and more, has been replaced by sub-suburban 'order': alien saplings, trimmed shrubs and smaller plants, manicured lawns, modish gazebos, shimmering swimming pools, stables, equestrian exercise yards, substantial 'staff accommodation' and not least, a rash of outlandishly ostentatious 'county seats'.

All building on the site is governed by specified 'design criteria'. They, we are told, are enforced by a quaintly named 'Aesthetical Committee', the members of which have, I imagine, endorsed the frequent departures from the document's often ambiguously phrased strictures.

Once through the tight security ring, one is in a quite unremarkable Johannesburg housing layout. Single plots for individual dwellings are accessible from roadways that deny the contoured terrain. There are no terrace houses, clusters, squares, open commons; no parades of local shops, churches, community halls . . . libraries. All is strictly private; certainly no provision for communal, for public life. There are, though, distinct Celtic references: street names that cite Land's End, Camelford, St Ives and that enduring Cornish connection, Aloe Koppie.

Then the houses, the buildings of which one might, Cornish fashion of course, say 'my home is my castle'. Plenty of that, indeed, one hundred per cent. This is where Cornwall Hill comes into its chic, country estate own.

Here the underlying narcissism of conspicuous consumption is sovereign. An array of uninhibited, pompous, puffed-up façades – medleys of imported, randomly snatched architectural features – announce that the owners, through their architects, have worked hard at their material achievements. They have arrived, and are eager to exhibit that presence.

We found a range of Gone-with-the-Wind, decidedly un-heavenly mansions. Was that – surely not – Rhett Butler loudly cornering a sleek Alfa Romeo? We stopped in awe of bogus Teutonic turrets and towers; abstracted, apparently, from their Rhineland origins. We gasped at tall, purportedly Tudor windows to grand stairways behind. Is that a Gothic Revival corner, Augustus Pugin at it again? Note those buttresses, that stretch of cottage windows under the eaves – C F A Voysey still at work . . . on Sesmyl Spruit? ('Six-mile Creek').

While on site, one is repeatedly alerted to inept touches of Charles Rennie Mackintosh, Philip Webb, W R Lethaby, Norman Shaw, Edwin Lutyens – I counted. The estate offers precise instruction on appropriating, on misappropriating these and other admired contributors to a specific vernacular; one more than a century, and several climates removed. Susceptible clients kindly steer clear.

So this is how the well-heeled respond to rampant poverty and its attendant ills – meagre welfare, educational and health services, xenophobia, under-employment and violent crime? If only in their mind's eye, they yearn for Provence, Tuscany, Cornwall; anywhere but here.

Corporate country seats in neo-Georgian Johannesburg – choose your stylism and settle in for a stay in supposedly swish office environs – all frightfully English public school, you know.

Office parks – not quite cricket

> There's a breathless hush in the close to-night –
> Ten to make and the match to win –
> a bumping pitch and a blinding light,
> An hour to play and the last man in.
> . . . his Captain's hand on his shoulder smote –
> 'Play up! play up! And play the game!'

We are firmly in *Boys' Own Paper* dreamland, north of Johannesburg at the Oval office park in Epsom Downs, corner Meadowbrook and Sloane Streets. The buildings are imitation cricket pavilions from the home counties, circa 1890. They have fake-timber balustrades and concocted hand-carved trim on the balconies. There are hammed-up window and door details, a roof lantern plus clock and, of course, a wind-vane. It is phony throughout; the accommodation, the interiors, the furniture and equipment. The entire ambience is as removed from ye olde village sward as one can imagine.

This synthetic stuff, including chock-full parking lots, is clustered about an oval-shaped cricket green, complete with pitch, sight-screens, scoreboard. It is kitsch, about as facile as Disney Land. There is, though, no duck pond or, to my knowledge, resident yokel in a manor house grotto.

The cliché dream takes off. White flanneled, square-jawed chaps emerge from their offices to watch and the more active, to play straight-batted strokes or to deliver swift, clean-cut bowling. Some crouch dutifully in the outfield. It is wholesome recreation, jolly good fun. They are, we all know, indulging the quintessentially gentleman's game. The ladies serve tea, sandwiches, home made cool drinks: the women – receptionists, secretaries, telephone operators – know their place.

Top to bottom: doing the rounds in the land of sham office buildings - this is all the rage.

Occasionally, a stalwart snicks a thick edge or stops a bouncer 'you've got to take the good with the bad, cricket is cricket, that's the way it goes'. And, from the office units encircling this counterfeit close, one catches a far-off echo, 'business is business, that's life'.

The fun is not available to all. Some, expressly those who are socially and financially distant from the affluent cricket buffs, are not impressed by far-flung office parks. They must live with acute transport difficulties. Without a motor-car, how does one get out to lunch or personal meetings, to a doctor's surgery and the many other places that working folk need attend? Where can they shop around for household necessities? How do they escape, put work and petty office disciplinarians behind them, if only for a half hour? They are stuck, allowed out at night and on weekends. Office parks, like other specialist enclaves, defeat the heterogeneity of city life.

Shams like the Oval are uncommon. Other office laagers are less imaginatively dressed-up; they deceive architecturally without providing sporty on-site diversions. Their designers concentrate fixedly on stylistic borrowings – from anywhere, everywhere: the models should, ideally, be overtly 'historic' and preferably from abroad. Their architects, however, are not especially faithful to what they filch so readily. Verisimilitude and scholarship are not on their agenda, images and surface effects are.

Epsom Downs and the surrounding areas – reaching southward into Sandton, up to and including Rosebank and Houghton – are natural habitats for these compounds. Arterial highways like William Nicol Drive, Rivonia Road and most other select northern boulevards are well supplied. Visit or, depending on your architectural stamina, shun them. The latter, though, is becoming increasingly difficult. The affliction is spreading – east to Northcliff, west to Bramley and then further. On which, among this embarrassment of choice, shall I focus?

Greenacres, corner of Rustenburg and Victory roads in Greenside, is probably as apt an instance as any. The buildings are muffled Georgian, but far, far removed from the urbane, the exact proportions of their eighteenth-century antecedents. The façades are coarse, without the subtle modelling of the original or its precise juxtapositions of neighbouring buildings. The interiors are mean; though showy, their materials and workmanship are less than spendthrift. The landscaping is perfunctory; it certainly does not compensate for the left-behind vibrant street life of the city which the bosses have fled.

That flight has become futile: constant motor traffic, polluting exhaust fumes, penetrating noise have followed the rush to suburbia, as has the hyper-nervous dread of criminal attack, the bogey of bar-room and dinner-party chat. As this regular exercise in mutually endorsed fear suggests, electrically charged fences, electronic gates, armed guards in block houses have not bought peace of mind. Outer and inner suburbia are fast becoming replicas of downtown Johannesburg.

Our next anxious stockade against criminality is on a smallish site facing Athol Avenue, off Jan Smuts in Craighall. Sparsely landscaped, Willowview contains buildings of no less than three stylistic types: a pared-down, crudely proportioned, faintly Palladian 'palazzo' plus a disturbingly unorthodox portico; then some vaguely colonial blocks with oddly paired windows that march in military fashion across their joyless façades and the apogee, Umbilo House.

Umbilo House's probable claim to an African title lies in its curious evocation of an ancient Egyptian temple, *via* a washed-out resemblance to 1940s MGM film sets. I do, though, recall another possible precedent: the ever-so jokey façades which the ever-so amusing British architect Terry Farrell planted on the buildings he designed for the TV-AM channel in London. Tiresome, boring as those 'jokes' soon became, they were at least intended to raise a laugh. Not much evokes even a forced smile at ponderous Willowview.

Finally, The Riviera, a compilation of discordant office units at 66 Oxford Road. Elements of this are, I imagine, consciously adapted from a sub-sub-Edwardian exemplar; selected perhaps from the expiring phase of that style. The stolid brickwork, simplistically divided window lights, bogus quoins, false arches and mock dormers may well be clues. But, frankly, I am out of my depth. I suspect, though, that the bourgeois office life and the construction technologies of Edwardian times bear as little resemblance to those of late 1990s Johannesburg as do the climatic conditions.

This wearisome parade of childish *ersatz* does not, patently, constitute architecture. Like all the cheery bucolic names, it smacks rather of cultural confusion, of adolescent make-believe,

> The voice of the schoolboy rallies the ranks:
> 'Play up! play up! and play the game!'

Top to bottom: the slippery aesthetic of gratuitous plagiarism – childish *ersatz*.

A meeting with Oom Paul at Hendrik Verwoed Plein, Pretoria – even the business of history is business.

Sammy Marks Square, Pretoria
– impressions and obsessions

I, a 'political returnee', write a piece for *Architecture SA* on the buildings – but since then completed – coming up at Hendrik Verwoerd Plein (Square) in Pretoria. Weird, *snaaks*. The Editor 'There's been a lot of controversy about this . . . as a newcomer to it, you can be objective'. Me, a neutral commentator? Hardly, but one can try.

So off I go, filled with the non-partisan fervour of a 27-year absence from South Africa. Off to browse about the building site, its environs and much of central Pretoria. Off to see the Director of the City Planning Department, architect Fritz Kraehmer; to interview members of the two design firms, Stauch Vorster and Studio 3; to visit some dissenting practitioners.

Soon that tenuous impartiality is under pressure, beginning to erode. Rose-tinted views seem, in our sweltering capital city, to melt readily away. Particularly in the context of a building project costing, I was told, 'approximately R220 million . . . the biggest in the history of Pretoria'.

First the accommodation. What is going onto this huge site? An entire block, owned by the City Council, bounded west and east by van der Walt and Prinsloo streets, on the north and south by Vermeulen and Church. A depressingly disjointed institutional and civic location: facing a humdrum, dispiriting, commercial strip to the west; the unblinking, aloof tower of the South African Reserve Bank opposite; that phlegmatic, sub-sub-sub Miesian municipal block on the north; and across Church Street, the bunker-like, crouching State Theatre (courtesy of Kenzo Tange?). And inescapably, that most frightening import from Brazil on Strijdom Plein. What is being inserted into this symbolically charged but visually scrambled aggregation? Sadly more incongruity.

Top to bottom: was Nachtmaal ever celebrated in this fake, sub-sub-Italian set-up – I doubt it.

The site is split, about fifty-fifty; a private sector, commercial zone on the western portion and to the east, a municipal area which is connected over Vermeulen Street to the oddly named 'Munitoria' building. Public and private, a joint venture – the long arm of Thatcherism reaching into the heart of the city. The commercial chunk (designers Stauch Vorster), almost 64 000 square metres of it, will consist of three separate sets of office accommodation, extensive shopping (national chain stores as well as small boutique-type premises), five cinemas, a games arcade and refreshment area, a major restaurant and other smaller eating places. All linked by three banks of lifts and stairs to basement parking for 870 cars.

In short, yet another of the ever present, larger and larger, city shopping centres. Complete with the now obligatory barrel-vaulted arcade, shop-lined open space – Sammy Marks Square – and of course, a Highveld–Mediterranean campanile. Everywhere inexorably the same, each unfailingly designed to offer some dredged-up, applied distinctiveness.

But, as I was told in the Planning Department and by the designers, 'the project . . . will extend the CBD shopping area in an Easterly direction'. Why? Who needs, desires the extension? Strange, gratuitous questions: it quite simply, self-evidently, is – that is how things are.

We are on familiar territory. Shopping malls: sanitised, neat, encased, supposedly secure; readied for use by those who are equipped and seek to spend in such coolly unchallenging settings. In South Africa they are usually white. With, on occasion, a few others whose incomes enable them to indulge sufficiently. But outside, indeed on an opposite pavement, the street vendors are busy; helping to make inner Pretoria like central Johannesburg or Durban. Bustling African cities, open, dynamic, vibrant, often untidy, even chancy.

Well then . . . an informal market on a portion of Verwoerd Plein? Similar to, but more imaginatively designed than those buzzing stalls on The Parade, Cape Town? Nice idea. Where, though, are the hefty investments and the juicy returns from relatively inexpensive market places? Not, apparently, in CBD areas; where they may well be needed.

So a central site, earmarked for public space, 'open and park-like in character', in 1966 and again in 1973, has become one more standard consumerist palace. Except for the other half, the 52 000 square metre municipal zone designed in the Studio 3 offices.

Here the accommodation is no less, perhaps more incongruous. There is to be a spanking-new, commodious mayoral suite and a capacious, well-accoutred civic and conference centre. Both claimed to be necessary replacements to existing facilities; although those sceptical of the anticipated costs point to the under-used City Hall facing Pretorius Plein further south. There will also be – and this is where the questions crowd in – a City Library that covers four generous floors; a Tourist Information Bureau ('all the latest for overseas visitors . . . the most sophisticated in the country') and a central Health Clinic that occupies two major upper storeys plus space on two basement levels. And more: footings plus lowerlevel columns are in place for a 'prestigious five-star' hotel (20 or more storeys) for which potential developers are currently being canvassed – which by 2003 had not been built. All to be accessible from basement parking for about 560 cars.

This bountiful – some have said overblown, opulent – clutch of civic amenities is, doubtless, intended for all the people of Pretoria. Beyond question. Join me in picturing the citizens of, say, Atteridgeville and Mamelodi townships abandoning their many grandly appointed local libraries and clinics for these welcoming facilities. See them sweep by car into the underground parking, ascend to the mayor's parlour, the conference hall, to sumptuous hotel bars and terraces, the international tourist centre – where they reserve passages to Bondi Beach, San Fernando Valley . . . Hawaii. Join me also in questioning whose needs are expected to be fulfilled by, whose aspirations realised in this off-beat assemblage of municipal accommodation.

Municipal, a key word: in an open society this must mean public. But which public? Even then, now, with the structure barely at second-floor level, the question hangs over Hendrik Verwoerd Plein/Sammy Marks Square. Is this the 'people's place' mooted in City Council documents *circa* 1973? Most people are likely to want a deal of convincing on the relevance of that description for them. As they may well do about the recent, somewhat expedient change of name. Are other timely, conciliatory changes to come: Mahatma Gandhi, Nelson Mandela or Sol Plaatjie Plein?

Turn now to the façade treatment, the public face presently seen only on the architects' models, sketches and worked-up drawings. Once more we are on familiar ground. Echoes, yet again, of Robert Venturi's quirky, non-structural arch at Guild House, Philadelphia; of Aldo Rossi's penchant for arcane, punctuating towers; of all that voguish, arbitrary mingling of trabeated and arched openings. Façade design as an exercise in stylistic borrowings, distant and local. In this case taken chiefly from the on site, retained – thoroughly gutted and 'recycled' – Kynoch Building of the early 1880s and far more so, from the admired (heavily over-praised?) Sammy Marks Building, 1909.

The method is architecture as romance: 'romantic in character' and 'a people-friendly place . . . reminiscent of a more romantic era'. The theme, I was told repeatedly, is old Pretoria, 'a bit of old Pretoria'; with, as admix, the well-worn piety 'but essentially contemporary'. Two recurring emphases: 'basically romantic' and 'sympathetic to old Pretoria'.

Which old Pretoria? The *nagmaal* (holy communion) village, the capital of the Zuid-Afrikaansche Republiek (ZAR), the seat of British occupation, the early nineteenth-century town growing into city status? Or, a more telling question, whose romantic old Pretoria? Not, I venture, the people-friendly image of the historically excluded majority, or of the Indian traders who once occupied parts of Verwoerd Plein. Nor, I imagine, the allusions – romantic or otherwise – of the many who have been confined for so long to outlying townships. Not, for instance, the romanticism of the only black people shown on the four plaques at Paul Kruger's feet on Kerk Plein. Those two ill-clad bystanders, a servant and a young lad watching passively as history is made by others. An earlier assumption and symbolic depiction of who will and will not be admitted to citizenship, of who is and is not counted a member of the public. Which public?

None of this unsparing comment diminishes one's respect for the way the pragmatics of the project have been handled. It certainly does not negate the technical command, the sureness of decision evident in the drawings and on the models which the architects, ever courteous, shared with me. The two firms have worked in tandem with obvious sensitivity. Moreover, they have done so in the taxing context of an awkwardly divided site; one encircled by a socially significant but aesthetically aberrant collection of public buildings. That, though, is another story; my focus has been different.

I expect to be charged, as a matter of embedded ritual, with the singularly South African offence of dragging politics – expressly 'racial' politics – into architecture. I plead guilty in advance. For me political life is pre-eminently about social power, as is the appropriation, the shaping, the use of space.

In stressing this I have an accomplice, probably unwitting – the sole interviewee to stipulate that his words may not be attributed. Responding to my query 'In what ways do you think the project will fit into the new South Africa?' he said, 'No, the initial idea was not to target the black market and even today that's the case. They [the buildings] are not black market orientated . . . they were never meant for the black in the street . . . You see we've got the swankiest interior designer in the country. He's UK trained'.

Sammy Marks Square: the refurbished and retained front of the past.

Bank City, central Johannesburg – a pompous, weighty repository of misplaced architectural symbolism – see it to believe it, then pinch yourself.

Taking a step back

It is big – Bank City, in downtown Johannesburg. From Harrison through Fraser and Sauer streets to touch on Diagonal Street. From Jeppe through Kerk to Pritchard streets. Seven city blocks, a major building envisaged for each. First National Bank's new head office is, we are told, to be 'the biggest banking complex on earth'.

Very likely. Some 50 old and new buildings have been or will be cleared to make way. There will be about 5 000 bank staff members, plus many others from extensive retail premises; more than 1 000 parking bays for the initial four buildings. The central axis, Kerk Street, which is closed, like Fraser, to motor traffic, will be widened to become a pedestrian mall and further west, an 'informal' market. Pavements on the perimeters of the buildings, planted with fully grown trees, will merge with the colonnaded, double-height arcades that are to front the shopping spaces.

It will be big. Even now – Spring 1991 – the two buildings being completed and a third, still a structural skeleton, are decisive insertions into the city. The promise of consequences is patent; of impacts as telling as those of the sleek Carlton Centre further east and that sullen Standard Bank complex to the south. Public response to a project of this order is clearly appropriate, necessary.

Much can, must, be said in analyses of the emerging colossus. Its effects on the local economy, the commercial balance of the city; the repercussions for traffic – pedestrian and motor – of such a concentration of people, vehicles; the implications in an undifferentiated, dull street grid of a forcefully axial plan for this large area. And more . . . the perks granted, presumably, to the bank in exchange for the open spaces 'given' to the public. These and like matters should, long since, have been aired; argued, perhaps contested, amended. Preferably before the event, but now *post facto*, as guidance for subsequent developments.

Top to bottom: domes, colonnades and stick-on stonework – not a few steps from the City Hall, also

Not least among the relevant issues is the stylistic, the formal treatment of the buildings and environs: their visual impact. Partially stripped of those robust, work-a-day cocoons of scaffolding, this is now becoming evident. It is now, belatedly, up for general discussion. For, one trusts, analytic, critical consideration. For comment that reaches beyond the fawning eulogies, the casual recyclings of publicity material that have, to date, occupied the popular and the architectural press.

Here, then, is a contribution to such debate; an opening shot, some probing remarks.

External appearance, aesthetics: no marginal matter for the bank or the designers - as the latter have documented and confirmed in conversation. Not surprisingly. Bank City will be a national (even wider?) headquarters; the flagship guiding a massive, powerful institution's journey into the new century. For senior executives in the organisation the complex must surely, epitomise this image, this symbolic appeal to public consciousness. For them, issues of corporate imagery are not peripheral.

These factors have also affected the architects' conceptions of the project. They, though, declare an additional commitment; one made explicit in other work they have undertaken recently. For them, the precepts of classical design – those underpinning the façades now revealed on the initial two buildings – comprise an, probably *the*, authentic contemporary approach and style.

Bank City – a weighty repository of architectural, of social symbolism.

How has this affirmation of classicism been expressed? First there is a call on universality, on a purportedly inherent human constant. So, quoting from a contemporary British classicist, the architects state that 'real architecture . . . is instinctively understood and recognized by ordinary people having evolved as part of the common language of civilisation over 3 000 years'. Transposed to southern Africa, this biological given, this venerable language, offers an apposite, a civilised (civilising?) idiom. It is, for the architects, 'an appropriate architectural expression'; suitable, indeed, 'for what amounts to a little less than [the] one kilometre of building façade . . . [to be] presented to the public'. A major architectural statement.

So, following the 'rules and erudition' of classical design, the façade consists of three principal elements. The arcaded colonnades at ground level form a base with the similarly treated, rusticated, mezzanines above them. The six-storey upper surfaces of symmetrically disposed solids and voids (walls and windows) are 'articulated' by vertical openings to the atria of each block and by horizontal, colonnaded loggias. This formula, the foot/body/head maxim of formal classicist architecture, is completed by a crowning cornice. All capped by a recessed seventh floor and curved, semi-vaulted roof. In another nod to neo-classical canon, each outer street corner is marked by a domed tower-like form.

As regards historical continuity – a further characteristic which the architects associate with their design – they acknowledge two specific sources, one from abroad and the other at home. Both are almost a century old. The former is depicted briefly as 'some of the truly elegant office buildings built in Vienna, Paris and New York before the First World War'. This was elaborated in discussion by reference to the Post Office Savings Bank (1903–6) designed for Vienna by an internationally renowned architect.

The local influence is described in similarly broad terms. It embraces buildings from the year 1905, when the Bank's nearby, present head office was erected, and includes more recent neo-classical work: 'what we have done . . . is to take a step back and look at the model of a more graceful Johannesburg. We have tried to imagine what might have occurred if . . . the period of Lutyens, Baker, Gordon Leith and others, had been allowed to develop . . . into the twenty-first century.'

But, they note, classical images and models are not confined to this period. Quite the contrary. They are 'universal and constant elements . . . as valid today as they have always been'. Accordingly, they assure their clients, 'this timeless and enduring expression drawn from the long continuum of classicism will present a sound and lasting image . . . as fresh and undated in 50 years as it will be in the 1990s'.

This commitment, this view of how architecture should be made, is bound by specified precepts, rules. It calls on a range of pre-determined, abstract design criteria for realising 'real architecture' on, for instance, the tenets of proportionality, symmetry, axiality. When observed, the code leads, in appearance at least, to neo-classical buildings. It results in architecture that is held to embody such classical ideals as equilibrium, synthesis, wholeness. It constitutes a design language which is, we are told, 'intelligible to the public, which, in the context of Bank City, bears an understandable resemblance to the best of Johannesburg or South Africa's architecture'.

I am sceptical, if not incredulous. I question this doctrinal, this reductive view of architecture and especially of so diverse an endeavour as classical design.

Claims for a specifically universal, timeless architecture can scarcely be sustained, even as rhetoric. Unless, that is, the categories 'real architecture' and 'civilisation' are deemed to exclude vernacular building, world wide; to banish pre-historic as well as much of, say, Mycenaean, Arabic, Gothic, Mogul, Arts and Crafts architecture . . . and that of other historical periods, civilisations. Calls on the suspect sociobiology of an instinctively recognised classicism are no more persuasive, even when reference remains within this tradition. Unless the non-axial, asymmetric, plans and, on occasion, buildings of, say, Hadrian's Villa at Tivoli, the Piazza del Quirinale or Michelangelo's Piazza del Campidoglio in Rome also fail the test of reality/civilisation. As do those presumably anomalous structures the Erechtheion and Propylaea on that icon of classicism the Acropolis at Athens – another irregular, asymmetric, non-axial layout.

Historical continuity: in southern Africa such assertions are, must be problematic. Take, as a case in point, that vision of a previously more graceful Johannesburg. Grace? For whom? For mine labourers displaced from the land, for tough and rough immigrants, small-scale entrepreneurs? For them as well as for the well-heeled with aspirations for status – mine owners, stock brokers, top banking personnel? Which cultural continuities? Those represented by non-classical Great Zimbabwe, those, like 'expressionist' Tswana architecture, of African settlements throughout the region, indeed the continent? Of our small-town Main Streets, our Hindu temples, of summarily demolished old Fordsburg in Johannesburg... District Six in Cape Town?

There are also those historically validated, 'time-honoured' elements of classical building. Here too there is room for scepticism. For example, the sweeping arch over Kerk Street: suspended from rather than, as in classical precedent, supporting the structure above (with space in the quarter-circle void at each corner for some three Soweto houses). The deep loggias, porches, of Caesar's Rome – suited to varied use in that, and our, climate – have become vestigial; narrow balconies or niches the width of the columns they accommodate. Those columns: stripped shafts, bald relics of the structurally decorated 'orders' of classicism. The rusticated walls: thin, applied granite panels that resemble but do not match the solidity of the prototypes they emulate. Tower and loggia effects on the façades that seem arbitrarily related to the office spaces inside. The scenery of classicism is set, the substance eludes.

Then axial planning, pre-eminently a device of the mid-fifteenth through to the sixteenth-century Renaissance in Italy – an earlier, formidably confident, neo-classicism. This was signorial space: stretches of medieval cities razed – the occupants dispossessed – to make way for the new order, the anticipated future. Space in the service of grandeur: geometric *piazze*, squares; straight and wide avenues; large finite buildings... commanded, controlled, ordered. The 'ideal city' of the Quattrocento: impressive, triumphal urban vistas.

Not quite the prospect presented in the inauspicious setting of Bank City; from, for instance, the hanging arch. Look eastward: in the distance, one of the more coarse of our many boorish office towers; closer, the bland extension to the Supreme Court, with a snatch of that building's cramped neo-classical façade. To the west the Turbine House, which is a fine remnant of industrial Newtown... but a mere glimpse from the complex – chiefly of chimney, sadly too small from this spot. A classical 'ordering... by the use of symmetry and strong visual axes'? Hardly more so than the amorphous vistas of nondescript buildings on view from the secondary axes of Sauer, Fraser or Simmonds streets.

On these and like counts the imagery of neo-classicism seems questionable; particularly the social symbolism of our local, Edwardian–Classic office buildings. Imported, stylistically, at or soon after the close of colonial rule, they bear the marks of the period – late Victorian pomp, declamatory grandeur, ponderous formality, self-conscious solemnity and of course, social exclusivity. Many of the models from which they were drawn are, after all, in the City of London; the home, then, of economic dominion, of imperial banking. There, as here, these buildings represented power, social sway. They were and remain seats of establishment. They helped to legitimate a divided social order, Disraeli's 'two nations'. Clad with the approved insignia of a supposedly authoritative past – expressly that of ancient Rome, an admired earlier empire – their already considerable symbolic authority was endorsed, reinforced.

This, as the appropriate means of bringing order to the crass, the gross competitive individualism of building in Johannesburg? This, as the relevant means of according symbolic meaning in an open, multi-cultural, pluralistic South Africa? Seems unlikely.

Bank City: 'a sound and lasting image', a reaching for 'the best in . . . South Africa's architecture'? Or yet another facet of a world-wide crisis in professional design; one in which architecture is being reduced to mere styling, to contriving forms and images that 'sell'? Often, as in this instance, these are adopted from selected pasts, from the imagery of historically dominant social groups.

There have been two major challenges to such practices during this century. First the democratically orientated, short-lived, summarily suppressed projects of Constructivist design in Poland, Hungary and specifically the USSR immediately after World War I. Second the successive minority efforts since the 1960s – in Western Europe and the US particularly – to forge socially responsible architectures: communal, democratic, participatory practices whose adherents seek to respond to popular desires and simultaneously, to admit of social change.

Together, fused in a searchingly critical continuation of Modernism, these offer the prospect of a distinctively contemporary and constantly evolving architectural language.

Such a prospect can be glimpsed in the work which the architect Giancarlo de Carlo has carried out with the co-operation of trade unionists in Italy and among many others, that of the Edward Cullinan collaborative in Britain, of Aldo van Eyck and Hermann Hertzberger in Holland. Work that is echoed in the buildings for which, also among others, Rodney Harber and Dennis Claude are responsible in Natal, of Jose Forjaz's designs in Mozambique and those which Joe Noero reveals for us on the Witwatersrand. Architectural work that indicates why Modernism, shorn of its 'internationalist' fetishes, remains pertinent. Work that suggests how, licked into local shape, Modernist exemplars like the Hillman Engineering Building on the Wits campus or the 1930s pair at 233 and 235 Bree Street, Johannesburg, might yet be developed to fulfil the early promise of that approach.

An archway that hangs from rather than supports the superstructure. Banal.

Keeping the pretenders at bay – rushing by a good-looking pretence; a modernistic, rather than neo-classical, false fr

Counterfeit facelift

What a delight, in our aesthetically bereft city, to come across building improvements which are just that, enriching refinements. How exciting, among the derivative new structures that spring weed-like about us, to have one's spirits lifted. See it for yourself: the Dunkeld Crescent development, corner of Jan Smuts Avenue and Albury Road, directly opposite Hyde Park centre.

Perhaps I was too ready to be impressed. I had, minutes earlier, driven past freshly turned sods on Outspan Road, Morningside – at a site being readied for another cluster of luxury homes. Access will be *via* a grossly ostentatious suburban archway; an Arc de Triomphe or, much earlier, AD 81, imperial Titus' commemorative arch in Rome? Or, most probably, another Italianate homage to up-market pretension? The term weed-like is advised, there are many more like this. They flourish in our rich soil. See nearby Sandton, where the streets and byways are awash with shop-soiled architecture. See the woebegone attempt to ennoble that architecturally barren Michelangelo Hotel with the spurious dignity of a filched *quattrocento* gateway.

Or visit the entrance to The Georgian Manor on Hyde Close, Hyde Park. Georgian? Throughout its daring revisions of classicism, the likely model – Osterley Park House (1761), Middlesex – does not indulge this crass boorishness. There is, assuredly, no homage here to designer/builders like Robert Adam, who was responsible for Osterley. No, this coarse parody is, in its own right, testimony to the debased state of our present architecture.

To return to that smiling site on an otherwise glum, advertisement-laden hill in Jan Smuts Avenue; hardly a setting that promises a worthwhile building renovation. Yet here, thanks to Francois van der Merwe of Design Partnership, Pretoria, is a local precinct that sings.

Top to bottom: a trio of fine views – if only they bore some, marginal, relation to that now deprecated notion, functionalism.

This was a drab group of four office blocks, each containing two stories of accommodation: dry-as-dust speculator–modern without the wit even to be unobtrusive. Lumpish, dull, inept are the depictions that spring to mind – van der Merwe speaks tellingly of 'that previous bunker'. It is now transformed, made over into living architecture; into buildings unburdened by mock-historical references. But some of the earlier bleakness remains. Though newly landscaped, the limited open spaces cannot mitigate the dreary stretches of asphalt, the serried rows of car parking. They are embedded in a singularly botched piece of urban planning: a public roadway which, quite arbitrarily, divides the accommodation into pairs of separated blocks.

This contrasts markedly with the engagingly, imaginatively re-planned interiors. They readily permit cellular as well as open plan offices, each type being as spatially stimulating and attractively finished as the other. And each is augmented in the extensive premises occupied by such avowedly publicity-conscious tenants as advertising, public relations and personnel agencies. They, in the architect's words, are 'dynamic, new economy companies, definitely very alternative'. Their executives require 'buildings to act as publicity generators', as indeed these have.

In this respect, the remodelled exteriors, their carefully reconditioned façades, are wholly convincing – handsomely so.

The four main entrances excepted, the previous forms have been retained; their continuous plaster bands stripped, reworked and plastered in tandem with the larger expanses of external brickwork. New windows and the altered entrances are in place. Colours are restricted to light beige and earthy-blue walls, black-anodised aluminium windows and metal-grey entry porches plus, notably, the sharp white finish to the 'sunshades' attached to all north- and south-facing façades.

That crisp white is as striking on the steel shades as it is on the V-shaped canopies which hover at roof level to signal each point of entry. Together, these command immediate attention – whether from the site, its adjacent environs or from the approaches on the Jan Smuts and William Nicol highways. Their fastidious detailing, their balanced, elegant proportions dominate the entire renovation. They are its central meaning. They are, to cite the designer again, its message of 'marketability ... the image which represents the interests and the distinctive features of the type of tenants'.

Then, on close study, comes the shock to design fidelity. The prime instance: sunshields that do not, are not intended to shield. Sufficient, the architect says, that they make for precisely patterned shadows, that they give illusory 'depth' to what were flat, featureless frontages. Sufficient that they add 'interest', extraneous sparkle; especially on south-facing façades which the sun does not reach. Sufficient that the V-shaped roof structures are also purposeless, except that they too provide 'a bit more depth'.

Form without content. We are in make-believe-land, where surface effect, 'what it looks like', is paramount, where image is in command, where architectural whimsy, ironic inference is all. This, as the architect volunteered, is a postmodern idyll – 'it looks good'.

A similar, an at least as accomplished and unreservedly authentic, revamp has recently been completed on the west campus at Wits. Here, the architect, Henry Paine, was confronted by an even more nondescript, exhausted package of accommodation; one left from the Rand Easter Show when, years ago, that occupied the site. Paine re-jigged four levels of cheerless interior to provide buoyant, tailor-made spaces. He fixed effective sun protection to the vulnerable north and west fronts. Now, purposefully rehabilitated, the building stands confidently among its amorphous neighbours – an appealing exemplar of what they too might be.

There are, I suspect, many local buildings of this nature: sows' ears waiting to be transmuted to silk purses or, if not quite that auspicious, to liveable internal volumes which are enveloped in cogently designed façades. Congenial surroundings would also be advantageous. Their intrinsic benefits aside, urban environs of this nature could well be seed-beds for growths of distinctive, of outstanding architectural quality.

Too much to ask? The trick is, surely, to identify potential of this order and that done, to muster the resources, material and social, for exploiting it. Both call for design insight, for architectural foresight.

A concluding note: since spotting that incongruous archway in Morningside, more of its attention-craving ilk have presented themselves – frequently, tediously. They are taking weed-like root, from lower Houghton to Johannesburg's northern boundaries . . . and beyond.

The Rand Club, off Loveday Street, Johannesburg – sometime exclusive retreat for what William Morris called 'the stinking rich', now a struggling institution.

Forsaken glory?

The Rand Club, some time emblematic seat of power and privileged social dominance, now stands quietly in Johannesburg's old financial centre. There, facing Fox, Loveday and Commissioner Streets, this relic of our imperial past is an outlandish anomaly: Antonio da Sangallo's and Michelangelo's Palazzo Farnese (1534) brought from renaissance Rome to the highveld, *via* an eighteenth-century London club.

As a newly graduated architect, I passed its then bustling entrance daily – to and from my work in the contrasting Art Deco splendour of nearby Loveday House. A radically dissenting twenty-something, I, like all women, black peoples and other supposedly lesser breeds without the law, dared not enter. That was the preserve of gentlemen: randlords, city merchants, senior mining personnel, commissioned military men, other practitioners of moneyed exclusivity.

Now, fifty years on, I am welcomed, invited in, taken on tour of interiors occupied, but forbidden to outsiders since 1904. What has changed? Is it the intensity of my dissidence or the spent might of what, in the *Rand Club centenary album, 1887–1987*, is lovingly depicted as a 'refuge for gentlemen'?

That call on gentlemanly status is a preoccupation of the contributors to this arcane publication, a text that descends frequently into the nudge-nudge sniggers of callow undergraduates – Oxbridge of course. These are usually occasioned by the mention of women (ever 'the ladies'), politicians (those 'noisy fellows'), dedicated boozers ('convivial imbibers') and their socially invisible attendants, their silent 'minions'.

In this, as in much else, the book resonates with the building, especially its interior decor. Here one is enveloped in the ritual

Top to bottom: the magnificently decorated, domed central hall, reminders of 'Jock of the Bushveld' hunting days; one of the many dignitaries on show in the nooks and crannies of past glories.

snobbery of the well-heeled English minor gentry, the home counties crowd. This stretches from the paintings, drawings, etchings, original and reproduced works that cover the walls; from the expensively bound, printed and illustrated books that line so many of the rooms; to the carefully crafted, exotic hardwood fittings and bloated leather furniture that fills these timber panelled spaces. It even reaches the collections of bric-à-brac that occupy so many not-quite-stately county homes.

All is either grand and compelling or comfortingly snug, cosy; everything secure in its designated place. Propriety and decorum are in uppermost.

But – and here is the rub – many of these pictures, books, furnishings and spaces are fine instances of their type. As witness, Thomas Baines' sure hand in the club's collection of his evocative sketches, or the grand stairway so precisely modelled on Sir Charles Barry's design at the Reform Club, London. These and similar treasures are well executed, thoughtfully selected, attentively tended. As are the other splendid interior spaces, the work of Frank Emley and the enigmatic W Leck, architects who were practised in the imitative stylisms of the time.

Notably though, in the transfer from sixteenth-century Italy, via Britain, few concessions were made to local climate, custom, craftsmanship or culture. The building survives as decidedly provincial, worshipfully borrowed architecture, an unquestioning offshoot of empire – of England, home and beauty.

Unlike those of its many neo-classical neighbours, the façades to the Rand Club warrant no special attention. Ponderously repetitive, they edge disquietingly close to architectural banality: deeply incised ashlar plaster-work and rows of uneventfully proportioned window openings spread across three frontages on each of the five main storeys. There is little effective recognition of orientation, of the two all-important corners, of the façade ends. The bulbous roof-line alone offers some distraction.

The heavily modelled walls and window surrounds, the latter's bracketed overhangs and stolid pediments dominate. They constitute the exterior's claim to such mention as this exercise in frantic fenestration may warrant. That might well have been otherwise. The solid masonry is deceptive, it is not necessarily load-bearing. The building, like its exemplar, Barry's Reform Club (1837), is said to bear its load of mock stonework on a steel-framed structure.

Then there is the barely acknowledged entry off Loveday Street. Here one negotiates a narrowly recessed opening that, in gentlemanly reticence, carries no identifying name-plate – save the minuscule words 'Rand Club' on the escutcheon of a bell-push. Those who need to know, know.

Given all this, there can be little doubt that it is the commanding internal spaces which call most for attention. The gem is the domed atrium that houses the magnificent great stair, the double-legged upper flights of which open, *via* a powerful ambulatory of teak-clad columns, onto the main dining floor. There one glimpses an array of inviting, tranquil sitting spaces. With or without the portrait of the youthful Elizabeth II as its centre-piece, this is a majestic, a regal space. I lingered to relish the unforced dignity, the dedicated attention to detail, while satisfyingly running a hand along the polished brass handrail.

Then the main dining room: a muscular rectangular space punctuated with sequences of paired columns that support a solid cornice and a ceiling of quietly decorative plaster-work. Access to the robust, urbane qualities of the room is through an imaginatively conceived oval lobby which is lit by stained glass windows. These depict all the signs of the zodiac bar two. We learn from the centenary album that, 'neither women [signified by the Virgin] nor bearers of water [Aquarius] . . . had a place in the Rand Club'.

The other reception, dining and sitting areas, the meeting rooms and galleries, are as architecturally rewarding. As are the immediately inviting library, the much lauded 'longest bar in Africa', even the tiny room in which members unobtrusively black-ball undesirable applicants.

Creative spatial enclosure lies at the heart of creative architectural design. This skill has touched these confident interiors. In that context, affected comment of the type that I cited earlier is of little but passing concern.

What will happen to these handsome spaces? The club's membership is reduced to 1 000, they are currently linked (attached?) to a euphemistically named 'branch', le Canard restaurant on Rivonia Road, Sandton. Are Leck and Emley's classic volumes to be demolished or, possibly worse, retained in mausoleum-like inertia? Or can they be sensitively adapted for wide social use – surely an exacting challenge for imaginative developers and designers?

The Reserve Bank in Johannesburg, off President Street – a lesson in filched architecture, a thoroughgoing mixture of borrowed architectures.

The dreariness of ostentation
– Johannesburg's Reserve Bank

Many new buildings seem insensible, alien to the people who experience them. This is particularly the case among recent additions to our architectural stock. They obtrude on us, we cannot dodge them; they out-stare us, impassively. On occasion we encounter instances that turn so dismissively, so truculently from us as to be downright contemptuous. Their designers have heavy reckonings to make with us.

Take, for instance, a pre-eminently public building in a key area of Johannesburg: the newly completed branch of the South African Reserve Bank, corner West and President Streets. With the much-mooted Newtown development, this marks a new emphasis in the city's west-end; a thrust toward Soweto, Johannesburg's long neglected neighbour. The branch is no common off-the-shelf local office. Decidedly not. It is a purpose-designed, richly finished, hugely costly enterprise. Do not be misled by the stoic exterior: those dour façades conceal princely, fulsome interiors.

Early in my discussions with the architect, he told me that he is not permitted to reveal the cost of the building, 'that's confidential information'. This in what is, surely, a project of public interest! Later, though, in an apparently inadvertent aside, I heard mention of a sum 'in excess of R90 million'. The outcome of this splurge became evident as I was escorted through the spacious and, at the time, under-populated interiors.

The materials are, let us say, immoderately costly. They comprise select, polished granite/marble cladding to walls and floors, massive arches and other wall surfaces of purpose-made 'Roman'-sized bricks, chunky stainless steel balustrades, highly finished steelwork and externally, heavy aluminium sun-screens. They include many, many square metres of expensive imported timber. Canadian maple doors,

Top to bottom: a series of purportedly imposing views – each as sterile, as ill-matched as the other, the architecture of manipulated imagery.

floors, skirtings, plus the ceiling panels and meticulously crafted grill-pattern maple screens that are installed throughout the upper storeys.

These materials are, as the architect commented, 'of high quality'. They provide, he added, an 'ambience of elegance and dignity'. Mere citizens – were they to penetrate the guarded entrance – might see their liberal use as profligate, as wanton indulgences on his and more significantly, on the part of the Bank's mandarins who endorsed their use.

Adherents of the latter view may well consider this aesthetic of spendthrift glitz to be an abuse of quality. They might regard the interiors – not least, the arched 'Roman' circulation gallery – as pretentious and coarse rather than elegant. They are likely to judge what has been depicted as the 'strong Roman architectural overtones' of this arcade, this structurally contorted stage-set, to be inappropriate rather than dignified. The relevance of that arcane allusion to ancient Rome may well escape them, especially in the miscellany of accommodation which opens, certainly without classical clarity, off the arcade.

They could be baffled rather than moved by that fanciful medley of plan forms: a wedge-shaped Head Office suite, a rectangular auditorium squeezed into a circular drum, a toilet block pinched incongruously in a semi-drum, elevators and a stair-well pressed into linked square and triangular-shaped forms. In culmination, a skewed rectangular Money Market with offices above.

Readers may wish to note the purpose of the plush Head Office unit. These seven spacious offices, with separate kitchen and toilets, are for the Governor and his attendants when, on occasion, they venture from their Pretoria base to the branch.

Vertically, the building is in two distinct parts. The office and ancillary accommodation which I have mentioned are on the upper levels. As are their associated elements: a lounge, Executive Dining recess, Labourers' Dining Room, games room, gymnasium and change rooms. Together they rise through four storeys. Below there is a basement and a ground floor. The former contains areas for sorting and storing bulk cash and banknotes, access bays for delivery vehicles and of course, its share of the ubiquitous security accommodation. The ground level is used for parking, plant rooms, stores, an armoury, a shooting range and further security compartments.

This division is made explicit on the exterior. The upper façades are set back from the site boundaries to sit on what the architect describes as a 'podium'. That comprises the ground floor, which occupies almost the entire site and a screen wall at first floor level. Like much else in the building, the wall is a piece of *ad hoc* design; there is no call for accommodation at this level to be screened. The Bank, however, insists on a ten metre high run of secure walling around the site. How did the architect provide for this?

Well . . . he extended the sloping ground-storey wall by adding an otherwise extraneous vertical screen; one that reaches beyond the first floor to the required height. He allowed for planting to cover the awkward junction of the slanted and the upright walls. He arranged for landscaping to relieve the stretches of bleak flat-roofing between building and screen.

Doctors, one hears, bury their peccadillos. Architects plant creepers.

The podium is, the designer claims, 'pedestrian friendly'. I find it raw, aloof, forbidding. It offers none of the bustle, the engaging interest of the off-pavement shopping in the neighbourhood. It can scarcely be said to be enlivened by the monumental entrance: an over-scaled relic of 1930s Hollywood film sets that is anything but inviting. Nor does the granite seating at the foot of the podium, a clumsy gesture to human need, hold much promise of animation.

The façades are, in a word, sterile.

Consider, now, the superstructure to the podium. The assorted plan shapes that open off the internal arcade emerge here; they surface as a pot-pourri of design titbits. There are snatches of the Brazilian architect Oscar Niemeyer, of Aldo Rossi in Italy, of Louis Kahn in the US, of the Festival Hall in London. The building will, I suspect, become a focus for student architects who, unsure of their design abilities, search out what they term 'unusual' forms into which they can push accommodation.

Then there is an enigmatic reference to the manner in which West, like Diagonal Street, runs at an angle to the local street grid; an external conjunction which, the architect explained, he 'exploited to produce a dynamic geometry'.

Accordingly, while other elements remain parallel to the grid, the auditorium drum, the lift and stair towers and the office unit are aligned along the oblique axis. Most passers-by are, I imagine, unlikely to rejoice in this abstract, cryptic response to an off-site shift of axes. A formal dynamic of this nature hardly helps to knit the new building into the life of the neighbourhood. It scarcely makes an uncivil, crabbed structure more congenial – for pedestrians or motorists.

Given the designer's apparent penchant for things Roman, his reliance on this esoteric device is bewildering. One might rather expect him to have called on the celebrated, the subtle play of geometric forms at Hadrian's Villa (AD 118) near Rome.

But I have probably missed something. Perhaps the building is a learned essay in post-postmodern ambiguity, in fragmented multi-valent imagery? Perhaps not. Perhaps it is yet another strained – and costly – exercise in being 'unusual'?

Nuggets in the dust

Notwithstanding the occasional heartening piece, included in an effort to buoy readers' spirits, the first three chapters have been heavy going. Not much to sustain one in the murky architectural gloom, not much to chuckle at, to engage one's affections for design professionals and their clientele. But then there is not much in our everyday built surroundings that supports architects' conceits apropos their self-proclaimed creative imaginations. Small comfort to think that we South Africans may well have the architects we deserve and less to suggest that they have the publics they merit. It is a sorry tale all-round.

But wait. What lies behind those two qualifying phrases, 'not much' and 'small comfort'? However little there may be, it needs be grabbed, clutched, cherished. And as the readings in this chapter illustrate, there surely are nuggets, many of which lie smothered in the dust churned up by the engulfing dross. As the readings also indicate, here, two notions appear to be specifically relevant: critical regionalism and user participation. Each calls insistently for attention; so, though their designers are Egoli-based, not all the following examples are in the immediate Johannesburg area.

Work in progress – a pre-completion view of the architect Peter Rich's always insightful interpretations of traditional Tswana architecture; at, on this occasion, Molatedi in North West Province.

Modest enterprise – worthy award

Peter Rich, a much awarded Johannesburg architect, has done it again. His modest thatch and gum-pole shelter at Molatedi village in the Makuleke region of North West Province has earned him an annual World Architecture Award.

Traditional Tswana building materials and methods of construction have been adapted to and re-interpreted for an appealing multi-purpose space – in ponderous officialese, the Bopitikelo Community and Cultural Centre. It is an unaffected yet distinctive structure: an elemental canopy of shade in a hot, dusty landscape on which, when the rains come, they fall with fierce vigour.

Rich is one of a steadfast minority of designers who have not succumbed to the modish succession of trends that has gripped so many of our architects. He has stood clear of the passing fashions that surround him and us. There are, in his portfolio, no glittering office parks, shopping malls or luxury cluster-house complexes – each dressed in ill-fitting imported clothing. There are no priapic glass towers baking in southern sunlight. There are no outwardly showy factories or warehouses with mundane interiors – aesthetic sensitivity is, in these, assumed to be beyond those who labour on the shopfloor! There are also no dreary attempts yet again to resurrect our imperial past.

Given the dismal state of our current architecture, these and like negatives alone call for respectful acknowledgement. To also design noteworthy structures is doubly meritorious. It is with this in mind that I have broken with my hitherto firm rule of reporting only on buildings I have personally visited and studied. Though quiet, contained and wholly unpretentious, this thoughtful Centre has forced itself on my attention; if only from Rich's telling sketches, his crisp photographs and focused explanations.

Top to bottom: the eminently appropriate Bopitikelo Community and Cultural Centre at Molatedi – crisp, neat and local, regional.

One would be hard-pushed to overstate the simplicity of the central element: an open, double-aisle shed under tawny thatch that is laid on homely king-post trusses. They, in turn, are supported on slender, close-centred timber columns. The raked roof sweeps benignly to almost head-height at the two outer rows of supports. And that is it, a rural awning, a spacious, grass-covered clearing in an apparently lightly wooded glade. And that is its appeal: seemingly guileless, immediately legible clarity; spare, austere, certainly lucid directness. We are in the presence of primary, of constituent architecture – a perhaps necessary antidote to present preoccupations with superficial, ineptly borrowed adornment?

The shed – in essence, an open village barn – gives overall shelter to lightly enclosed, semi-enclosed and unenclosed spaces; places that accommodate celebratory, recreational, educational and similar group events. The spaces, like the events, are likely to change over time. Built of cement and local earth blocks, they can be inexpensively altered, demolished or relocated. Maintenance aside, the over-arching roof on its independent supports will probably remain untouched.

Beyond this restrained, this dignified shed, there are semi-circular thatch-covered and rectangular structures. They are placed in relationships that are anything but arbitrary. Their spatial links to the barn, as well as to the open areas between them, are purposefully dynamic. They alternate between closely defined, intimate spaces and more expansive communal places, community arenas. This ordered spatial interplay is emphasised by the changing levels of the gently sloping site; changes that accommodate these traditional fore-courts.

Much of this is, I gather, associated with the designers' sustained relationships with the small village community. Rich reports that he and his professional assistants have enjoyed and reciprocated the creative, the co-operative confidence of their multiple client. This is explicit in the manner in which their designs differ from, but also echo, Makuleke customs. They have incorporated and extended the community's constructional practices. They have respected and identified themselves with the group's social practices. Each of which is echoed by, for instance, the many *khotla*-like meeting places that occur throughout our sub-continent.

Construction and social purpose, tradition and change: these are the dynamic fascinations of this project. They are its special merit. They warrant international recognition that acknowledges the ways in which local buildings have long been erected and used; one which is also, simultaneously, an exercise in open, innovatory design. Rich, his community participants as well as his professional colleagues have, surely, taken a significant step on the path to a distinctively indigenous as well as an unmistakably contemporary way of building. In that sense, they are all practised regionalists.

For more than two decades, Kenneth Frampton – one among a handful of design theorists who call for serious attention – has grappled with the notion which he terms 'critical regionalism'. Architecture, he argues, is being devalued, debased to a bland, corporate, international homogeneity. Downtown anywhere is much like downtown everywhere; as are the shopping centres, business parks, medical precincts and other newcomers to suburbia. Architectural design is being reduced to a packaged commodity. Once optimal rentals have been ensured – principally by means of standardised building plans – design becomes a matter of choosing façade patterns from an approved range of fashionable – and thus marketable – images.

Frampton advocates resistance. He describes a variety of instances, drawn from many countries, in which architects and their clients have sought to identify and acknowledge regional, often parochial forms of expression. These designers, whilst remaining committed to the now world-wide processes of technological modernisation, seek to resist the consumerist uniformity associated with those same processes. They seek to deploy contemporary building procedures, techniques, materials and to address localised cultures, rooted 'architectures of place'. They seek to engage critically with modern technology; to do so through self-conscious, deliberately cultivated regionalisms.

The issue is a pressing one, nowhere more than for the populations of southern Africa. Like other 'developing' societies, they cannot for long forgo contemporary technology. Yet such local cultures as remain to them are precariously fragile; expressly in the face of modernisation introduced from outside – often aggressively, even forcibly. They are vulnerable to new, to seemingly alien technologies and their often antithetical values. The contradiction is painful, acutely so: how to embrace modernity and also sustain cherished cultural continuities?

Molatedi, a resettlement occasioned by arbitrary forced removals in 1969, seems a singularly appropriate venue for testing a likely resolution.

Designed by white-as-white-can-be architects in Johannesburg, adapted and built by young local, black, volunteers in far-off Mpumalanga – their *in situ* community building and the better for the changes they made.

Almost barefoot on the Lowveld

In 1990, after a 27-year absence abroad, I came home to a students' design conference in Cape Town. There, I still recall with excitement hearing an address on bare-foot architecture by the insightful – and inciting – Mozambican architect Jose Forjaz. He readily transposed my long standing advocacy of what, in Britain, was termed 'community architecture' to our regional context. Since then, I have seen or heard of instances in various parts of southern Africa that approach his prescriptions.; few though, have been quite as telling as the tiny Zwelisha Environmental Education Centre in the Acornhoek area, Mpumalanga.

The building, like its neighbours in this scattered, maize-planted settlement, sits on the brow of a gently sloping, verdant hillside; an alluvial valley below, scraggy *kopjes* behind with tough, shady trees and skin-scratching thorn bushes here, there, almost everywhere. A reddish dirt road suggests other, distant villages and – I imagine – the anticipated allure of local towns beyond.

The nearby buildings, each on its hard-stamped clearing, are of adobe and block-work with eye-catching swashes of colour around windows and on timber doors. Mud or cement plastered walls, corrugated iron – the roofs weighed with hefty boulders – and rippling family washing hung to dry are pervasive on this humid, shimmering-hot lowveld. Though far from easy, quiet village life endures.

The plan is an elementary L-shape. The eastern wing contains an office, an indoor meeting room, a utility kitchen and two water closets. All are small but not unduly so. The southern leg comprises a similarly small resource room and an extensive covered, but not enclosed, meeting area. These spaces, the entire built accommodation, are linked by a covered way that flows from the roofed meeting place, past an entrance court at the junction of the two wings and then to one of two large corrugated iron tanks that collect and store rain-water from the overhead gutter.

Top to bottom: the centre – modest, simple, the community's own. And attached, the instructive rough sketch plan to which the volunteers worked.

Materials, construction and finishes are also basic. Floors are cement screed or the smoothed wood-floated surfaces of concrete floor slabs; walls are plastered and painted or bagged block-work; the roof is of corrugated sheeting on timber rafters and purlins which, for the covered walkway and meeting space, are supported by posts fixed to the surface beds. Items such as window and door frames, the gutter, water tanks and roofing materials are standard, off the shelf.

Construction work was also standard, straightforward, as were the guidance notes and building details on the architect's admirably clear drawings of the structure and its immediate surroundings. The latter include a southern courtyard, an open *kraal* with low-level seating of block-work, a central clearing for an external fire, mature trees and the probable location of as yet unplanted indigenous saplings. These will complete the suggested *lapa* formed by the existing marula and acacia trees and two wings of the building with, as backdrop, the silhouetted rock-strewn hills that enfold the village. The scene is Spartan, spare, restrained – engaging.

True to the community's goal, the centre offers explicit instances of environmentally conscious design and construction. These range from matters such as tanks for saving rain-water and inexpensive ceiling insulation through to shallow rooms for easy ventilation and more traditional concerns like orientating the little building for southerly shade and simultaneously, for catching the prevailing cool breezes. There is, in addition, the disarmingly simple device of shading walls from the powerful overhead sun by overhanging roof-lines and eaves; a now neglected practice that predates the much admired farmhouse *stoeps* and colonial verandahs of the region.

One needs no trained skill in reading architectural plans, sections and elevations to appreciate that the designer's drawings do not quite tally with the building as it now stands. This is especially evident in what the architect refers to as the 'ears and teeth' of the striking parapet walls that flank the east-west wing. Here we are at the core of barefoot-like collaboration between a responsive designer and whole-hearted community involvement.

Colin Savage, the architect, described something of this dynamic process.

From the outset he worked with, he was well-nigh a participant member of the client body, which consisted of young women and men, some teenage, drawn from the Zwelisha Youth Group. He was, one might say, a receptive – a reciprocating as well as an initiating – pencil in their hands. This did not mean abandoning his specialist knowledge or his well-honed design skills. Quite the contrary, these were repeatedly called for and relied on by his colleagues on the building committee.

Indeed, the idea of an environmental education centre, funded by the national Department of Environmental Affairs, originated in and was then built and managed by the people of Zwelisha. Volunteers from the Youth Group dedicated their time and considerable labour at no cost to the project. The architect, who was consulted throughout, helped to focus and facilitate their efforts.

When he discusses the process, Savage conveys his enthusiasm readily. It was, he reports, a delight to direct one's professional experience to the gratifying task of realising a collaborative, home built, environmentally sensitive centre. He points proudly to the creative changes which the building team made to his restrained, cost-aware design; for example, to the projecting purlins, the 'teeth' and traditional Shangaan ear-like profile of a gable wall.

He recalls his admiration for the eagerness with which the young volunteers devoted themselves to their new-found building tasks, for their inventive desire to learn new principles and procedures. He and his associate Heather Dodd are currently engaged in similar participatory work; on this occasion with taxi and street trading organisations in heavily populated urban settings.

Now, two years on, he still relishes the opportunity he was given to play a contributory part in promoting local 'job creation and a return to rational water management and indigenous planting'. He still cherishes the low-key nature of the project, 'no posturing, no flag-waving, no politicising, no fanfares'. He still looks forward to seeing the large-scale mural that, after the building works were completed, was to have been carried out by school children from the village.

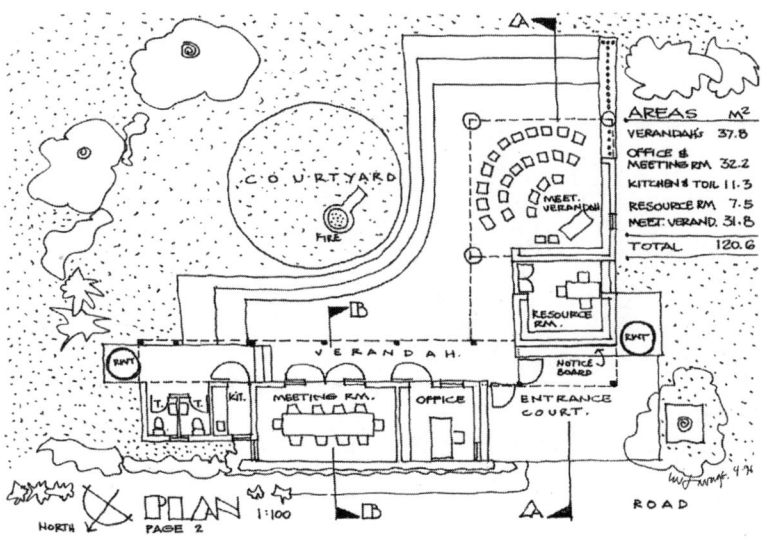

The traders' market on Rockey Street, Yeoville – an urban layout in an urban setting, traditional, contemporary, South African.

Architecture as backdrop to life

There is a realm of design which differs from grand ARCHITECTURE, from declamatory design statements, eminent celebrations of high-minded values. It is the vast world of everyday housing, workplaces and recreational buildings; of places which people occupy or call on regularly. These include public and semi-public venues such as shops, markets, schools, clinics, sports arenas. That, I submit, is where especially accomplished design is usually unobtrusive; where notable architecture is a designed backdrop to daily activities, a discreet setting in and against which they are enacted.

Such a place, an exciting one, has recently been completed in the commercial area of Yeoville. It is the new urban market on the block bounded by Cavendish, Hunter, Bedford and Rockey streets. A sliver on the north-west corner apart, the entire site is filled by Yeoville Central Market. That narrow exception is occupied by a nondescript multi-storey apartment building, the main façade of which has long been exposed to the merciless western sun.

There are no echoes of this inanity in the new buildings. Quite the contrary. Their disposition on the plot, their welcome devices for sun protection, comprise thorough as well as attractive responses to the highveld climate.

In other respects, the designers – Urban Solutions – have further acknowledged their surroundings, expressly the traditional low-rise ambience of this modest commercial area. This is particularly evidenced by their insistence on building up to the perimeter edges of the block. To that end, they have located trading accommodation at pavement level where it opens directly onto the four street frontages.

Other trading stalls, of which there are many, open off two open courtyards, one of which straddles the spinal passageway that runs from Hunter through to Rockey Street. The other, with its raised platform at the east end, is intended to be a 'performance courtyard'

Top to bottom: more and more of that up-to-date traditionalism.

for audiences of 200 people. At least some of the shows are likely to be presented by the street entertainers who currently perform in Rockey Street, a long-favoured venue.

The decision to bisect the market place by a lofty, double volume passageway has been decisive. This gives immediate access to and through the entire block for the many actual and potential customers who use the parking recess for taxis off Hunter Street – Yeoville is a daily destination for people travelling from Alexandra. It, the central corridor, leads to and past the internal trading spaces. Their occupants need not rely solely on pedestrians using the four encompassing roadways.

Visually this striking element knits together the two major, the eastern and western sections of the overall accommodation. Each of them penetrates it spatially, vigorously. It forms the core, the armature of the dynamic shed-like volumes which comprise the market place; all with their open mono-pitch roofs supported by elegant light metal tie-trusses.

The sheds warrant further mention. Initially the buildings abutting the southern courtyard were to have been double-storey. The upper level was intended for flats rented to traders and later, for manufacturing spaces occupied by shoemakers, carpenters, carvers and other artisan–producers. Funding restrictions intervened, the enterprise was reduced to single-level premises throughout – the sheds. They consist of sturdy buttress-shaped piers that carry the upper walls and lean-to roofs. Roller-shutter doors fitted between the piers provide easily manageable security on the street and courtyard frontages.

That, in essence, is the accommodation: secure, straightforward, robust, readily erected and maintained shelter. It is neither intended to be, nor is it tightly weather proof; excepting, of course, the closed-off cooking and food sales cubicles, a large area for storing traders' wares during closing hours and the men's and women's bath/toilet areas which are managed separately. Handsome, tough simplicity prevails.

This also applies to the imaginatively pragmatic way in which the sheds have been detailed. There are, along that powerful spinal corridor, the galvanised metal shoes which house, locate and secure the long gum-pole columns supporting the roof. There are, on the stocky brick piers that carry those columns, the inset tiles which give scale to the steeply sloping passageway. There are the numbered trading spaces indicated on the sheet-metal plates to which wall-mounted light fittings are attached. There is the slender steel rod bolted to each rafter-end that ties it to the wall below. There are the vertical and horizontal timber rods that provide shade where required and simultaneously cast shifting shadows on the surfaces beneath them. There is everywhere the sure sign of sensitive, alert designers at work.

Little of this adeptness is marred by its occasional lapses; by oversights such as the inordinately high bath house facility and storage room. Happily, the building wears errors of this nature comfortably. The architects, presumably, are anticipating opportunities to refine their confident first attempt at designing a local market. Meanwhile, they can surely be heartened by this unforced building, this quiet background against which animated, ever-changing scenes are played daily.

There is, however, a less sanguine, more far-reaching public issue at stake here. Is the new Yeoville market a socially suitable means of confronting the widely – the usually self-righteously – mooted 'problem' of street trading? In the clumsy new-speak that peppers official discussion of these matters, are such places acceptable 'inner city street trading management strategies'? Recent resistance by traders suggests profound disagreement.

If one accepts the research reports and business plans I was shown, the strategy is comfortingly relevant. But, as I could scarcely avoid noticing, these documents start from the apparently self-evident, unarticulated assumption that street trading does indeed call for a managerial tactic of this nature. They are grounded in the conviction that the trade is disorderly, unhygienic, unsightly, threatening, a civic menace which must needs be uprooted or banished to controlled off-street venues.

Given the undiminished pressures of widespread poverty that prevail currently and seem likely to persist, expectations that the promise of earnings from informal trading can be confined to officially sanctioned market places appear, at the very minimum, to be dubious. I, for one, shall not count on the now tidily cleared, lifeless, Rockey Street area remaining that way.

An architect's office in his garden; look to the detail, the architecture will look after itself – not quite there but approaching sound advice.

Heavenly detail

The bold assertion 'God is in the details' has been attributed to many architectural idols, especially to each of the modernist giants Le Corbusier, Frank Lloyd Wright and Mies van der Rohe. The notion is, though, far from modern or necessarily theistic. It lies in the venerable conviction that craft-like skill in construction lies pre-eminently in the seemly, the exact and elegant assembly of building elements and materials.

That is an essence, a litmus test of accomplished design; from even prior to ancient Egyptian or Japanese temples, to Maori long-houses, to the outstanding adobe buildings of northern Nigeria and the expressive gothic cathedrals of medieval Europe. It applies to fine building world-wide, across centuries.

This is one of many reasons why the extended coverage of glossy architectural journals tends often to be disappointing and vacuous. In their eagerness to convey glamorous overall impressions, they rarely focus effectively on detail. Other architectural comment – particularly that in the lay press – depends on less lavish, more pointed means. Here the critic/historian Reyner Banham who, throughout the 1950s and 1960s, wrote mainly unillustrated pieces for the *New Statesman*, was signally successful. He relied on descriptive imagination, as in his frequently cited comparison of an immaculate corner detail on van der Rohe's Seagram tower in New York with Stirling Moss effortlessly rounding a hairpin bend at Le Mans.

The Londoner Edward Cullinan has, in my view, long been one of the more polished of the designers who help keep this – regrettably now fading – skill alive. His work is simultaneously precise, appropriate and crisply instructive. So much so that he has been described as a contemporary constructivist: a designer who, through forceful and handsome detailing, offers lay observers a grasp of

Top to bottom: gems of workmanlike detailing – elegantly jointed roof members, glass and steel book shelving and a timber column on its base.

constructional intent, purpose and fulfilment. Here, in far off Johannesburg, Henry Paine, among others, practices a similarly explicit crafted clarity.

Paine's efforts are effectively illustrated at his recently completed small office in the rear garden of 35 Escombe Road, Parktown West. This Spartan little building accommodates three designers, their computers, drawing boards and storage requirements. The internal space spills readily, comfortably, onto a covered porch which doubles as an outdoor board room and lunch area. The setting, a quiet domestic garden, is embedded in dense highveld planting.

The detailing is impeccable, especially Paine's forte – points at which timber members are joined or fixed to masonry and like materials. So, there are the neatly wrought steel feet that hold the lower ends of his shaped timber columns in position and simultaneously obviate the likelihood of their end-grain edges rotting at pavement level. Then there are the steel brackets on which the rafters rest and are bolted to the rear wall of the porch. Internally, there are the memorably shaped, elegantly functional metal straps of the exposed roof trusses.

All this is echoed in Paine's quietly patterned, subtle floor tiling; in the restrained manner in which one is guided inconspicuously into the interior by a narrow, ladder-like suspended ceiling; in the sturdy, seemingly casual ethereal book shelving and other internal fittings. Nothing is ostentatious, rowdy, self-consciously *outré*. Thoughtful, careful, punctilious detail is paramount, everywhere.

I turn now to another of Paine's subdued, precisely detailed designs, the revamped premises for the newly instituted Graduate School for the Humanities and Social Sciences at Wits university. This occupies the second of two originally open-air courtyards in the old engineering block; that stately building immediately to the west of the declamatory central block on the east campus. Here too detailing is all.

A large seminar room has been won from a neglected, decidedly nondescript space. Sympathetic flooring has been installed; a coarse ceiling with crude fluorescent lighting has been exhaustively re-modelled; splendid double-leaf, four metre high hardwood doors are now in place; the blind arcades that embrace this volumetric relic have regained their earlier strength and grace. The space is now – in finish, proportion and symbolic meaning, in detail – a handsome place of learning, a refuge for debating diligently excavated, carefully evaluated knowledge.

This transformation is reinforced by a massive seminar platform, a huge gum-tree table from the hands of the carver Geoffrey Armstrong. With its chunky set of benches, this stamps and focuses the central purpose of the room as a venue of scholarly discussion.

That, of course, is the basis of postgraduate, advanced academic work – interrogating concepts and interpretations in detailed exchanges among colleagues who seek critically, analytically to explore the data presented to them.

One is immediately gripped by the restrained yet powerful ambience of this new setting for seminars. The neighbouring Hillman Block excepted, I doubt whether Wits has a more fittingly academic space.

While also finely detailed, the remaining accommodation for the Graduate School does not reach these expressive heights. An inviting entrance has been squeezed from an inauspicious nook under the main stairs. This leads into a reception area and then to various other student and staff rooms; including a printing and photocopying recess, a student forum and of course, extensive computing accommodation.

Paine has directly confronted the dilemmas of installing computing and other electrical services in an inflexible early twentieth-century, mock-classical structure. A continuous suspended cable tray runs along the major axis of the premises, while right-angled branches 'top feed' study and work stations that are located on shorter axes. The expanded metal trays carry service cables at a safe level, comfortably above head height. That, with judiciously selected wall colours – principally red, orange/brown and ochre – helps bring the volume of these over-lofty spaces down to human scale.

The School is a harmonious marriage across time and function. On the former count, long-past facilities have been skilfully adapted to meet recent academic developments. On the latter, bygone uses have been compellingly supplanted by those practised at present. These are apposite academic spaces. Their readily usable and symbolic impact, their aesthetic effect, has been comprehensively accounted for by carefully attentive design detailing.

Whether they are guided by presiding deities or skilled craftsmanship, designers like Paine lift us above the mediocrity that currently engulfs local architecture.

The shacks of Alexandra under the pylons and electricity lines into which the people were, until recently, unable to tap – taxation with amenities.

Shack settlements
— architecture without architects

Architecture has long been and still remains the privilege of the privileged. For millennia most people the world over have designed, constructed and lived in buildings without calling on specialist designers. Historically, the architectural profession, a product of the unprecedented occupational specialisation that occurred in mid-nineteenth century Europe, is a recent phenomenon. It sprang primarily from the medieval craft guilds that were associated with building work and later, from the *bodega* system of craft and artistic production which Filippo Brunelleschi, an early art entrepreneur, initiated in fifteenth-century Florence.

Happily or otherwise even now, the majority of buildings escape professional architectural attention. Unlike state national health and in some instances, legal aid provisions, open public access to specialist design is offered principally by a handful of non-governmental organisations (NGOs). This impinges on indigent people with special force; usually they cannot contemplate paying professional fees for what to them are traditional processes of self-help.

None are more subject to this restricted recourse to professional designers than the many millions of shack dwellers in Asia, Latin America, south east Europe, Africa and not least South Africa. They must and do rely on their own resources, on their own design skills. These, I suggest, are considerable; particularly because they are rooted in first-hand knowledge of what is needed and viable in the daily lives of the people affected.

Armed with this thought and heartened by the recent newspaper publicity given to 69-year-old Elvis Dube's remarkable double-storey home in Ivory Park, I resolved to visit some shacks in and around Johannesburg. His imaginative use of scrap materials was a foretaste of the ingenious, self-built structures that I found.

Top to bottom: township vignettes.

I was reminded constantly of earlier calls, over almost seven years, on people who live in what are often described, somewhat aloofly, as 'chaotic squatter camps'. The layouts of the settlements which I saw are far from unplanned, formless. They are certainly not, another common depiction, 'all higgledy-piggledy'. Quite the contrary.

They are arranged, apparently by common consent, to suit everyday usage. The deliberately positioned shacks are linked by major and lesser paths, some wide enough to form roads. These designated pedestrian and vehicular ways are, of course, directional. They lead to specific, functional, destinations such as *spaza* shops, communal water outlets, open spaces, taxi ranks, political party offices, points of access into and out of the settlements. They lead to places of public assembly, to places of social encounter.

Although customarily crowded into small areas, the shacks do not usually block paths or intrude physically on neighbours. Limited as it may be, there is space about them; space for neighbourhood activities such as watching casually over children at play, trading with hawkers at local stalls, maintaining informal surveillance of the area and – commonly – exchanging views with people from diverse backgrounds.

There is, in other words, space for many of the congenial attributes of urban, as against suburban, life which planning commentators like Jane Jacobs have ascribed to the local residential areas of cities throughout the world; of, for instance, downtown New York, Rio de Janeiro, Bangkok, Paris . . . of Hillbrow, Johannesburg.

These informal and consistently effective physical arrangements are matched by similar, seldom officially recorded, social compacts. My most readily illustrative instance occurred when, in 1991, a colleague and I visited a section of Orange Farm shortly after it had been established. Civil turmoil was, at that time, held to be endemic to sites of this nature.

Arriving at the outskirts of the settlement, we were approached by four young men who enquired about the purpose of our visit. My friend explained that he was showing me – an architect who had recently returned to South Africa after many years abroad – the circumstances in which self-built shelters were being erected and occupied. This done, they offered to assist us, first by indicating where his car might be parked in safety and shade.

While one of the group remained with the vehicle, the others guided us about the settlement and introduced us to people living there. Among a range of matters, householders were invited to tell us why, how and when they had come to Orange Farm, to clarify the site layout for us and to indicate how they had constructed and were now using their homes.

There is, we soon realised, a shared understanding of how life on the settlement might be conducted in an orderly, mutually satisfactory manner. We learnt that the physical and social arrangements are not fortuitous: they are communally negotiated, clearly articulated and endorsed by informal peer pressure and a written code of conduct. As key aspects of public life on the site, they are appropriately, if not conventionally, civic.

Turning to the arena of private life, the shacks themselves, one finds that, despite the persistently adverse conditions in the settlement, most shanty-homes are maintained in a similarly ordered fashion. Given its social connotations, the German word *gemutlichkeit* seems an apt depiction of the regularly swept earth forecourts, the serried rows of neat washing-lines and the similar signs of attentive household trimness which are visible to passers-by, even from vehicles speeding past on adjoining highways.

A corner of orderliness is, I imagine, an acutely perceived necessity in a world of unmanaged urbanisation, of seemingly entrenched unemployment, racial tensions, unrelieved poverty and the lofty indifference which 'respectable' society manifests toward the privations of 'squatter' life.

Most of the shacks which I have visited are constructed of corrugated and/or sheet iron, of plywood boarding and often of plastic sheeting. In the main, these adaptable, portable materials are fixed to metal or, more rarely, to timber frames. A few dwellings stand on concrete surface beds, but the majority are not founded solidly. Roofs are sloped slightly to discharge rainwater and frequently, held down by rocks or similarly weighty objects.

Unlike the picturesque adobe and thatch of the homes which many shanty dwellers probably occupied before coming to Egoli, these materials are industrial products. That they have been assembled by people who have adjusted rapidly to urban operations and methods is reflected in the structures; especially in the cockney, the proletarian adeptness of their construction.

As in all meaningful design, this proficiency links pragmatic and aesthetic issues. Here, as a case in point, I have in mind the resourceful dual use of standard 'up-and-over' garage doors. On a number of shacks, these serve as an external wall at night or during poor weather and in sunny conditions, as the tidily tucked-away fourth side of a now open verandah. This down to earth inventiveness is reminiscent of how, in the 1940s, the north American designer Charles Eames sought to exploit off-the-shelf, prefabricated materials for utilitarian and aesthetic ends.

The ubiquitous sheet or corrugated iron surfaces offer another instance. These abstract arrangements of rectangular planes remind me of the British artist Ben Nicholson's precisely controlled geometric compositions. As such, they evoke the powerful architectural aesthetic which the modern movement designer/architect Gerrit Rietveld pioneered for the living quarters and garage grouping he designed in Utrecht, 1927–28.

There are other examples: from the quilt art curtains that provide visual privacy in some shacks to the imaginatively contrived shelving and *ad hoc* containers for storing clothes and other domestic items. And they include space management: the carefully devised procedures for assigning the grossly inadequate space that is available to household activities such as washing, ironing, cooking, sleeping . . . and school homework.

Whatever else shack settlements lack – and that is a great deal – they are not without creative planning and design talent.

Growing up in pervasive poverty – future citizen.

One of the four peripheral lighting masts that slip through the bleacher seating to carry that semi-suspended structure.

Royal Bafokeng sports stadium

One of the SA Institute of Architects' annual awards for excellence has gone to a sports complex in Phokeng near Rustenberg. This is a twin success: collegiate recognition of a fine building and public acknowledgement for a socially responsive client, the Bafokeng Tribal Council.

The architects, Waterson Weyer Roon of Pretoria, are to be congratulated on the former. They will, doubtless, be envied for the latter. As appreciative bystanders, we can all relish confirmation of the hoary maxims *people get the architecture they deserve* and *handsome is as handsome has done.*

The new football and athletics stadium grew, I gather, from an informal soccer pitch around which heaped soil from nearby roadworks provided makeshift seating. That rough berm is now, a decade later, a powerful but also gracefully enfolding oval of raked bleacher seats on a sturdy reinforced concrete structure. The site allows for a taxi rank plus extensive motor-car and bus parking in glades of newly planted trees. Shaded stalls are intended for informal vendors on pedestrian ways that lead inter alia. to an established tree-lined picnic area by a dam.

The accommodation includes open and covered seating for about 39 000 spectators, executive suites for 140 VIPs, a large hall with kitchen and bar facilities and spacious halls for gymnastic, boxing and aerobic performances. There are, of course, change-rooms, food and drink shops, clubrooms, offices, maintenance workshops and storage spaces.

Additional facilities are located just south of the stadium: separate change-room and ancillary accommodation for four tennis and a like number of netball/basketball courts plus another phalanx of the same for an Olympic-size swimming-bath and an adjacent chil-

Top to bottom: three views of the precise detailing that marks this rural, but clearly, urbane stadium – immaculate precision and polished sophistication throughout, a right royal building.

dren's paddling pool. Each of these has independent sets of bleacher seats. A portion of this area has been earmarked for a multipurpose hall of approximately 5 000 square metres.

Even a casual visit affirms the spirit of the description *Royal Bafokeng Sports Palace* that was used in the citation for the award. The complex is, in its small-town setting, regal. That though, does not allay the feeling of incongruity one experiences on encountering such a customarily urban facility in what is – notwithstanding the local shopping complex and school to the immediate north – an unambiguously outer suburban area.

There is evidence of craftsmanship throughout, expressly at the stadium. Here advantage has been taken of the plastic quality that characterises concrete; a material which takes on the form and texture of the shuttering into which it is poured. That being sheet metal in this instance, the concrete surfaces echo the rectangular shapes and central fixing plugs of the individual sheets. The resulting smooth surfaces are given close-up intimacy by the randomly spread patches of exposed stone aggregate that pepper them. As an ever-present setting for the burnished metal balustrades and similar fixtures, as well as for occasional timber elements, this sophisticated finish provides a restrained backdrop; one that is eminently appropriate for a heavily trafficked, necessarily robust structure.

The unforced directness of built form and materials complements the craggy highveld *kopjes* of the surrounding hills. So, as a case in point, the recognisably saddle-shaped skyline of the stadium – occasioned by the emphatically raised east and west grandstands – parallels the undulating profile of a distant double-humped hillock. Happily, this and similar views of the rugged landscape beyond are framed in openings off many points within and on the stadium.

Then there are items that call for particular mention, two of which engaged my rapt attention. First, the four peripheral lighting masts that are cast of the same material as the main structure. The pair to the west stand free of that structure, each on its separate concrete base. The eastern couple pierce but do not touch the outermost edge of the stadium to hoist their huge lighting installations high above the sports buildings, the nearby houses and immediate landscape. Rising from powerful conical footings of concrete, these two slip effortlessly through oval openings in the perimeter rim of the building. The four are strikingly visible vertical elements of an inescapably horizontal structure.

The contrapuntal effect of this towering quartet occurs elsewhere; principally in the light, floating roof structure at the upper reaches of the western grandstand. This consists of nine latticed, tubular steel supports that are secured to the external wall of the stadium and cranked to cantilever over the uppermost tier of seats. These light beams carry cross-braced steel members onto which corrugated iron roofing is fixed from below. The ensemble provides a structurally confident, breath-taking sweep of shade and a welcome modicum of shelter from sudden summer downpours.

The rhythmic beat set up by the nine supports is as gripping from inside the stadium as it is from the approaching pathways. And that pulsating pattern is repeated on the opposite, the unroofed eastern stand as well as on its northern and southern neighbours. Here, though, the steel frames are inverted to form cantilevered supports for the top tier of seating. In the daily shifts of light across its contrasts of solid off-the-shutter concrete and open metal lattice work, the building is animated by a countervailing dance of the two materials.

The complex is, one gathers, informed by a pervasive social commitment, one that passes beyond sports entertainment and the ever-pressing local employment prospects it might engender. It is, I was assured, part of the tribal authority's investments in schools, clinics and similar socially pertinent projects – a trumpeted altruism that has been radically questioned in recent newspaper reports. Those investments are made possible by hard-won courtroom struggles for Bafokeng ownership of mineral rights in the vicinity, especially for the rich platinum deposits.

Why, then, focus on a costly – some may argue flighty – sports complex rather than on undeniably worthy needs such as more schools; needs which the young king-to-be, Kgosi Lerulo Molotlegi, and his tribal councillors claim to have sought consistently and are still seeking to address? Well . . . like people the world over, the Bafokeng do not live by or for bread alone. They too call for the pleasurable qualities which this rare development so patently offers.

Sturdy, durable, a handsome shelter for a local street-side marketplace – nothing makeshift, no cowboy workmanship here.

Wayside containers, local shenanigans

The more an architect cares about her/his work, especially the product's eventual use, the more he/she is likely to become embroiled in public wrangles. So much, then, for those specious but constantly trumpeted claims that architecture is socially neutral. Anticipated or not, desired or otherwise, one is rarely able to remain aloof from collisions that, for some, may seem extraneous to design activities. To be committed to architecture is to be enmeshed in its disputed uses.

Memories of this homily were renewed when I visited the wayside market on which the Heather Dodd and Colin Savage design partnership has worked over recent months. There, at Orange Farm Extension 9, on the R551 between the Golden Highway and Meyerton, one finds a handsome group of newly erected roadside structures. Their sturdiness contrasts immediately with the makeshift, the flimsy shelters that usually cluster about outlying mini-bus terminuses. In this instance, their muscular appearance is as fascinating as are the issues surrounding their occupancy.

The necessarily pared down construction – finance is tightly limited – centres on three related elements: adapted metal containers that serve as lock-up sales cubicles; Y-shaped steel joists that support butterfly canopies of galvanised roof sheeting, and sturdy concrete slabs that rest on solid cement-bagged brickwork. The low-slung horizontal effect is punctuated by a segment that runs at right angles to the main accommodation. Beyond, there are toilets with generous tub-like sinks.

These, with the many refuse bins on the site, are essential elements of hygienic street markets. They are surely what Johannesburg's unjustly maligned pavement hawkers yearn for: nearby toilets, cleansing water, adequate waste facilities, durable work-surfaces, sheltered and secure stalls. The paved areas, carefully considered stormwater drain-

Top to bottom: the market and its steel containers that provide lock-up stores and shopping cubicles; then, the lower two shots, the nearby Ubuhle Buyeza Children's Centre with its adapted, classroom containers.

165

age, the bright colours and cheerful signs, the tender green saplings signal a cared-for, a designed ensemble; one to which its users will, I imagine, respond in like manner.

Dodd and Savage have imported pre-fabricated, industrial products into an informal settlement. They have set such machine tooled items as steel containers and shaped joists among *ad hoc* hand-built, rudimentary shelters. This was done under the immediate charge of a self-made contractor, Johnstone Motsane, who backed-up these manufactured installations with a team of local, informally trained building workers. Unsurprisingly, that labour force, whether directly employed or sub-contracted, called on detailed, frequent attention from the architects. Their time and didactic interventions far exceeded customary professional services.

That was not the designers' only unscheduled involvement. They were also challenged by other responsibilities; by tasks far more tangentially related to daily architectural practice. For instance, during an initial visit to the site, I found the architect at the centre of a pressing crowd. This, I learnt, comprised prospective vendors who were reinforcing their claims for rented stalls by offering detailed information about their wares and themselves – data which he was required to record accurately. Architectural work, apparently, embraces estate agency . . . and more.

At the time, Savage was also conferring intensely with the occupant of a stall to be vacated for the new premises. The latter argued that since, like his indigent colleagues, he was trading rent-free from a self-built shelter, he should not be required and could not afford now to pay council rents. Following that, a variety of seemingly consequent threats and intimidatory acts had to be weathered. This too appeared to be an unquestioned architectural responsibility; as did repeated canvassing for additional resources, arranging for repairs due to petty vandalism, balancing the contending manoeuvres of local political bosses, negotiating between other affected parties. The architects were, I learnt, acting as general go-betweens – as letting and funding agents, mediators, umpires, socio-political fixers.

Not far off – at the Thula Mutwana shack settlement, some 38 kilometres from Johannesburg – Dodd and Savage's architectural colleague Peter Rich's experiences have not been dissimilar.

Despite his confident assertion that 'we worked hard to get the politics right from the beginning' and the local 'participatory dynamics' which he helped to set in train, he too reported problems of a predominantly political nature. These centred on what he termed the 'brokered deals' negotiated for some 750 families who had been removed from a temporary settlement opposite the Johannesburg Oriental Plaza. The special facilities now being afforded to them by European donors have, apparently, provoked damaging jealousies among residents of less favoured settlements. Rich spoke in the heightened terms of 'social upheaval' and even 'civil war', avoidance of which demanded a deal of time, energy and social skill.

Rich also used three metal containers as the core of his design for the complex, the Ubuhle Buyeza Children's Centre. As had occurred at Orange Farm, he too dismissed reservations that these un-insulated boxes are ovens in summer and winter chill boxes. Here they are encompassed by tall gum-pole structures that support shaded outdoor areas. They provide lock-up storage and homework rooms; all of which are in comfortable proximity to a covered creche, a proposed planting court and garden, a basketball pitch and a children's play corner.

Set among fragile shacks, the centre is an evocation of purportedly African forms. Where Dodd and Savage sought to turn industrial products to local purposes, Rich has attempted to recast traditional materials, to bend them to contemporary intentions. Each is embedded in current reality. Acceptance or otherwise of these differing approaches, as of many others which come readily to mind, calls for widespread discussion. Like other crafts, popular architecture resonates with publics who have some grasp of what is involved in its production.

In these and similar matters, the efforts which caring designers make need to be examined widely, to be analysed openly. That could enable them, with their less committed colleagues, to reach beyond the facile borrowing that marks the generality of present South African design.

Without public discussion – critical as well as appreciative – everyday architectural work cannot but remain in thrall to market-besotted speculators, to 'development managers'. Without such a broad reference, locally rooted architectures are unlikely to escape the sterile grip of postmodern discourse – our effete counterpart to the languid comment that passed for analysis in the aesthetic salons of the past.

Strength and grace, ancient and contemporary – the supple geometric order and subtle sophistication of the new mosque in central Johannesburg, a peninsula of serenity in an over-burdened inner city.

Serenity in clamour
– the new Mosque, Johannesburg

Central Johannesburg has long been architecturally bereft. In a city still locked into the crude grid of a mine camp, few of our stolid, modern towers – relentlessly borrowed from downtown anywhere, everywhere, nowhere – warrant sustained attention. They seem indifferent to us, as we have become to them.

Intriguing that these numbingly bland environs should have been taken over, appropriated. The inner city, a site of compressed urban density, is now patently African; pulsing with open, daily celebrations of activity. A spirited public place. The earlier genteel, skin-deep, enforced tidiness gone, replaced by a local, kaleidoscopic, often threatening, vitality.

Occasionally, all too seldom, a downtown building grips the imagination. One's heart floats, breathing quickens, attention is concentrated. Architecture comes into its own – an engaging, engrossing public activity. Such encounters are infrequent: Patidar Mansions in Ferreirasdorp, Aiton Court on Hospital Hill, that prescient 1930s-modern pair at 233 and 235 Bree Street . . . and – now gone – the bravely innovative 20th Century Cinema, opened in 1940 to be razed, in Jo'burg-style commercial vandalism, some 30 years later.

Now a new, a traditional building of distinction, perhaps the most notable of all – Johannesburg's Jumah Masgied, that August mosque which has been growing off Sauer Street. Architecture at last, designer Muhammad Mayet's singular addition to the city.

Clearly, I am an enthusiast. Architecture of this quality, buildings that evince such loving design and construction are hardly everyday currency. Why, then, restrain one's so rarely excited joy, wonder, respect?

An admirer, but an outsider. I've no basis for commenting authoritatively on Islamic precedent, on the sacred antecedents of this *musjid*, mosque. I can, though, recognise that it stands as an artefact which evokes admiration.

Top to bottom: a thought-provoking trio of alien elements – alien only in their confident, quiet dignity, in their respectful recall of tradition.

Externally a powerful, handsomely proportioned building with, fortunately, each of its four precise, confidently controlled façades visible at present. Internally the spaces are similarly comely and functionally exact. Dignified volumes in which revealed, unadorned, structure is poised in dynamic juxtaposition to robust, yet delicately patterned, plasterwork. And what structural elements they are: muscular arches, sinewy fan and cross vaults, sturdy squinches, enfolding pendentives and to cap it, a fine dome. What plasterwork it is. What a sure, subtle application of traditional Arabic craftsmanship. Shades of the complex geometric patterns and stalactite plaster vaults of the Alhambra (1309–1354) in Granada, Spain.

There it stands, a tribute to the religious, intellectual, social, political, the mercantile contributions made to Johannesburg life by Muslim peoples. There it is, a signal to the enlivening cultural diversity of this vital city. A serene place, in clamorous surroundings, for exercising personal and communal faith, for meditation and prayer.

What lies behind these calm, reassuring façades? At basement level, two crypt-like prayer halls of immediately sensed strength, of contained structural energy. The larger has a square floor plan, comprising nine vaulted bays, with a *nimbar* (pulpit) recessed into the massive north wall. This hall, like the major volume above, has been shifted marginally but appreciably off the street grid in order to face Makkah (Mecca) directly; and thus to add a vitalising tilt of orientation in the axes of the floor plan. To the south there is a smaller, plain rectangular hall lit by three centrally positioned roof-lights. It contrasts with and complements the stable, earth-tied solidity of the bigger hall.

Both these spaces are separated from the toilet area by a foyer/lobby that extends north-south through the building and also occurs on the upper level. There the lobby forms a break between the Main Prayer Hall and a *wudhu*, an ablution chamber in which worshippers wash exposed parts of their bodies that might touch the floor of a prayer room. At other, higher, levels access is provided to residential accommodation for the *Iman* who conducts services and the *Meuzzin* who summonses people to prayer.

Now to ground-floor level where the major, the domed Main Prayer Hall is situated. Here too there's a call for keen admiration. This, the central space of the building, sails upward through almost fourteen meters with something of the airy ease of, for instance, the medieval Lady Chapel at Bristol Cathedral. Four elegant columns plus their pilaster counterparts rise through the cube-like volume to carry the arches that span the hall – and – in a dramatic off-centre position, to rise to a higher arch in the dome opening.

Excepting the lofty foyer space at the Baxter Theatre in Cape Town, I cannot think of another such enthralling volume in a contemporary South African building. This is architectural enclosure – space skilfully manipulated for people's physical, emotional and further, their spiritual well-being.

Then there's the minaret ascending through and above the structure to present, with the dome, a familiar mosque silhouette. Extended by the slim spire beyond its strongly corbelled balcony, the tower reaches over 48 metres above pavement level: an expressive call to prayer, an emphatic piece of city-scape.

In all, it's an exciting ensemble of contrasts: powerful repose and buoyant tracery; an earth-bound and immediately above, a gravity-defying prayer hall; weighty, dense brick walls and seemingly weightless, gossamer, plaster-work; a compact, firm masonry base and a lean, sky-piercing tower . . . sacred and profane places.

The plaster-work comes from the deft hands of visiting Moroccan craftsmen. They, I learnt, were born into or brought up in this venerable tradition. It shows. Their work is geometrically intricate and wondrously inventive within strictly bounded, hallowed custom. It's as alive with the signs of human skill and imagination as machined work is so often impassive, lifeless, dull.

Here, however, I've a reservation; it concerns the external treatment of the mosque. Superb as the plaster-work is, I prefer the uncovered, sturdy brickwork that has been so evident during construction. These rooted masonry walls offer, in my view, an instructive glimpse, an understanding, of how the building has been made – an unforced public lesson in fine brick construction.

In a brief comment on the project, the architect noted that it was designed for load-bearing brick in order to 'reintroduce the scientific and artistic superiority of brick technology and its economic use'. This demonstrative, didactic purpose marks a happy change from what occurred in the case of other, older brick buildings in the area.

It differs, for example, from the School Clinic Building in nearby Jeppe Street, and from the coolly accomplished 'Georgian' instance on the north-east corner of Joubert and Jeppe Streets. In these and similar cases, the joy of proficient, proudly executed labour departed with the craftsmen who had been brought here – chiefly from Britain and the Netherlands – expressly to work on the buildings. When they returned to Europe, their craft went as well. It was not, categorically not, shared with the majority home population; with people from different, more rural, more impermanent building traditions. This loss is what Muhammad Mayet now, about some eighty years on, seeks to counter.

In the passage which I cited above, he argued that brick technology surpasses 'the prevailing ill-adapted technology of reinforced concrete'. Sadly, he has himself demonstrated the point. The Main Prayer Hall has two balconies of this material, one above the other. They project obtrusively, awkwardly, as alien trabeated elements, into the hall to negate part of its spatial integrity. Had this not been the case, the soaring thrust of this arched, confidently proportioned volume would, assuredly, have been *the* exemplar of deeply moving architectural interiors in Johannesburg.

Islamic worship has taken place on this limited, 740 square metre plot for well over a century. An attractive formal structure was erected specifically as a mosque in 1918. Five years ago, that building was demolished – too small and structurally unsound. Hence the project now nearing completion.

Given the shifts of populations from inner to outer areas that have come to characterise Johannesburg, like other cities, this centrally located site could pose problems for future attendance. Worshippers pray, preferably in congregation, five times each day; historically occasioning settlement within about a fifteen minute walk from mosques. Need one now fear falling numbers as a consequence of this continuing urban relocation; increasingly perhaps over the coming decades?

Further, the constrained site has contributed, I suggest, to the monolithic form of the building; it has imposed a convergent design. A plan without, regrettably, even a vestige of the inviting open platforms, the forecourts, courtyards or walled gardens of the Great Mosques at, say, Bukhara, Cairo, Cordoba, Delhi. It could, concomitantly, have resulted in a probably unintended feeling of introverted exclusion.

Despite ready accessibility – the *musjid* is open to all Muslims at any hour – there may be a perceived turning from others in the city. A remnant of bruised sensitivities engendered by the cruelly offensive, the damaging deprivations of the Group Areas Act and other, now also abolished, discriminatory practices?

Serene, in dignified repose.

A triumphant, flattish dome that sits astride splendid stretches of face-brick work, curved and arched, to rival the very best in Johannesburg – and elsewhere.

The Hagia Sophia
on Wolmarans Street, Johannesburg

The Johannesburg Great Synagogue, built 1913–14, now stands unused; in all too evident decline. Though ever closer to dereliction (perhaps to demolition?) it remains high, wide and handsome. Will, should the building be saved? Could it be put to purposeful use?

The *schul* fills the entire block bounded by streets with names that trumpet the city's mining origins: Claim, Quartz, Wolmarans and Smit. Excepting the areas at the three round-headed arches of the forceful main entry and at the administrative entrance off Smit, a stout brick wall with cement copings and rhythmic grilles encompasses the now scrappy gardens, the ragged trees, the forlorn annexes. These scruffy surroundings notwithstanding, the building rises powerfully, confidently.

The palette of materials and forms is limited, convincingly so. Principally, they comprise flat and curved planes of finely crafted and laid face-brick, cement insets to deeply recessed window and door openings, copper clad half-domes, barrel vaults and a robust concrete clerestory drum beneath the shallow main dome. That is capped by a slender lantern and surmounting six-pointed Star of David. There are unmistakable shades of widely admired contemporary buildings; like Hendrik Berlage's outstanding Stock Exchange (1897–1903) in Amsterdam, or Josef Olbrich's accomplished Kunsterkolonie (1905–7) at Darmstadt near Frankfurt.

Twin stair towers of the same reddish brick-work flank the major entrance. They too are domed and covered with green-oxidised copper sheeting. There is little applied ornament. This massive yet elegant structure is restrained, quiet, monumentally serene. At present, it sits unruffled among coarsely designed blocks of flats, noisy postmodern fancies, a glitzy 'nite spot', raucous advertising. It is as unmoved by the fume-spewing motor traffic on the encircling roads as it is receptive to the bustling pedestrians of the area, particularly the street traders who line the sunny northern front.

Top to bottom: the dome, the main, south, façade and, shamefully, a house of God now given over to casual, kerb-side trade – all still under the hallowed Star of David.

The interior is no less impressive: an over-arching volume of plain-plastered wall and dome surfaces; the full-muscled arches and pendentives that carry the strong curves of the hemisphere poised above; sweeping timber pews on the male-only lower level and upper balconies for women; a grille-covered choir gallery; the cantor's raised *bimah* of sturdily detailed timber; the sudden outbreak of rich marble and mosaic around the marriage platform and Ark – a sacred tabernacle that, until recently, housed the holy *torah*.

It is a strikingly simple interior; a coolly enfolding space of immediate dignity. That is not surprising. The architect was, he said, moved 'to design something on the lines' of the sixth-century Hagia Sophia, the 'divine wisdom' of Santa Sophia in Constantinople. That extraordinary Byzantine church and later mosque, was described, with widespread agreement, by the historian Banister Fletcher as 'the greatest glory of early Christendom'. Though not, to be sure, as magnificent, the synagogue is indeed something on those lines.

Built to the competition design of a Swiss engineer–architect, Theophile Schaerer, it bears many marks of *fin de siecle* European architecture. Not least, it exemplifies the uneasy, the not-wholly-convincing bourgeois confidence of Edwardian Britain. During my recent visit to its soundless lobbies and halls, I was reminded repeatedly of buildings such as the Adelfi Hotel, Liverpool or the Ritz of London: solid materials and construction; grand foyers, imposing spaces, heavy door and window fittings, marble inlays, weighty furnishings, thick-piled carpeting. The focus is one of seemly, respectable homage to rapidly passing dominion, power, wealth.

Respectability, propriety, fitting behaviour: these are exemplified in the precisely incised Hebrew and English words on the large marble plaques at either side of the Ark. They announce ingratiating fidelity to the purportedly benign rule of 'our sovereign Lord, King George V and gracious Queen Mary, Alexandra the Queen Mother, Edward Prince of Wales' and other imperial worthies.

My discomfort with that self-conscious rectitude is, chiefly, what came rushing back to me as I sat on the hard seat (adjoining my grandfather's and father's) which I had occupied on high festivals from boyhood to late adolescence. There I was once again, looking to the women's gallery for my mother, grandmother, aunts; they who sat among many similarly jewelled, best-frocked, heavily furred wives, daughters, sisters. Again, among those serge-suited men, I heard whispered concern about current affairs, scandals, tragedies, business deals. Again I realised how readily one is schooled to distinguish nuances of status: which convoluted subtleties set the established apart from the newly arrived and both from the least well-heeled. There I, like others the world over, was exposed to fine gradations of condescension and such lean charity as was dispensed.

There were other lessons; stemming mostly from communal intimacy, shared histories. These, as I sat on that tough bench, seemed to focus on the celebration of my coming-of-age, my barmitzvah, when a nervous thirteen-year-old at the *bimah* was guided tenderly through his public reading of the law for that day.

Such respectful compassion did not, to my knowledge, reach beyond the *schul* to our many, many needy fellow South Africans. Like other devotees of imperial decorum, the congregation was not renowned for challenging prevailing dogma; particularly the Kiplingesque precept that the people on whose toil the city's wealth was centrally founded were 'lesser breeds without the law'.

Is that an indicator of a possible future for the building?

For my part, I have no doubt that the Great Synagogue must be preserved. It is a building of cultural import, of historic value, of considerable architectural merit. To what purpose might this fine relic be put? The answer seems self-evident – to the service of its surrounding inhabitants with, of course, active sponsorship by their predecessors, who, after all, are unlikely to return as congregants.

Customary uses come readily to mind: in the annexes, a creche, nursery school, community hall and associated offices, a clinic, day centre and meals-on-wheels kitchen for elderly residents. Space is plentiful. And, in that great hall of worship? I envisage a community market, a further facility that could make real the many past prayers to universal humanity.

There must surely be other, more imaginative suggestions – especially those which, if asked, the currently excluded neighbours might offer.

A happy complex of buildings at the Cradle Game Reserve, just north of the Crocodile River – the restaurant and its breath-taking panorama, with bustling meal servings.

Straightforward and good

As others celebrate each year-end in Johannesburg, one cannot but think in anguish of the city's most recent annual crop of built grotesqueries. No longer. Since the birth of the much heralded twenty-first millennium, the term *grotesque* has been made obsolete: first by the monstrous Montecasino complex on William Nicol Highway, then by the mooted 108-storey block adjacent to Alexandra Township. Our tolerance for freakish buildings must, surely, be spent.

That new Montecasino is, the developer's chief executive officer tells us 'perfect in every detail . . . a Tuscan village'. Its medieval namesake in Italy – site of a particularly murderous battle in World War II – has been transported across time to the Italian Renaissance, there to be decked with 'beautifully replicated' façades. Those humbug fronts cover, among other things, a massive shopping hall, restaurants and not to be missed, facilities that 'will move the gaming experience . . . beyond the expectations of its visitors'. The bizarre Lost City comes to town.

If not, consider the 'beacon of the African Renaissance' proposed by the Maharishi development corporation. A 488 metre skyscraper costing R20 billion and more will be snatched from its Kafkaesque nightmare to be nothing less than 'the tallest building on earth'. All this, and reams of cloying hype about a 'luxurious, environmentally friendly development' on a site abutting the ever-spreading shacklands of Alexandra.

Enough? I shall spare you more by turning now to something that is, indeed, celebratory – the clutch of buildings designed by architects Enrico Daffonchio & Associates at the Cradle Game Reserve, off D F Malan Drive (now Beyers Naude Drive) immediately north of the Crocodile River.

Top to bottom: three of the many felicitous details in the restaurant building – the central being the effortlessly framed view as one enters.

There are, at present, three structures in the visitors' precinct: a smallish conference unit, the sturdy manager's house and the restaurant, Cornutti in the Cradle. Each bears the stamp of imaginative design, of sensitive architectural planning. None more so than the restaurant block.

Visitors soon find themselves rid of their enveloping Johannesburg shams. Having parked one's car on a plateau overlooking the reserve, one descends to the restaurant *via* steps carved from the rocky hillside or by an electrically powered golf cart. The panoramic views of verdant bush, sunlit hilltops and shaded valleys from that acropolis and throughout the descent, are majestic. They demand repeated pauses during this and the upward journey when leaving the reserve.

It is the ever-shifting, constantly gripping southern African highveld in its most impressive splendour. The prospect and reality of encountering wild game in these sublime surroundings is a bonus. On both scores, my companions and I were not disappointed. Nor were we in the least displeased by the buildings. Quite the contrary.

The restaurant building lies along the contours of a steep, rock-strewn hillside facing a now focused view. Approached from above, one looks down onto a large mono-pitch roof that, in a huge bird-like sweep, seems poised to float over the valleys below. That impression is reinforced when, later, one stands under the wide, daringly cantilevered canopy over the north-facing terrace. Here the impulse to take wing in hang-glider fashion is as striking as is the scenic parade below and beyond.

Back to the entrance. This is made across low steps, or a gentle ramp, *via* a space which appears to have been scooped out of the built-up, earth-filled, turf-covered rampart that, a series of high-level windows apart, comprises the entire southern façade. The drama is emphasised by the hovering slice of raised roof which, having marked the entry point, carries through a bridge-like lobby into the body of the dining area. The veld views ahead beckon all the while.

Utilitarian spaces – kitchen, stores, scullery, change rooms and toilets – occupy the southern portion behind the long rectangular dining volume and its centrally located, elongated bar. A further dining space and lounge are similarly placed to the south-east, across the entrance lobby. That and the main, rectangular, dining area open onto the covered terrace, which is of comparable size. Tall, full-height, fold-slide-and-roll-away glass doors enable the staff to throw the terrace and the interior dining spaces together in fine weather. On these occasions, the place filled with the buzz of fellow diners, the tangible sybaritic bliss makes one's head reel. Metaphorically, one floats off over the undulating landscape below.

The building is without counterfeit pretensions. It is self-confidently modern – steel, glass, timber, concrete, clean-cut furniture, contemporary fittings and decor. Handsomely laid stone walls – expertly hewn *in situ* and immaculately set by Ben Mpapani, a local craftsman – help tie this airy construction to the earth. The contrast with game park buildings across the country is marked. The homely cosiness of the ubiquitous thatch and gum-pole has been foresworn for the structural steel, the metal sheeting and toughened glass of nearby industrial Johannesburg.

'We wanted simplicity and beauty' says Daffonchio. He and his design associate, Anna Claude, have realised just that.

Though much smaller and less dramatically situated on this magnificent site, the conference block wears the same distinctive aura of responsive architecture. It too rides the contoured hillside with elegance. It too fits snugly, without self-effacement, into that rocky slope. It too frames views and sunlight through a shady terrace across the north front.

That verandah, the familiar southern African stoep, is but one aspect of the architects' work which makes it so searchingly contemporary: a readiness to adapt traditional building elements – enduring cultural practices – to long-lasting regional conditions.

The manager's house, like the gate lodge through which one enters and leaves the reserve, results from a different, though related, use of building materials. While each celebrates the local stone, neither precludes contemporary items such as steel windows and door frames, industrially produced fitments and thoroughly modern installations.

Both echo, but most decidedly do not imitate, aspects of Le Corbusier's innovative lesser works. The gate-house resonates distantly with Maison aux Mathes, Corbu's delightful family holiday home of 1935. The manager's house summonses his designs for the even more modest dwellings, *circa* 1952, of Chandigarh, the Punjabi capital city, India. Fleeting as these, my personal, architectural associations may be, they tower above the increasingly banal grotesqueries of urban Gauteng.

The central, administrative block at Siemens on the Pretoria-Johannesburg road – Teutonic exactness in the sub-tropics?

Gropius comes to Midrand?

When you are next on the N1 from Johannesburg to Pretoria, slow down on approaching Halfway House, pull over to the left. Look, please, for two handsome new buildings. You will not miss them. They are beacons of quality in the ribbon of architectural dreariness that straddles this, probably the busiest stretch of highway in southern Africa.

First there is Pilkington's PFG Glass Centre: a swashbuckling cubist essay in sheet glass and smooth wall planes, an architectural *tour de force*. Then, a half kilometre on, there's the more restrained classic modernism of Siemens Park, local head office of the huge corporation in Germany. Here, on our rolling highveld, you'll encounter a poised *ensemble* of imported, *Mittel Europaische* buildings.

The Park is a late twentieth-century homage to 'total architecture'. It is a salute to 1920s Neue Sachlichkeit, the new objectivity: the rational design which architects like the pioneering German modernist Walter Gropius taught and practised. That touch is everywhere: from a crisply articulated site layout to the urbane, clean-cut white buildings and, once inside, from the precise stainless steel trim to the sensuous, semi-suspended central stairway. It is all of a piece: a designed totality.

The wedge-shaped site descends steeply from the south along Ben Schoeman Highway. Two parallel rows of building, separated by gardens, pathways and a tumbling water cascade, step down in measured pace from the wider southern end. At present – the Park was opened in March 1996 – there are five standard blocks plus a 31 metre high, six-storey drum on which the complex is firmly pivoted.

Plans for phase two of the project, which will bring building costs to over R120 million, show four further units to the south. These include an apse-like curved block to close the tightly composed vista

Top to bottom: controlled, minimalist, precision detailing – whether at a bow-window, a signpost or the effective, built-in sun-visors.

on the powerful north-south axis. The promise is enticing: a dynamic symmetry of eight linked units contained between an enclosing upper semi-circle and the robust off-axis drum at the lower level.

Over a third of the site, at the northern end, is given over to serried, regimented rows of car parking under shade cloth. The relentless order will, the architect assured me, be mitigated by the indigenous trees which have been planted. Currently, though, the unmistakably martial feeling of this vast area (for over 800 cars) amplifies the taut severity of the façades. Perhaps the landscaping, as yet undeveloped, will help soften these unbending effects.

The 'white' architecture of early modernism was, in the main, realised in painted stucco; a finish that cracks, flakes and discolours readily. The Siemens designers have opted for a more enduring – and costly material: machine crafted baked enamel panels of specially strengthened sheet aluminium that are fixed to the frame of the building by means demanding punctilious on-site, craft-like skills.

All the structures – the drum, the two main wings and even the gate house – are clad in these precision-made, square (882 x 882 mm) powder-coated aluminium panels. And throughout, the sound-dampening double-glazed windows are framed in the same white material; as are the variously sized sun-screening devices that are mounted on all north, west and east façades.

The buildings gleam and sparkle in their uniform, engineered whiteness; breached only by the blue logo SIEMENS on the upper level of the drum and high on a southern face. In our lively highveld light, the changing shadows are exact; especially those cast by the open fire escape stairs that march across the east and west façades. The white architecture which, among others, Le Corbusier promoted in his 1920s *maisons blanches* has come of technical age.

The symbolism is unambiguous. Siemens, its multi-national interests rooted in the cross-national electrical, electronic engineering and atomic industries, is nothing if not an assured worldwide enterprise. Whether at its recently erected office buildings in Munchen and Manchester or here in Midrand, the machined white corporate image speaks, in subdued but confident tones, of up-to-date organisational and technological expertise, of industrial competence and above all, of order.

The designer has done this by means of a finely balanced inversion of effects. The more restrained the quiet monochrome aesthetic, the more luxuriant the impact: conspicuous consumption dressed in chaste white enamel.

Now pass under the daringly cantilevered canopy, through an ascetically unadorned entrance hall into the central foyer of the drum. It's white, all white. There are though, in strategic places, stainless steel handrails, matte finished waste paper-cum-ash receptacles and glossy frames to bulbous black leather, Le Corbusier-*manque*, armchairs. A white spiral stair with black carpeted treads ascends through six floors to a domed roof light high above. Black and white, the primary non-colours, in austere impeccably contrived juxtaposition.

This purity of form and colour, pre-eminently white, permeates the interior of the drum ... and beyond. There is a security enclave, executive offices and dining rooms, open-plan suites for office staff, an auditorium that seats 300 people, plus attendant toilet and other service areas.

Not least, there is a sweep of immaculate cafeteria space for 600 diners that overlooks what will soon be a lush garden. The pervasive white finishes in this restaurant-like, splendidly equipped area are relieved by two boldly coloured walls: deep metallic blue and cadmium yellow.

One moves directly from a large lobby at the base of the drum to the first of the five identical L-shaped blocks. Each of these comprises a semi-basement, three upper storeys and a landscaped courtyard. The basements house laboratories and/or workshops; the upper levels are for offices, mostly open-plan but with five or six enclosed units per floor. These work settings are all purposefully planned, well lit, spacious, comfortable. They are methodically arranged, businesslike, shipshape. White, not surprisingly, is the predominant colour.

Here, as elsewhere on this well-ordered site, in these trimly designed buildings, the image is insistent: a celebration of functional effciency, industrial exactitude, corporate control.

This is not reflected in the customary behaviour of the 1,050 members of staff, nor of visitors to the Park. They, like most of us, are not uniformly neat. They wear unmatched clothing, discordant colours; their executive pin-stripe suits are soon creased. They are not unremittingly engaged in productive work. They leave open books, loose papers, floppy discs, half-finished coffee cups on none-too-tidy desks. They lean casually against clean white walls, they slump on pristine black chairs.

They are not designer-human: they obtrude constantly on the vitreous clarity of the architecture. A local Charlie Chaplin or Woody Allen would surely relish and no doubt embellish the contrasts, the ironies.

Siemens Park is, I submit, architecture of a fastidious, a refreshingly welcome order. That, though, does not preclude queries about aspects of this recital of modern design ideals.

Why, for instance, choose a site so polluted by exhaust fumes and traffic noise as to necessitate environmentally costly air-conditioning and double-glazing? And why, in the hot sunny Gauteng climate, clad buildings in metal; in a material that calls for the elaborate insulation installed, perforce, at the Park? Why, in short, use scarce resources with such off-hand profligacy?

Clearly, the corporation's precedents in Bavaria and the English midlands need not, in the hugely different circumstances of southern Africa, have been adhered to with such determined dogmatism.

A cool cascade on a summer's day.

Well chosen face-bricks and smoothly finished reinforced concrete blocks – a song of architectural harmony at the old Woodmead School, north of Johannesburg.

Architecture to sing about

The northern rim of outer Johannesburg is, many will probably agree, not where one might expect to strike architectural gold. So when such a find occurs ... well, that is definitely something to sing about. Since stumbling initially, at an earlier stage of construction, on a group of imaginatively designed school buildings in Nooitgedacht, beyond Craigavon, I have been captivated in the thrall of its rhythmic pulses.

At the periphery of pretentious suburbia, tied into humming highveld grassland, I came across Woodmead School: an ensemble of buildings in a whispering bend of the Jukskei River. Hush! That is surely Miriam Makeba's click song, a staccato Hugh Masekela chorus? Listen! Whose taut notes are those long-ago echoes of Kippie Moeketsi's incisive, swinging sax?

Enough! These are new buildings, not the recycled jam sessions of nostalgia.

First, and the basis of all else, there is a happy congruence at Woodmead, a long-held design goal made real: a fusion of form and content. To adapt a phrase from the pre-modernist designer, architectural historian and theorist William Morris, there is a reaching for an architectural ideal 'Those externals of a true place of learning can only be realised without affectation by the life to be lived in them being reasonable and fit for human beings'. In short, there is here a binding harmony between the buildings and the life that goes on in and about them.

Reasonable and fit for human beings! In South Africa that has to be multi-racial, cross cultural. As the condition for other humane pedagogic goals, it must mean a firm refusal of racial segregation, of cultural separation, of apartheid 'own affairs' and similar notions, not to mention divisive practices.

Top to bottom: more harmony, memorable melody – in the fine assembly hall, a passage way to the classroom block and an overview that sings of sensitive adaptation to local climate.

Those who struggled for, who founded and ran the school, have worked toward that end since its inception in the mid-1970s. They did not do so *via* heroic, dramatic gestures but quietly, persistently, ingeniously. To that purpose, they sidled past legal obstructions, they turned from impeding bureaucratic minutia, they eased parental doubts.

For years now, they have wrestled with the devastations of 'Bantu' schooling, of white cultural dominance. They have battled for a representative, an as yet not fully balanced complement of black and white, of male and female pupils and teaching staff.

Teaching is emphatically learner-centred and – judging by past examination performances, markedly effective. Coercion is taboo, especially corporal punishment; there are no detention classes, no obligatory standardised uniforms. The governing students' council is elected, self-discipline and peer discipline are encouraged, cultivated. There is, an older pupil told me, 'plenty of space to be an individual in this unauthoritarian community'.

Over the years, people from the surrounding area have attended literacy and especially supplementary classes at the school. This well-endowed, privileged institution's facilities were and are shortly again to be available, over weekends and during vacations, to the more indigent neighbouring children.

To this visitor, the school community is unmistakeably democratic. It is also open, civil and dedicated to responsible civic values. Happily, my outsider's impressions were readily endorsed in discussion with the current and former pupils whom I met. None of whom seem, incidentally, joylessly weighed down by their citizen-like expectations. Sounds good? It is. Committed efforts have been and are being made at the school. In our divided, macho, race-befuddled society, that alone is something to sing about.

The buildings and their layout are integral to all this: there is a continual interplay between this insightfully designed physical setting and the everyday life of the school. Wherever one is, indoors or out, there are views of pupils at work or play, of indigenous trees, plants, grass, the buildings, the river, the veld beyond. There are the sounds of school children, of laughing, talking, of their music. There are songs of the wind, of the tumbling river spilling over a nearby weir.

There are busy walkways, open paths and covered corridors; sheltered places to sit, informal places for learning, chatting, larking about, thinking, dreaming.

On this the staff and pupils seem unanimous: the positive factors of their social and educational lives are matched, are reinforced by what a teacher spoke of as 'the rich, the life-enhancing qualities of our buildings'. For members of staff, the architecture is, quite simply, part of their teaching programmes, of their working and personal relationships at the school. 'We teach and connect with each other in different and better ways here. The buildings help our teaching'.

For the pupils: 'the Hall is a lovely building to enter and be in' the library is 'a magic centre of attraction, it's not enclosed and claustrophobic, you can always look outside'. The classrooms are 'not like cells, we do not hate them like at other schools   ... they're designed to argue in democratically'.

In sum: it is an open, generous school in open, generous surroundings; reasonable and fit for human beings. And what Morris referred to as 'those externals' of a true place of learning, the architecture?

This is not another self-conscious design, another striving for grand ARCHITECTURE, for modish gestures, stylistic borrowings; for the noisy rhetoric that so often passes for architectural creativity. Woodmead is quiet, consistently modest, fitting; a helpful framework for school activities. There is no grandiose, pompous overall plan: no hierarchy of spaces, no sequences of formal, frontal perspectives, no major and lesser axes, forced symmetry, imposed systems of proportional relationships. None of that histrionic baggage.

The cluster of buildings at Woodmead is, rather, an example of a straightforward architecture of growth, of accretion. The central focus is, appropriately, the communal core. Situated at a major entrance to the community centre, which is also the school hall, it comprises a sturdy raised platform flanked by robust columns. They bear part of the load of the tiled roof to this lofty meeting place. In addition, the columns carry the symbolic weight of this ceremonial place of assembly, of this intimately scaled heart of the school.

Other buildings have been or are being disposed about that nucleus in a subtly revealed spiral. The inner areas are for learning/teaching: classroom units, the library, a students' council office, an administrative block and similar office spaces. The next segments are allotted to boarding accommodation, a dining and kitchen complex and common rooms. The outer rings of this organic, spiralling form contain staff cottages, a workshop, sports and outdoor facilities plus, distinctively, the enfolding curve of the river.

One passes through and between these places in continually awakened attention, in constant appreciation. Is this what a 14-year-old meant when he said: 'The buildings are great, you can climb on the roofs. It's mountaineering'? Or is it, as his presumably horse-loving companion exploded, 'simply marvellous, it's as good as a pony trail'?

The designer's informal spatial control is everywhere, like the quietly unifying appearance of the buildings, their variegated brick and red tile roofing. One finds its imprint in a restful classroom quadrangle that, unusually, is entered diagonally, dynamically. The layout and buildings are redolent with imaginative spatial juxtapositions: at, for example, a crossing of passageways from which the symbolically emphasised opposite corner of a courtyard is glimpsed but is not directly accessible.

Walking about the site, I was repeatedly alerted to this confidently handled spatial interplay: at, in another instance, a viewpoint which is intriguingly off-centre, as is the planting about it; at the irregularly shaped grouping of the girls' dormitories. The later is a particularly notable set of buildings. Following regional African, especially Tswana tradition, each 'house', with its articulated sleeping and living spaces, is fronted by a walled forecourt, a *lapa* that clearly demarcates private and public places.

There is more, much more: the handsome library building where, open but distinct, horizontal and vertical spaces are gathered under a sweeping raked roof to provide discrete spaces for individuals and groups at study. There are, here, adeptly inter-related upper and lower storeys, sensitively varied floor levels, crisp laminated tie-beams and rafters. There are nooks, reading carrels and window seats; from each of which the songs of the stony-bedded Jukskei may be heard.

And still more: just south of the hall there is the recently completed, colonnaded art and drama building with its two linked open spaces. One of these is an expressive, inviting forecourt for display and like activities. The other, also a delightful space, is more narrow and directly utilitarian. The southern prospect from this complex is always exciting: the major rooms face a white-watered reach of river over undulating sward, khaki in winter and green during the summer rains.

I understand that when and if finances are available, a music department might well be added to the built ensemble. This would certainly be apposite; there is, after all, much to sing about on the Woodmead campus.

A Woodmead vista: composed drama.

Overhanging eaves, the forgotten or abandoned essential for shading in our basting sun – here seen in the appealing simplic of Casa Bedo, surely one of the more important of the modernist houses built in the late 1930s.

Sometime too hot . . .

> Sometime too hot the eye of heaven shines,
> And often is his gold complexion dimm'd
> (William Shakespeare)

You have surely noticed. There was first a quiet infiltration, then a stampeding influx. Now whole crops of squat, monolithic, casbah-fashion imports are flourishing in Johannesburg's green suburbs.

There are pompous and less posh walled-in villas, groups of bleak shops, a severe office park or two and quite the most evident, the present full-blown eruption of sub-Mediterranean townhouse developments

You know them. Chunky stuccoed cubes, in white or often colour-card hues of terracotta, with dollops sliced out for balconies and *moderne* corner windows. Raucous, usually pastel-painted slender pipes that offer dubious structural support. Vague, plaster applique references to keystones, gables, arches; irrelevant icons abstracted – filched – from long-forgotten architectural history books.

Furthermore, unforgettably, there is the bizarre rash of incongruously chambered parapet walls that conceal flat roofs; which, by the way, are singularly prone to leak. Whether they are pretentious villas, swanky clusters or lowly terraces, these modish strangers epitomise a curious, a wilful indifference to climate.

Why, but for shallow fashion, ignore time-honoured pragmatics? Why else deny the widely recognised diurnal effect of the powerful, the insistent sunlight in hot and even in temperate climates? It is pretty obvious. If they are left unshielded from direct overhead sun, masonry walls absorb, accumulate heat; heat which, in cooler night-time conditions, they radiate. They may well transfer warmth to already uncomfortably hot interiors; such as sleeping areas.

Top to bottom: Casa Bedo as it was when erected and, bottom, as it now stands – plus, on a following page, the architect's refined cross-section and floor plan.

So shield them. So, in different cultures across time and space, walls (especially those of stone, brick, concrete) have customarily been protected by overhanging eaves. They've been shaded. Suitably modified, extended, this simple device has a further advantage. It can be used to provide covered, desirably cool outdoor spaces: porches or loggias such as the familiar verandas, the *stoeps* of southern Africa.

In this respect at least, one must acknowledge the hard-nosed sense of most settlers to the region, successive groups of colonists included. Much can be learnt from how, adapting local pre-colonial practices, they have tended to house themselves. There is certainly more than can be gleaned from casbahs.

The lessons are all about us. From the verandah houses of, among others, the Venda and Tswana peoples; from, for instance, the front porticos of hut dwellings in KwaZulu; from the homely early-Johannesburg *stoeps* of, say, Bertrams, Yeoville, Vrededorp. Moreover, similar precepts are on offer in the late-Victorian and Edwardian grand mansions of Parktown, the Houghton Ridge and old Doornfontein.

As they are in the lean-to roofs and expansive all-round verandahs of estate homes in, for example, the Howick, Karkloof and Dargle areas of the Natal Midlands. As they also are in the wealthy suburbs of Harare and Lusaka; in the eminently practical corrugated-iron awnings of German colonial buildings in Namibia.

Shielding walls from the sun as it approaches and moves from the daily zenith has long been a characteristic of the region; expressly of its domestic architecture. Not necessarily, though, for enthusiasts of casbah and other postmodernisms. For them this is naive functionalism, an aspect of modern movement ideals which they have demonised.

Let us, then, consider an instructive example designed in the late 1930s; one which, six decades on, still merits attention. When, in December 1962, I wrote about Douglass Cowin's Casa Bedo, I described it as 'a development towards a regional South African domestic style'. That, I believe, remains the case.

At this, the architect's own home, significant steps were taken to meet the specifics of the locality. The low-pitch hipped roof was probably the most notable of these measures. Cowin had earlier abandoned the mandatory flat roof of orthodox modernism. The roof fits onto the building like a lid, resting at the north-west corner on an unobtrusive colonnade of elegant columns and for the rest on the brick or concrete perimeter walls of the house. Its edges are extended to form one metre deep eaves that throw storm-water off the built fabric.

This overhang permits an apt use of a major feature of the local climate. The latitude of Johannesburg is such that wide eave projections can shade windows through the summer months, when the sun is high in the sky and yet allow sunlight to penetrate rooms in winter, when the sun is relatively low on the horizon. That is to say, Cowin adapted a traditional form to provide for living in a climate of hot summers and for winters of chilling winds but warm sunshine (he allowed shelter from the winds by screen walls). These functional uses of the low, projecting roof-line augment the comforting feeling of a roof that appears symbolically to tie the house to the earth.

Turning to the interior, one notices that selected walls start deep inside the house to then extend beyond the eaves into a small garden. These have not been chosen arbitrarily. As well as screening a covered porch and a generous verandah from the cold prevailing winds, they help to define and provide privacy between bedroom, living and service areas.

The roof, yet again, is the key. Seated only on the outer walls, it allows ceilings and internal partition walls – non-supporting, enclosing surfaces – to be carried outward and so to connect inside and external spaces visually. As a case in point, the verandah becomes an extension of the internal volume of the sitting-room; an additional liveable area that is private, on the sunny side of the house and shielded from winter winds.

Internal space is handled in a like manner. The interiors at Casa Bedo are related dynamically, they are not static sequences of compartments. Where appropriate, walls or wall-fittings (cupboards) are treated as planes, as surfaces for defining specific volumes, rather than for sealing rooms off from each another. They are secure, sound-insulated screens that suggest and where desired, reveal spaces beyond. In this context, the wall-to-wall windows, enfolded as they are by wide eaves and screen walls, intensify everyday connections to the world beyond. They help to relate internal and external spaces.

Immediate small-scale views, nearby garden foliage and distant glimpses are brought into the house. As are the sublime summer cloud formations that, almost daily, sail galleon-like across the highveld sky.

All this in select Waverley, in a modest suburban home. One that celebrates the informal outdoor/indoor life-style so readily realised in temperate climates. One that still, despite the security bars added in later years, speaks of easy-going domesticity. Also, it must be emphasised, one that bears the same social scars as its overblown neighbours: the back space, tucked away, minimum sized, crudely finished 'Boys' and 'Girls' rooms of Cowin's – and our – times.

In these more favourable days, we probably need to revisit our Casa Bedos. We certainly need the thoughtful planning and skill in relating spaces which they embody. Free of tacked-on styles, of mannered follies, they could well mark a way to our regional architectures.

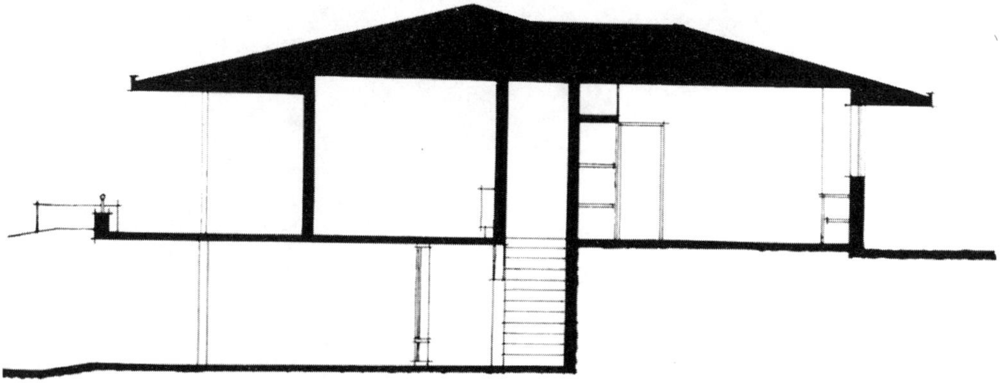

section ▲▲

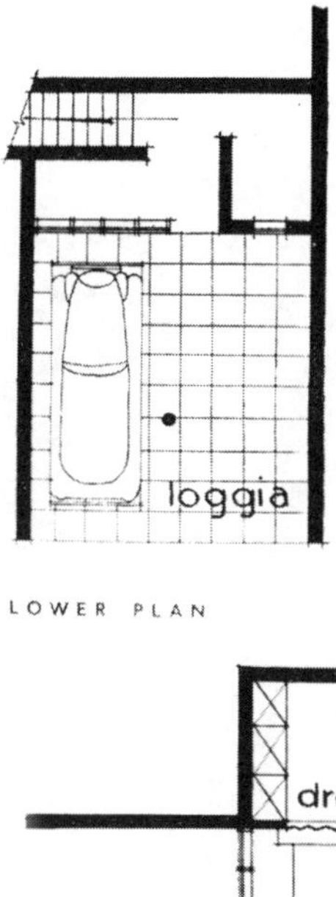

LOWER PLAN

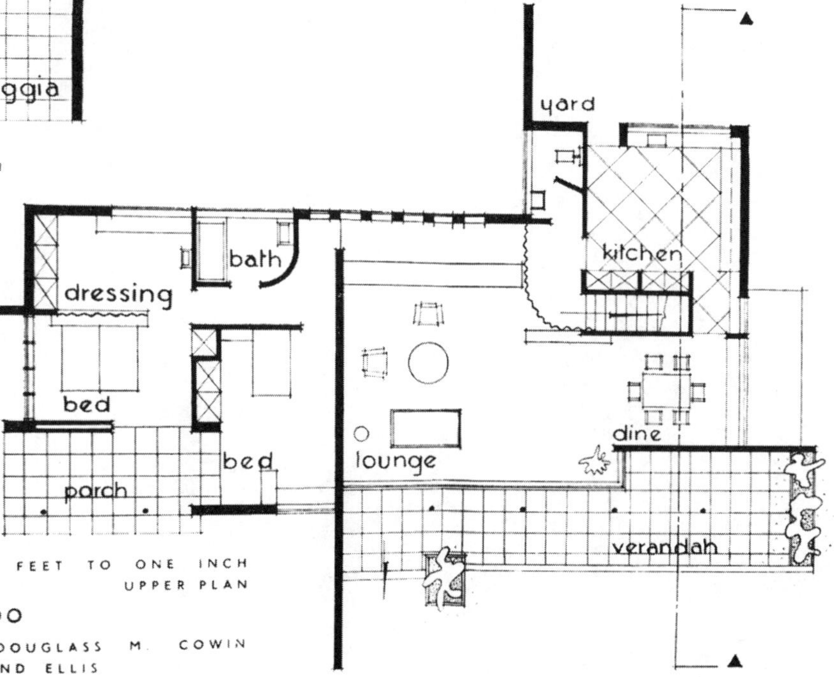

SCALE EIGHT FEET TO ONE INCH
UPPER PLAN

CASA BEDO
ARCHITECT DOUGLASS M. COWIN
OF COWIN AND ELLIS

Simple barns, sheds – often the most appropriate structures for our urgently demanded, our short-changed, socially directed stock of buildings; and, contrary to popular opinion, like this example, they need not be clumsy, inept, coarse.

Handsome sheds, elegant dignity

St Paul, Covent Garden (1631–38), one of London's finest parish churches, was designed by Inigo Jones to be barn-like; as Elizabeth I is reputed to have said 'The handsomest barn in all England'. Instructed by his client, the Earl of Bedford, to erect a church as inexpensive as a farmyard building, Jones responded imaginatively. By simple means – a rectangular basilica, widespread eaves, a plain Tuscan portico and pediment – he produced a dignified building; a quality which Bernard Shaw exploited for the opening scene of his social comedy Pygmalion.

Although the noble Earl's injunction smacks of the customary demands made by local clients, to my knowledge none of our buildings matches St. Paul or, indeed, the adjoining arcades of what used to be Covent Garden Market. After years of trying, I search still for a handsome architect-designed shed in Gauteng, let alone all South Africa. Occasionally one is partially rewarded by contenders for a similar but less royally endorsed accolade. This occurred recently at two new community clinics: in Yeoville, Johannesburg and in Kagiso township near Krugersdorp.

Access to the new Yeoville clinic is off Kenmere Road, immediately north of the swimming pool on Raleigh Street. The site is part of a dishevelled park; one which also contains a dreary police station, dull tennis club building and a forlorn recreation centre. Excepting the new building and the pool – a crisp example of early municipal design in the city – there is little on this bleak space to engage one's attention, architectural or otherwise.

The young architect, Paul Schlapobersky, told me that he views the inauspicious setting as a challenge, an opportunity to highlight forcefully the impetus for positive change which bold design must, he claimed, bring to a neglected area. That, patently, is what he and his colleague Jennifer Sandler sought for this socially utilitarian building.

Top to bottom: three glimpses of the clinic off Kenmere Road, Yeoville – an exterior shot and two interiors; not great architecture but also not negligible.

The plan is orderly, rational. Accommodation calling for direct public access – the reception area, eight consulting rooms, a baby-weighing space, an emergency dressing room – has been distributed on the four sides of a central, rectangular waiting area. This, the core of the building, also opens onto an uncovered public courtyard and a multi-purpose hall. The latter will be linked to a future wing, a maternity unit. Staff facilities, such as kitchen, utility and storage spaces, are less directly accessible from the waiting area. The courtyard excepted, all this is covered by mono-pitched roofing; by a shed-like corrugated iron roof that sweeps upwards to the north where it meets a similar lean-to which slopes in the opposite direction.

The entrance, on the north-west corner of the clinic, is unmistakable. It is marked by a steel canopy cantilevered from the building and a towering extension to the main roof. The hovering planes of the canopy are juxtaposed with a neatly designed security fence and automated gateway; each of which is a regrettably necessary addition to an otherwise welcoming building. The projecting roof that now soars over the reception area will in future cover additional office accommodation at first floor level.

Externally, the structure is finished in face-brick and painted plaster, the surfaces of which are modulated by functionally and rhythmically placed window openings. Where appropriate, windows of disparate size are linked by panels of ceramic tile which reinforce that rhythm and the prevailing proportions. Taken as a whole, it is a colourful shed, a sparingly but effectively decorated barn.

The architects have also exercised their bold sense of colour internally. This is especially evident in the waiting area. Here non-institutional brightness holds sway; especially through the green, yellow, blue and maroon surfaces that harmonise brilliantly with the natural timber of the lattice beams which support the sweep of the roof.

This is a striking volume; not least because of the lively clerestory light which penetrates from the north and from the roof lights overhead. That, plus items such as a cheerfully tiled drinking fountain and sculptural clock as well as a spatially dramatic view through to the upper level, lifts the building into something other than a conventional shed.

There is a similarly engaging spatial imagination at work in the extensions Henry Paine designed for the clinic on the corner of Kagiso Drive and Emdeni Avenue, outside Krugersdorp. Here a dismal, barrack-like nonentity has been transformed by internal alterations and an additional wing of almost equivalent area. And here too attention focuses principally on waiting space, a central issue for community clinics.

Initially, an inadequately sized internal waiting room was supplemented by an even smaller south-facing verandah at the public entrance to the building. Extensive participatory reference to medical and lay personnel at the clinic indicated that the new accommodation – five consulting rooms, toilets and an emergency suite – required well over double that waiting space. This was provided in three ways: an additional internal area in the new wing, a covered space in the open link between the old and new premises and an extensive walled garden with trees, planting, pergolas, built-in seating and a children's play area. The two open-air spaces were intended as and soon became the social and visual kernel of the clinic.

The architect argues that the local climate invites such waiting space. If adequately shielded from the prevailing cold winds, it is pleasantly usable throughout our sunny winter. Of course, shelter from our sudden, usually late-afternoon summer showers can readily be found internally or under the roofed link.

Moreover, as may be appreciated by visiting the site, the ensemble offers exciting vistas: from the new wing, across the garden, to the wall beyond which one enters the clinic; from the shaded, open-trussed, link to the wings on either side; from the play area, through the link, to a far courtyard; from the wall enclosing the garden on the north to the pergola abutting the new wing.

Inigo Jonesian barn or not, this pair of subtly related sheds constitutes anything but happenstance, unintended farmyard naivete. Like the very different Yeoville clinic, it demonstrates the enduring qualities of simple, inexpensive, consistently gimmick-free design.

An existing municipal swimming pool in Linden, Johannesburg – recently heated and covered with an over-arching envelope of structural sheeting and tracery that spans between two majestic columns; demonstrating the economy and dignity of fine, atter design.

In the swim

It stands out: the design touch that matters, that lifts the everyday beyond our currently pervasive mediocrity, that points to anticipated possibilities – perhaps probabilities. It is distinctively architectural – a feel for building design that, while rooted in the quotidian of daily life, reaches to the far, far side of dross. It excites much of Italo Lupini's work. He is a locally born architect some of whose elders may well have migrated with the shared design ethos of the Italian peninsula. They travelled, it seems, with recollections of their origins in stunningly beautiful Bergamo. Bergamo, just north-east of Milan, a hill town where before, during and since its medieval glory, fine architecture has been commonplace.

I stumbled unwittingly on that welcome legacy as a serendipitous consequence of my wife's and my determination to indulge our daily swim on a recent, closed-down Easter weekend. Temporarily denied access to our customary heated pool, we visited the municipal facility in Linden, on 11th Street. The immersion in shiver-proof, pellucid waters was splendid. The dominant visual scene even better.

One leaves spankingly clean changing rooms to approach an arched steel construction that sweeps across a standard 25 by 25 metre pool and its immediate paved surroundings. The profiled sheet metal, barrel-vaulted roof leaps from appropriately stocky concrete buttresses on each of its two opposite sides to rest on an elegant central steel girder that spans confidently from front to rear – in this instance, north and south. The latter is, in its turn, carried by a pair of impressively powerful, yet shapely, concrete columns to which the trussed, overhead girder is attached by means of studiously detailed steel collars and struts. That triangular truss pushes above the curved roof sheeting to provide a central strip of glazing which, with the two huge window elements at the open ends of the vaulted structure, saturate the interior with light. Sliding glass doors give access to inviting gardens on either side.

Top to bottom: swimming in exhilarating surrounds – exercising body, mind and aesthetic sensibility.

It is an all-weather, straightforward, engagingly unencumbered, effective public amenity. And there are two more in the Gauteng area, one in each of Coronationville and Pimville. Others, I am told, are shortly to be built in Durban and East London. The model is geographically mobile.

That all-weather depiction means more than comfortably enclosed swimming in poor as well as fine conditions: it also represents gently heated water in similarly comfortable, enclosed surroundings. The second is realised ingeniously, and simply. The vast external exposure of un-insulated sheet metal roofing makes for a glass-house internal effect – ambient temperatures that are supplemented by the warmth from heated pool waters and of course, the generous expanse of north-facing glazing on the precisely orientated structure.

This, though, carries with it the ever-threatening consequences of rapid corrosion from condensed moisture on metal surfaces throughout the structure. These are obviated by passive, that is, not mechanical, ventilation which Lupini describes as 'creating a "Cathedral" effect displacing condensed air through continuous openings over the ridge beam [the central girder]... the heating of the non-insulated roof covering creates high-level ventilation thereby eliminating condensation on this surface'. Further, he notes that 'the combination of the high span profiled galvanised roof sheeting and single centre spine roof truss have minimised surface areas onto which any condensation and dust could accumulate causing undesirable precipitation'.

Its 'Cathedral effect' notwithstanding, the structure is no place of solemn worship, hedonistic sunbathers and fitness devotees apart. It is, though, a delightful, handsome pleasure dome; one which is readily accessible to all in the neighbouring community. And, as Lupini subsequently demonstrated, this addiction to thoroughgoing design and detailing is not alien to his work.

In addition to describing other of his built designs, he took me on an extended visit to two probably representative examples: the campus currently in progress at Naturena, Soweto, for the Kaiser Chiefs football team and then to a newly completed house in Saddlebrook – an unabashedly up-market, haughtily horsey residential area on the showy far northern outskirts of Johannesburg.

The site for the soccer players snuggles into a characteristically magnificent rock-strewn highveld *kopje*. That overlooks, it commands a clutch of refurbished buildings, including a crisply converted new clubhouse and a shed for storing the team's gear. These step down the slope toward the pair of well-watered iridescent green football pitches on the lower reaches. A recast version of the structure at Linden is shortly to accommodate the team's gymnasium and related accommodation. This will be linked to the newly erected changing room blocks by extending the immaculately detailed series of subtle arches that currently mark the walkway leading through these ablution units to the soccer fields.

It is this small, low-slung, appropriately symmetrical building which hints insistently of the qualities which the campus is likely to display: sensitive, clean-cut urban and building design, imaginative yet chaste detailing and most telling for me, a readily demonstrated love affair with arched, with curvilineal forms of roofing. Here they echo the smoothly weathered curves of the boulders on the *kopje* behind.

We then drove across the city to the Saddlebrook estate, Kyalami, where the well-heeled are busily entrenching themselves and their equestrian gratifications. I am not given to commenting on costly villas for costly folk – there are, I believe, many, many more pressing South African design issues for contemporary architects. But, one must confess, this more than comfortable home will not lightly brook my prejudices. What I have referred to as 'the touch that matters' is, here, too evident.

In this house – in all respects more muted than its coarsely ostentatious neighbours – commitment to design becomes a personal apotheosis, a present realisation of goals that reach beyond an individual designer. If you are able to, drive briefly past the corner of Ascot and Saddlebrook drives to relish – even if only through the rhythmically contrapuntal external façades – an innovative, an exhilarating and yet always controlled work of ordered design, of architecture in dynamic repose. Would that similar qualities touched the lives of most of our fellow citizens, of those who stand in urgent need of attentive, fine design.

A small office building on the West Rand, Florida – inventive design, innovative installations, a comely resolution; one dare not wish for more, especially in view of its gross companion in Johannesburg.

Highveld offices — doing it in style

Architectural thinking in South Africa, as elsewhere, has been in persistent agitation these past decades. Look about you, note the successive flurries of modish façades, of purportedly new styles. These replicate exotic, not to say esoteric imported trends; like metabolism, neo-rationalism and most favoured, free-style classicism. For many architectural theorists this is just dandy: we are, they argue, enjoying the benign pluralism of our consumerist economy — anything that sells goes.

For others, bemused practitioners and their bewildered publics, it is another reason for being chary of contemporary architecture. Why cherish the work of designers who seem preoccupied with fads lifted excitedly from regular consignments of glossy overseas journals?

These generalisations should be made specific. Consider, in illustration, two examples, both office buildings. The first is a recently completed instance of the style-as-looks school; the second, by way of contrast, is a building from a designer who has resisted the surface fashions introduced *via* Europe, Japan . . . wherever.

The head office for Thebe Trust stands at a bend in Jan Smuts Avenue, a major entry to Johannesburg's classy northern suburbs. Clothed in re-interpreted classical elements, the building offers few concessions to its dull setting. It is distinctive: a sore thumb distinction that is confined to the main, the west façade. The prospect from Keyes Avenue to the east, like the north and south fronts, is as mundane as the neighbouring façades.

What are those additives from classical architecture; impoverished, stripped-down Etruscan, Roman, Palladian? Anything goes, bald shaft-like columns on coarse bases, choked metal-band capitals — relics of a recently excavated anodised aluminium Doric? What is one to make

Top to bottom: the grace and unaffected directness of tough-minded design and, below, by way of extreme contrast, the off-hand coarseness of Thebe House on Jan Smuts Avenue, Parktown North. No vote called for.

of the three storeys of stacked columns that stand so firmly on . . . nothing, on cavernous garage entrance-ways?

Then there are the two symmetrically disposed pediments, each with a circular recess – blind openings to nothing. And more: a pair of concealed, squashed entrance stairways leading to a cramped portico with its own curiously emaciated pediment. The latter appears to rest on two sets of columns that support an extraordinarily ungainly entablature.

The whole thing is of a piece; especially that supposedly classical ordering of the façade – the hackneyed foot, body, head imagery comprising a sandstone base, four storeys of banded brickwork and the overhanging eaves of a Mediterranean-type tiled roof. The superficial, the trite has been made obvious, lucidly so. Beyond these trappings of past glories lies the accommodation: two levels of parking and three floors of offices topped by penthouse flats. The finishing materials are of a high standard, particularly where visible. There are no inhibitions here about using polished marble, burnished timber and other indulgences of a similarly costly order. Anything impressive goes.

The occupants, what do they say of their local Palazzo Uffizi? They confess to admiring it. Of the dozen with whom I spoke, all concurred with the evaluation 'it's really nice, even our clients say that'. Try as I did, I was unable to probe this off-hand assessment: 'it stands out, it's right for the client, it's nice'. Nice, very nice.

The architect is more explicit and disarming.'The client wanted classical, the Union Buildings and Bank City. That's not a problem for me. I like all architecture, so I give them what they want.' The building is 'an advert . . . the classical is really skin-deep, it's all in the skin to reflect a certain image . . . a plan behind a false façade'. Any damn thing goes.

One cannot but recall the debates of over a century ago, when designer/critics like John Ruskin and W R Lethaby engaged with fashionable gothic revivalists such as Gilbert Scott. Rejecting the 'root absurdity that art [is] shape and not substance', Lethaby described his adversaries as people who, 'follow the movement – backward . . . rather than settle down to perfect a science of modern building'.

That striving for a humane, sensitively reasoned approach to design marks our second focus of attention, a modest two storey office block on the West Rand, bordering central Florida. Situated on a narrow domestic site with a deep north-south axis, the inevitably linear building faces east and west. On the hot, dry highveld that is a major problem; one which the similarly orientated fake-classical example fails to confront.

Here the building is planned to respond positively to its environmental setting. Penetration by the powerful western sun is controlled, limited, by adjustable louvres of semitranslucent shade cloth. The less troublesome eastern aspect is moderated by a horizontal, fixed-angle screen and vertical fins which also direct northern light into the offices. External surfaces exposed to the sun, including the metal roof, are painted white to reflect heat. The extensive glazing on the east and west fronts provides comfortable, natural cross-ventilation.

The designer has devised an inexpensive evaporative air-conditioning system. Fresh air, drawn by fans across wet wood pulp, is cooled and humidified before distribution through the building. This is realised through, on the upper level, an attractively sinuous set of exposed ducts that runs immediately below a continuous central roof light. Occasional winter warmth is provided by electric heaters along the perimeter of the accommodation. The design is direct, straightforward, inventive. And, I was assured, costing about half of conventional air-conditioning.

These and the other practical measures that are deployed so imaginatively – like the easily erected framed construction with light-weight panels – are appropriate, pragmatically relevant. They flow from committed efforts effectively to reconcile social, environmental, constructional conditions. They echo an established tradition in architecture.

While comment from the classicist designer had remained fixed on surface effect, now discussion centred on matters of purpose, method, procedure; on design principles. "One works with environment, with the climate. That gives exciting opportunities for innovation, for exploring dynamic responses to things like sun and shade.'

That is the nub. Whereas the building on Jan Smuts Avenue is a product of relentless image-making, the block in Florida arises from struggles to marry form and content, to unite shape and substance. There is, of course, nothing new about this in the story of twentieth-century architecture.

Up to and during the 1920s the pioneers of the Modern Movement rejected what they argued was the stylistic fetishism of Victorian design. Committed, as many were, to social activism, they sought to harness industrial technology to societal upliftment. To this end, they forged a new, a principled architecture based on function and need; one that would be integral with efforts to meet changing social relations.

John Berger, artist, critic and poet, clarified this view with characteristic insight: '[A] style in art mediates between form and content. It offers a method and a discipline to apply to the search for unity. It is not a formal quality but a way of working. A new style . . . evolves . . . to meet the problem of treating new content born of social change'.

There have been at least two modern architectures. The first appears in scholarly books as works of inspiration, the outstanding buildings of modernism which few of us see, let alone live or work in. These are the avant-garde buildings of the early twentieth century when, for the first time, architects grappled with the issues surrounding mass populations, industrial production and technological innovation. This is an architecture of change, of social hope. The second is 'modern-styled' architecture; mostly flaccid reproductions of surface borrowings from the innovative work of modernism.

And since World War II, architecture – so bound up with structures of power – has been reduced to a consumer good. It has become subservient to the overriding preoccupation with packaged, surface appearance. Once again, John Berger: 'Consumer goods are artificially rendered obsolescent by each new model being given a different "look" from the preceding one. The content usually remains the same. The "look" is arbitrary in relation to the content; its only meaning lies in its difference from the previous look.'

Style as surface concern – current neo-classicism is but one expression – defeats the possibility of an evolving architecture. It feeds on the familiar in order to reproduce . . . the familiar. It pre-empts that critical observation of what exists on which efforts to derive alternatives rest.

Florida, West Rand: decorous and effective sun-protection.

An often quirky, always inventive design set in the staid surrounding of Johannesburg's Rosebank and its ancillary dreariness – a welcome relief in this inauspicious setting.

Rosebank relief

The Rosebank shopping precinct offers little relief from architectural bombast. So, when a modest structure of worth appears, one celebrates. Not least when it signals a co-operative hand from the local authority; in this instance, a successful road closure. Those who endure the pomposity of the area, will surely recognise what I am referring to: the new African craft market on a now traffic-free strip of Cradock Avenue.

This is a high spirited building from an architect, Kate Otten, who seems unable to design anything that does not sparkle with her patent zest. Here, in this decidedly unpropitious setting, she has done it again. None but a killjoy could fail to respond with a lifted heart.

The roadway – from the dull parking lot opposite the main mall to beyond Biermann Avenue on the north – has long been a place for street traders, many if not most of whom brought wares from across our borders. Here one found smoothly crafted goods in exotic hard-woods, carved traditional head rests and chess pieces, intricately wired armatures in the form of motor-cycles, helicopters and similar icons, brightly coloured beadwork, flowing cotton shawls and other distinctively African craftwork. Daily, this open-air venue rivalled the regular Sunday market on the roof of the adjoining mall.

This made for a bustling excitement and not a little dexterous dodging between passing vehicles. One's attention was constantly arrested by the items on sale and, as engaging, the good-humoured banter of practised salesmanship. It was a jostling street theatre – beguiling, tempting and warm.

Now, after this additional structure, it is also a more humane centre; one that accommodates the necessities of African marketing: shade, lock-up facilities and nearby ablutions. Bully for those whose vision has, until recently, rarely veered from openly expressed antipathy or,

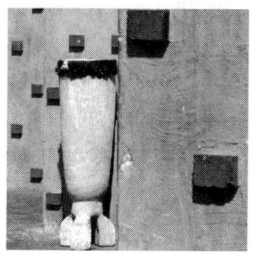

Top to bottom: some light, Antoni Gaudi-like details which the architect handles with an engaging, an ever light-hearted sense of delight in her work – an affliction that she passes on to those prepared to attend the work.

at best, aloof suspicion. There is now a touch of magnanimity in tough-minded Rosebank, place of the hard sell.

The commercial reaches of Cradock Avenue and its environs are prime instances of contemporary architectural confusion. There is here no overarching design framework, no pre-colonial consensus about building materials, construction, functional uses. Nor is there the urbane unity in diversity of, say, Gothic or Georgian concurrence about such matters. There seems to be no scope for like subtleties in this and similar suburban enclaves of consumerism. In Cole Porter's telling phrase, anything goes – the more flashy the better. Here designers have attended chiefly to their personal drives for built publicity and/or to those of their mainly corporate clientele; neither of whom customarily care for companionable architecture.

How does one design an attentive, neighbourly building in this clamour of incompatible façades? How to coexist with, for example, the noisily abrasive implacability of the FNB premises to the north, the clamour of the nearby Standard Bank, the risible mock-classical rumblings on Biermann Avenue, the yawning mall and open car park to the immediately east? How to acknowledge this brash babble? Add to the din, close one's ears, slide silently away . . . what?

Otten, with admirable restraint, has sought another way; one marked by her characteristically affable humour. She has taken refuge from this rowdy setting in perhaps the central, but now modishly dismissed modernist commitment to design veracity, a simple but far from simplistic notion.

Briefly, she has sought, with her distinctive imaginative energy, to release the architectural form of the new building from what is available to her – materially, structurally, functionally. These, her main technical means, are interlaced with the humane values, the abstract meanings which she ascribes to this modest public venture. Those range from a broad concept of physical shelter to less tangible, more abstract ideals. They reach especially for the goal of offering a neighbourly, welcoming hand to people who are demonised in our often fiercely expressed xenophobic bigotry.

The building, a lineal addition to the parent mall, abuts the indoor parking area on the eastern frontage of that massive, faceless structure. It accommodates two new trading levels, with above head-height partitions to the lower stalls and a continuous open-plan reach on the upper storey. The latter is served by three easy-going stairways and an internal street-like atrium that rises through the two lofty floors. There, at roof level, this spacious double-volume filters natural light from a lattice of close-packed wattle branches. They are fixed above a full-length roof light. The inter-linked volumes – those that are over-looked and those from which one looks down – are entrancing, as are their relaxed links to the outdoor areas.

All in all, the interiors are delightful. They are marked by design: from the dappled lattices above, the 'street-way' through the building and its sturdy internal finishes, to many of the hand-crafted goods on display.

Then the exterior. The façades are playful without a whiff of frivolity: brightly coloured balustrades of welded steel, engagingly undulating handrails, more undulations across the east elevation, a cluster of three handsome light standards at each end, a double curved balcony on the northern edge. The latter catches the reinforced-concrete frame of the entire building in mid-dance. Masonry surfaces are painted in strong earth colours, the steel structure in charcoal blue, the all-important wattle rods are finished with natural varnish.

This is not a building for orthodox purists. Each visit has revealed more seemingly *ad hoc* detail; from the tiny upward spotlights that illuminate the stairs, to the boldly sculpted treads at the northern stairway and on the east façade, the crisp 'positive' and 'negative' images cut from stainless steel plate. These are emblematic portraits of readily recognisable people, symbols, scenes from Africa. They add a characteristic Otten touch.

So, thanks to a sensitive design, one now indulges African curios in an inviting market; postponing, if only briefly, the crassness of Rosebank shopping. Whether this will persist is an open question.

Given the pressures of unrelieved poverty, expectations that informal trading can be restricted to officially sanctioned markets seem misplaced. I, for one, shall not count on the currently sanitised Cradock Avenue remaining that way; an occurrence which our citizenry might come to welcome as openly as they surely will this fine building.

The weight of bumptious design in Market Street – an open welcome to all who, under sufferance, dare to use this oppressive, boastful building. Would that we were spared such arrogance.

Jo'burg, that is the place for me

Sinatra is not quite my kind of guy; he is brash, overweening, ever ready to engulf his fans in syrupy bathos. Yet I take notice when he belts out 'Chicago, my kind of town'. Inner Johannesburg is similar. It is not lovable – as are old Delhi, Fez, Siena – but it cannot be brushed aside. Despite the ugliness, coarseness, menace, frequent violence, it presses on one. Like it or not, we take note; often a surprising fondness develops. However marginally, one begins to care.

So when local newspapers announce the Mayivuke project, a 'R2 billion kickstart for Jo'burg CBD revamp' and an 'African renaissance' in Egoli, I become agitated. What are 'they' up to now?

We are promised 'inner-city renewal': direct links to the airport and Pretoria via 'a high-speed rail network', a '600-bed hotel complex' near Jack Mincer Park, Hoek Street to become 'pedestrian friendly'. These, plus a string of other enticements, are described in the catchy phrases of newly launched official projects. We are even back with the tired story of 'Newtown as a cultural precinct'. The proposed scheme will 'bring [Johannesburg] into line with cities around the world'. Not, I trust, with central Detroit, post-war Warsaw, that urban monster Bangkok – with cloned inner city areas everywhere and nowhere.

Is this the 'upgrade' for which our too long impoverished, our unemployed fellow citizens yearn? Is this going to be an attempt to gentrify our bustling African city under the banner of, for example, 'regulated hawkers' facilities'? It is not as though our smooth-talking officialdom has engendered confidence. We recall too clearly the hugely trumpeted wonders of that ridiculous early 1990s Civic Spine.

Most of us, I imagine, would welcome even a partial realisation of Mayivuke's reported focus on urgent social issues, like housing for

Top to bottom: a random selection of architectural vanity, hollowness, banality – the weighty burden of misappropriated crassness.

homeless people. But, inviting as that phase of the anticipated renaissance is, lest they get lost in the current hullabaloo, we need also attend to more mundane matters. Perhaps a pause is called for, a time briefly to ponder less newsworthy concerns.

Take first a seemingly trivial matter, public seating – that everyday city amenity. A stroll through our central area makes the point: Johannesburg is almost bereft of places in which people can rest their feet; in which they can sit and indulge that always fascinating activity – watching the urban parade and being watched by its participants. There are few seats in the city; there are fewer ledges or other edges of buildings on which to perch; there are even fewer seats at sidewalk cafes, bars. It is, in the main, standing room only.

Having initially been colonised by people from drizzly, puritanical north-west Europe, our cities lack the urbane pavement life which enlivens the sun-doused sociability of north African and southern European countries. Rarely, even in our few traffic-free zones, do we sip at drinks, eat or casually sit in the throng of passing pedestrian life. Gripped as their managers are by security fears, our fast-food outlets, let alone coffee shops and bars, are frequently indoor, 'safe', exclusive.

Those who throng the pavements, mainly people from outlying townships, can seldom afford such places. They, the citizens who most need respite, are barred by an income-based apartheid. Where are they to ease their city-weary limbs, to relax in the human flurry? Bus stop benches are at a premium, casual seating is exceptional and the otherwise suitable surfaces of buildings bristle with spikes, studs – devices installed to repel 'undesirables'. Where to sit, to be still, to chat, to eat those take-away munches? Where are our Casbah-like eating houses, our versions of London's appealing city squares? Where is our 'theatre for everyday life', our variant of, say, the new intimately scaled seat- and tree-lined space on the crowded Via Croce Rossa in Milan?

That leads me to a related aspect of our crass indifference to human convenience and delight – the absence of informal local parks. I am not referring to major public spaces such as the vast grounds of Delhi's Red Fort or London's Hyde and Green Parks. These are alien to Johannesburg's mining camp origins. My reference is, rather, to smallish places like Paley and Greenacre Parks in New York or, the sole South African instance of which I am aware, Medwood Gardens off West Street, Durban. These contained, off-street spaces – with water, planting, trees – are usually found on sites that are squeezed between buildings. They offer shelter, sunlight, shade and above all, seating. They are partly paved to accommodate street entertainers and to minimise the damaging effect of regular pedestrian traffic on dry lawns, a constant concern in our highveld winters.

Now think of Joubert and End Street Parks, of that wasteland west of the Technikon, off de Villiers Street; dispiriting echoes of what city parks might be. Or think of the pompous spaces on either side of the old Post Office, Rissik Street: to the west a watery, pedestrian-shy traffic island and on the east, a comfortless setting for kitsch sculpture. There is nothing else in the city; save the sub-lunar landscape that links the Library to the Cenotaph and the ersatz-classic, mock-seigneurial courtyards at Bank City.

Seats and modest infill parks, these are but two of the amenities for a renaissance shopping list. There are others: outdoor sculpture and art exhibitions; sculpted play installations for children to touch, climb over, slide down; food kiosks and small open-air cafés with running water nearby; drinking fountains; arbors and creeper-clad trellises; secure facilities for parking bicycles; plaques and other symbolic reminders of our past, joyous and tragic. These and like objects could provide citizens with avenues for shared exploration; they present means by which, through joint use, we can the better identify with our fellow citizens.

And for the city's especially dislocated population – commuters from distant townships, from those spatially segregated, far-off dormitories? There are clear needs here: many, many more public restrooms and toilets; secluded rest areas for elderly people and weary parents with toddlers; accessible information centres for enquiries about transport, housing and most important, jobs; appropriately sheltered places for newspaper walls . . . and very likely, others of which I am unaware.

None of this is out of reach, forbiddingly costly or technically problematic. Indeed, a humble but telling pointer already exists. Make your way along Commissioner Street to the taxi drop-off area between Kruis and Von Wielligh Streets. There you will find a delightfully varied, finely crafted group of innovative pavement bollards. Simple things, bollards. Most of these are less than a metre high; they are fashioned of sturdy hardwood – probably the now easily come-by railway sleepers – that have been fixed to handsome metal shoes which, in turn, are secured to the pavements.

They offer pedestrian protection from fast-moving, jostling traffic. The designs, by local carvers, range from dynamic abstract patterns to figurative, usually comic representations: here a trudged-in boot, there a caricatured mini-bus or upward pointed finger, the customary signal to and by taxi-drivers.

In these celebrations of everyday life – contemporary, urban counterparts of Pieter Brueghel the Elder's humorous, fondly observed sixteenth-century rustics – one glimpses a future Egoli. Moved by a handful of bollards, one can imagine a downtown which is not drearily 'in line with cities around the world', which is not merely another commercially necessary destination, is not a place to be endured and soon escaped.

Hope sustained?

Clearly, the talent, the skills are to hand but not, seemingly, the will to use them. Open, democratic participation in the form of insistent public pressure to shift official inertia is surely our main hope. Reliance on the presumed good offices of the much discussed 'private sector' would be misdirected; the latter's members are, after all, the most consistent, unrepentant philistines. It is they who have sought and continue so coolly to despoil our world. What else might one expect from folk who – to call on a half-remembered phrase from childhood – appear ever to know the price of everything, the value of nothing?

And the great South African public, what will lift its members, that is, us, out of social, environmental, aesthetic apathy? I am not so bold (foolhardy?) to address an issue of this magnitude here. You who have remained with me this far will, perhaps, draw conclusions of your own. Or, probably more likely, you will join me in enacting the essayist Romain Rolland's terse prescription: simultaneously and energetically to exercise pessimism of the intellect and optimism of the will.

To that end, I offer this final chapter in homage to my fellow designers. They, like me, are probably engaged in life-long searches for what, in the initial piece, I have described as spatial imagination. They too must yearn for the positive outcomes which, in the concluding chapter, I refer to as *utopian*.

A relic of prior relics – pathetic recourse to purportedly universal symbols at the main entry to Wits University; pointless echoes of the crisp light of ancient Athens.

Spatial imagination

Whilst students, our most charismatic lecturer constantly reminded my colleagues and I that, in his words: 'Architecture is the imaginative manipulation of space for the convenience of man'. His gender specificity apart, the point merits repeated consideration. Later, under the title 'the three stages of architectural development', I read a little known elaboration of this truism by the renowned twentieth-century architectural historian Sigfried Giedion.

A caution: following Giedion, a Swiss scholar, I shall focus on western European architecture. Others may offer enlightenment in wider contexts; in, say, the exterior rather than interior spatial emphases of historic southern African habitats.

According to Giedion, the first of the three stages reached from ancient Egypt to the Pantheon in Rome (AD 120–24); the second from that singular dome to the beginning of the nineteenth century; the third, yet in its formative phase, is what he termed 'space–time' architecture. None, he argued, is self-sufficient; each has facets that draw on the past and, often simultaneously, point to possible futures.

Egyptian buildings were set in a seemingly boundless space; the apparent endlessness of the desert being a pervasive factor. Here, built spatiality developed through the unending interplay of planar surfaces, closely encompassed volumes and acute sunlight. Structures, such as pyramids, temples and palaces, were bounded by walls or analogous elements to displace the immanent, the continuous space about them.

That so-called displacement was central: interior volumes were closed off from their surroundings. They were formed of short-span beams resting on closely set columns that were symbolically and in some cases actually, connected to the inner faces of outer

Top to bottom: the Corinthian order comes south, far, far further south than the life and times that spawned it – borrowed, filched symbols to reassure potential students' parents, to endorse academic pretensions, to intimidate student neophytes.

walls. The massive planar surfaces were incised with low relief, almost shadow-free carvings. With their effect of impassive permanence, they, the ubiquitous planes, were paramount.

That changed in ancient Greece. Now temples and similar communal buildings were surrounded by open, colonnaded peristyles; the inner columns of Egypt were moved to the perimeter. Low relief carving gave way to high relief, even to fully three-dimensional statuary. In the crisp Mediterranean light, deep shadow and sharp sunlight were exploited to advantage. Though space now flowed about and through building exteriors, spatial imagination had not yet penetrated to their interiors. That occurred at the Pantheon, Roma.

This building, a huge hemisphere sitting on a powerful circular drum, is the prototypical scooped- or hollowed-out interior of Giedion's postulated second stage. The inner walls and heavily coffered soffit of the rotunda are modelled by shifting shafts of light that penetrate from an open 'eye' at the apex of the dome. This is circumscribed interior space; space in which the interplay of enclosed volume, mass and light is sovereign. The Pantheon did not bypass past spatial realisations; see, for instance, the pediment and triple colonnades of its huge portico. Elements derived from antecedent Greek structures were planted onto a circular temple. Witness also the markedly incised marble and stucco exterior surfaces of this monolithic form – a rounded, windowless evocation of the planar preoccupations of ancient Egypt.

The route from Hadrian's Rome to the early nineteenth century passed through many variations on the theme of hollowed-out interior space. Most may still be visited: from, say, the Byzantine church of San Vitale in Ravenna (AD 562) and the tenth-century Saxon basilica at Breamore, Hampshire to the four-domed San Marco of Venice (1063). Then, following the fecund Norman period (eg, L'Abbaye aux Dames, Caen, 1062), came the eruption of vaulted Gothic interiors: from the pilgrim church of Santiago, Compostela (1075) to the glorious fan-vaulting at Ely (1321) and the flamboyant south transept at Beauvais (1499). Even now, most are lit through stained-glass filters.

The next burgeoning of scooped-out interiors occurred during and shortly after the Renaissance. Here the route passed through the arched and domed buildings of, among others, Brunelleschi (1377–1446), Alberti (1404–72) and Bramante (1444–1514) to the undulating surfaces of baroque and later, rococo buildings. These are exemplified at, respectively, San Carlo alle Quattro Fontana, Rome (1638) and Ottobeuren in Bavaria (1748).

The third, certainly incomplete, phase leads over roughly some two centuries to recent spatio-architectural events. Although that proximity gives rise to much ambiguity, there are pointers. These lie in the quite unprecedented possibilities released by nineteenth-century industrialism – new building materials (such as steel), novel construction procedures (eg, prefabrication) and demands for hitherto unknown building types (eg, railway stations, aircraft hangars). Their potentialities were expressed in the related notions of simultaneity and transparency.

Designers were urged to view buildings and offered instances in which they had been conceived 'in-the-round'. They were to be acknowledged as fragmented entities whose various facets could be recognised simultaneously, much like the subjects of Picasso's cubist paintings. Space now flowed about, in and through buildings; a vision of spatial inter-penetration that was dramatically evidenced in Walter Gropius's group of structures for the Bauhaus at Dessau (1926). That vision was enhanced, made feasible, by the transparency of sheet glass.

Revolutionary as these and other aspects of this third stage of spatial development were, past elements persisted, though affected by what was now occurring. So, the swirling vortices of Baroque space were transposed to the elliptical dome, constructed of prefabricated concrete members, with which the engineer Nervi covered the Chianciano Terma in Italy (1952). So, the closed planes of ancient Egypt were burst apart at Gerrit Rietveld's Schroeder house in suburban Utrecht (1924), where Mondrian's two-dimensional, space-emanating planes were reassembled in-the-round.

Now, at the turn of another century, architecture is said to stand at another spatial threshold; one that, through techniques such as the computer technology used for the Bilbao Guggenheim (1997), will revise and probably reaffirm, the desiderata of simultaneity and transparency. On that the jury is out and likely to remain so for some time.

Though a careering gallop through history, Giedion's notion of spatial development – especially when read with his parallel concept of social imagination in architecture – offers a suggestive interpretation of the discipline's multiple pasts and possibly, of its wracking present dilemmas. But that, as the cliché has it, is another story.

Housing, homes – an enduring individual and social concern; a matter in which personal problems turn readily into public issues.

Housing – asking those who matter most

The word 'development' has come to permeate everyday talk in South Africa, especially since the inauguration of our first president on that tumultuous April 27 1994. Popular terms of this nature can seldom be defined readily; they are diffuse, not precise. On one matter however, there appears to be consensus: an urgent need in developmental procedures for open consultation with, for active participation by the people affected.

Consulting with, let alone inviting 'the people' to participate in shaping their futures, was, until recently, scarcely part of the official perspective. Now, in the heightened excitement of the new democracy, negotiation with community leaders is accepted as a prerequisite for development. Even direct involvement – not, that is, mediated through leaders – is advocated widely.

We are beginning, perhaps, to grasp the import of the affirmation which Thomas Jefferson, accomplished building designer and third president of the US, made some 200 years ago: 'I know of no safe depository of the ultimate powers of society but the people themselves, and if we think them not enlightened enough to exercise their control with a wholesome discretion, the remedy is not to take it from them, but to inform their discretion.' A rousing sentiment, even with that concluding touch of paternalism, which is not surprising coming from a Georgian patrician.

As we all know, housing is a huge issue; or, rather, a series of interlocked issues, of unyielding questions, numbing dilemmas, threatening problems. What sort of houses where, when, how .. for whom, built by whom ... funded by grants, by bonds ... guaranteed by whom, how, to what extent? We are mired in yet another entangled chunk of the whither-South-Africa conundrum. Novel analyses, recommendations, initiatives flood in on us. The debate is incessant, pervasive. Whether passionate or cool, engaged or detached, the advocacy on offer is awash with ideological twists, overt

Top to bottom: private homes, personal problems – three current or potential venues.

and hidden. The loudest centre on personal enterprise, private ownership: forward to a property-owning, stable future for all. The other highlights purposeful state intervention, public ownership; a major step toward the coming egalitarian society. And there are, to be sure, numerous stops between.

The experts, as one might have anticipated, are everywhere. Those who – in the persistent absence of grass-roots accountability, of popular control – pronounce, savant-like, from the upper regions of our social hierarchy. These are the housing pundits: expected, pressed, paid to tell us what we need and how to get it. They are the mandarins. Though seldom agreeing among themselves, they purport to be uniquely in-the-know; especially about 'what the people want'.

What do folk want; the dispossessed, indigent, homeless, the ill-housed, rack-rented and the over-crowded? What are the housing desires, preferences of that huge mass of our people?

Who can say? Not, customarily, the over-burdened leaders of on-the-ground civic bodies. They are often poorly housed themselves; they are beset by the exacting struggles of daily life, surrounded by indifferent, at times hostile, authority and unfamiliar with the techniques of thoroughgoing social enquiry – certainly not the long-entrenched bureaucrats of housing; officials in whom trust, confidence has long evaporated. And hardly those speculative developers who urge that such issues be settled in the market-place; where, they contend, consumers vote through their pockets. Far, far too many of their potential constituents are disenfranchised, their pockets empty.

So perhaps now at last, better late than never, we will turn to the people most immediately affected. Perhaps we will, as a matter of principled procedure, consult the prospective occupants of the houses so massively and urgently required for our as yet unrealised new South Africa.

In this context, consultation may broadly be depicted as free, democratic participation in the decisions that bear on one's life. That is something more than a consumer's opportunity merely to select from set, predetermined alternatives. Full public participation starts with, arises from the right, at the outset, to take part in formulating the choices to be made available, arguing them publicly and then choosing.

Efforts to approach this ideal, to enlist people's active control of what, in housing, might be relevant to them are not new. They have, since World War II, constituted an enduring thread in the story of house building across many industrialised countries. Starting with the dissident 'advocacy planning' activities of the 1950s and 1960s in the USA, this strand (often termed 'community architecture') links the work of, for instance, the architect Ralph Erskine in Norway and Britain, to that of Lucien Kroll in Belgium and of similar design teams in Germany, Holland, Scandinavia, India, Australia and many other countries.

Indeed, whilst disappointingly rare, participatory design is not wholly unknown in South Africa. There is, for example, Roelof Uytenbogaardt and his colleagues' Belhar Housing Project from the late-1970s at Bonteheuwel on the Cape Flats. There is the early 1980s Briardale scheme at Phoenix in Natal, where occupants exercised individual choices, largely about house-types and internal finishes, that were far removed from the bureaucratically imposed uniformity of, say, Soweto.

Generally though, public commitments to participatory procedures are more honoured in the breach than the observance. Their rarity, in private as much as in public sector housing, is associated with the bland, the indifferent manner in which they have been bypassed, ignored. Too often one hears that 'you can carry participation too far you know' or that 'full consultation takes up a lot of time, what we need is a strong decision maker'. Authoritarian attitudes and practices die hard.

Consider, as a case in point, the seemingly forgotten talk, 'Soweto on my Mind', which Professor Chabani Manganyi presented in 1977 as guest speaker at the Golden Jubilee Conference of the South African Institute of Architects. Manganyi, then living in Soweto, offered significant insights to his audience. One might expect that the crisply argued, immediately relevant observations of a graduate in clinical psychology would be noted, pondered on, attended to. Not a bit of it. His address seems to have sunk like lead in an ocean.

Where have Manganyi's pointed comments on the acute inadequacies of township housing been acknowledged in action? Where have designers responded to his reflections on how newly urbanised people perceive of what he termed their 'personal space'? Where have his arguments for consultation, for full participation by potential housing occupants been heeded?

Where have his calls for co-ordinated social research in these matters been taken up? These, of course, are and are likely to remain rhetorical queries.

I know of but one major, systematically conducted study: Mary Tomlinson's recent, 1996, report of householders' views of their newly occupied homes and of the procedures they were required to follow in obtaining them. There is plenty to learn from that document; for those who formulate official housing policies, those who are obliged to apply implement them, those who seek to fund them and not least, for those who yearn so desperately for decent shelter.

The question remains, it burns: what do ill-housed, homeless people want of housing? Unqualified participation and applied social research offer what may well be fruitful ways toward enlightenment. Other, probably more readily implemented approaches seem, to date, to have been sterile.

Participation presents an opportunity to break through the customarily closed relationship between client and designer; to include, as a matter of course, those who will inhabit and use the resulting buildings. It rests on a mutual striving – through shared control of resources and means – to plan for, erect and occupy built environments that are suited to, fit for the people and the activities they accommodate.

To these ends, applied social research – action research – will probably focus on surveying patterns of home usage, eliciting the needs and desires of future building occupants, analysing the relationships between the various parties who provide and live in mass housing and then monitoring the dwellings in use. The central purpose of such enquiry is publicly to reveal the knowledge that flows from it; knowledge that could help facilitate people's control of the location, production, type and form of their housing.

We are, not unexpectedly, back with Thomas Jefferson's clarity of vision; back, many housing experts may say, with impractical, naive idealism. Possibly. But not, I imagine, for the present and future occupants of mass housing. Nor, I suggest, for investors who look beyond the quick buck, the financial killing.

A nodding familiarity with participatory projects in Europe, north America and Australia plus some knowledge of research conducted there and elsewhere, makes me wonder what is holding us back. Not, surely, another instance of subtle retreat, on grounds of costs, from earlier undertakings? Banish the thought. Our national housing shortfall offers too many, disturbingly many, settings for participatory research and monitored building programmes. Gauged against the overall costs, social and economic, participation is cheap, a snip.

Folk who will, surely, soon yearn to be consulted, not tolerated.

'Adequate housing' – a human right? Reaching toward that consummation to be desired on the far east bank of the Jukskei River, overlooking Alexandra Township.

Alex, the far east bank

Last Christmas I received a welcome gift, an admirably clear, thoroughly researched booklet on affordable housing. A passage in the opening section, *The International Right to Adequate Housing*, has stuck stubbornly in mind.

Those few pages included references to national constitutions and citations from the usually reverential pronouncements of international organisations. Their grand rhetoric contains shared ideals which focus on the mutually endorsed sentiment that all people, universally, have a right to decent homes. None, surely, but the most oafishly indifferent might be expected to disagree; yet across entire continents that right is – and looks to remain – more conspicuous honoured in the breach than the observance.

There is wide consensus: from the United Nations Declaration of Human Rights, 1948, the Habitat Agenda of 1996 to the South African Bill of Rights: 'Everyone has the right to have access to adequate housing.' But these ringing phrases are rarely matched in reality. The nirvana of broad housing provision remains tragically beyond reach, especially in the so-called developing world.

Nonetheless here in southern Africa doggedly dedicated people have been and are committed to such remedial measures as they are able to forge. They labour to make even minor dents in the currently estimated backlog of three to four million homes. Locally, Michael Hart, Christos Daskalakos and their co-workers, who have been engaged in social housing for some years, are among the handful of these devotees. The two recently invited me to visit a project on the far east bank of the Jukskei River, overlooking Alexandra.

There is much one can mention about this as yet unfinished exercise: the encouragingly high levels of reliance on local entrepreneurs

Top to bottom: the march of uniformity in the 'model' black suburbs of Gauteng – 'you pays your money and this is what you get, like it or not'.

and craftspeople; the complex financing procedures instituted by government agencies; the varying types of tenure on offer; the shock of vacant, long-completed homes in an area scarred by supposedly temporary shacks. Debate on these and like issues press. They, though, are not confined to this project. What is fresh here is the overall housing disposition and composition.

This humane development departs sharply from the adjacent housing, the crass, relentlessly repetitive barracks built for the 1999 All Africa Games. Whilst the latter indulge the crude little box and garrison encampment blunders which so drearily disfigure low-cost housing across the country, Hart and Daskalakos have sought to break from that mediocrity. Their efforts rest primarily on the urbane layouts in which they have mingled a range of house types.

There are a dozen house plans that, with variations and combinations, are arranged in distinctive clusters, cul-de-sacs and similar groupings around open spaces which, at present, await landscaping. Other houses are built in terraces of varying length; they open directly onto access roadways and to the rear, face internal gardens intended, allotment-like, for cultivating vegetables and similar domestic crops. Occupied housing in a prior phase of the project has already been developed in this green, productively suburban way.

Dwelling units in the single and double-storey groupings can be extended as occupants' needs demand and their finances permit; a flexibility which is, clearly, not readily available to those in the three-storey blocks. There is a busy school nearby and is provision has been made on vacant plots for retail shopping, social amenities and community facilities such as parks. The overall settlement, now nearing completion, appears liveable, inviting.

Regrettably, the buildings are less accomplished. The designers' unimaginative use of standard fenestration, their ubiquitous choice of currently modish earth colours (ochre yellows, russet browns and dusty pinks), their frequent lapses into toy-town gables and porches are anything but encouraging. None of this is mitigated by the seemingly arbitrary changes of colour to roofs that offer sadly inadequate eaves protection for the wall surfaces below.

In this respect – appearance – the development is almost as dispiriting as the neighbouring Africa Games complex. Yet there are outstanding exemplars that could have served as points of departure: the recent housing at Cato Manor, Durban, Springfield Terrace in Woodstock, Cape Town and nearer home, Jo Noero's back-to-back houses on Alexandra's west bank. And for those seeking more venerable instances, there is the fine housing of fishing villages such as Arniston on the Cape coast.

All this raises a larger matter: the not entirely convincing relevance to local conditions of garden suburb imports.

Finding that they could not easily reverse the miseries of early Victorian industrialism, members of the then rising middle-class in Britain took flight from urban centres like London, Manchester, Glasgow. They scrambled for retreats on the leafy edges of their sprawling cities. There, they found pure water, space, quiet, semi-rural beauty. They found a relaxed privacy; one that slipped readily into the aloof isolation which now, as then, marks comfy suburban life.

So, the new settlements played their part in the de-politicising processes that spread as swiftly as the suburbs did. Intensely private, they lacked the close spatial concentration, the ready social co-operation, the shock and jostle of dense urban settings. Increasingly, more people lived more divided lives: home split from work, public entertainment from family recreation, production from consumption.

Then sections of the 'respectable' lower-middle and working classes were allowed in on the act. Relying on newly developed forms of transport, mainly railways, they too moved to privatised areas. They occupied sub-suburbs: a few essential shops, smaller homes, less space and greenery, much less clean water and air. This, with the whole suburban ideal, invaded southern Africa. Here we added a distinctive touch: townships that had been banished to the outer orbits of urban life. We ensured that space and greenery were further reduced, that water, sewers and other services were even less evident.

This is where our resources still go: to servicing the myth that 'my house on its private plot is my castle' to extending over-stretched electricity and water supplies, roads, rubbish removal, postal and similar services. An unsuitable pattern has been adopted as the model for millions of South Africans who yearn for decent homes near job prospects. And this despite our older, more compact housing traditions; like row or courtyard houses and clusters around communal open space.

Soweto – the textures of poverty, homelessness and the vivid vitality of the local muralists, commercial or otherwise.

Housing layouts

Recently, I encountered an imaginative housing layout in Alexandra township, a departure from the dreary rectilineal orthodoxy that prevails across the country. Since then, I have been pondering that joyless phenomenon. What more is there to say about the landscapes it has scarred? Why do so many of our housing commentators seem undeterred, perhaps unmoved, by these ubiquitous blots on the daily lives of so many people?

Why indeed? Consider, by way of illustration, two recently published, impressively authoritative manuals on housing, expressly self-build homes. Each is a thoroughly studied, well planned, an exemplary document. Each is written in crisp, unambiguous language. Both are presented with systematically formulated, step by step clarity.

They are usefully directed at their likely readerships: principally eager home-seekers but also so-called emergent, small-scale contractors, empathetic professionals and local or central government officials. They are rooted in urgent home needs.

We turn first to that untiring housing polemicist and campaigner Dominic Tweedie, specifically to his fine piece in *metroBUILD 2000*, a magazine published on behalf of the Greater Johannesburg Metropolitan Council. Here, in seven closely printed pages, he explains how to set about building one's own home, from start to finish.

Tweedie covers such often perplexing matters as understanding building plans and their associated drawings; measuring, ordering and scheduling construction materials; the implications of contracts with builders, sub-contractors, building merchants and others. He describes and explains 'the main parts of a building': walls, roofs, ceiling, door and window frames, floors. He covers the fun-

Top to bottom: texture, texture, texture – resistance to officially imposed uniformity.

damentals of estimating and controlling cash flows, time budgets . . . and much, much else. On these and like matters – the standard procedures and techniques of construction management – he is nothing if not reassuringly comprehensive.

Read with its companion paper by the attorney Claudia Noble, Tweedie's contribution should inform and guide the most inexperienced or anxious of prospective home builders. This thoroughness is, surely, the basis on which the magazine's editor advises that 'there is nothing about erecting a house that cannot be understood by ordinary people and that you, the reader of *metroBUILD*, cannot do yourself. Building your own house does not necessarily have to an exorbitantly expensive operation.'

All this accepted, one cannot but note that the entire issue of *metroBUILD 2000* rests on a salient, an apparently unnoticed, certainly an unquestioned assumption; one that is, though, made explicit in the drawings accompanying Tweedie's piece. A house is, it seems, a 'stand alone' structure on, usually, an orthogonal site. A home is one among serried rows of similarly disposed dwellings – 'you', the editor declares, 'erect your house'. Enterprising individualism is paramount.

My second example, the more wide-ranging monograph, *Towards the right to adequate housing*, published in November 1999 by the Built Environment Support Group, Durban, is founded on an analogous premise.

Among concerns such as identifying and defining land suited to residential development, this informative booklet covers matters which include housing tenure, health issues, preferred orientation, environmental pollution, affordability, services, harnessing solar energy . . . and a brief sub-section entitled 'Layout'. While that touches on curvilinear and irregular patterns, its focus and advocacy explicitly favour grid layouts; rectangular patterns which lend themselves to ranks of look-alike structures.

Patently, the authors recognise dwelling layouts other than the standard, the freestanding house on its individual plot. These, they suggest, comprise variations of row or terraced housing, including perimeter developments around urban squares and similar open spaces. However, elsewhere in their publication – indeed, throughout its remaining sections – the exemplary model, the implicitly endorsed standard, resembles what the majority of commentators appear to accept. With few exceptions, members of the housing establishment seem wedded to the deadening layouts which currently engulf us.

Of course, like other documents of this nature, the two I have referred to focus directly on what is commonly termed low-cost housing. As far as I am aware, detailed guidance of this order is confined to that sector. Except in the costly, fashion-bound glossies, homes for more affluent householders do not appear to call for detailed design guidance. Ready access to resources buys professional advice.

Our *deurmekaar* (mixed-up) economy is filled with these maddening contrasts. None more stomach-churning than the bald differences between the spacious settings in which planners and politicians live and the crushed layouts they tolerate, advocate, for their fellow citizens. Though each rises on the same scattered suburban pattern – single plots for single houses – what occurs on the ground is grotesquely dissimilar. Well-heeled individualism is screened by greenery, often behind fortress-like walls, while poverty brings regimented repetition.

To my knowledge, the first publicly mooted shift in this discriminative insensitivity was formally commented upon in early 1996. That done, the notion – let alone relevant action – was bypassed, dropped, dumped, forgotten.

The Star, 3 April 1996: 'Although people are used to living in single-storey detached houses, cluster developments and multi-storey housing could enhance the social fabric of the community.' This report followed an earlier editorial in the same newspaper (March 21). That endorsed a yet earlier call for 'a break with the Soweto gridiron layout . . . for a movement towards multi-storey – though not high-rise – development'.

The editorial highlighted some key disadvantages of rigid orthogonal layouts: for instance, spatial profligacy, high maintenance costs, extended amenities such as roadways and sewerage services, water and electricity supplies. On the other hand, in circumstances of dense occupation, cluster layouts enable public transport, services and maintenance to be rationalised. They allow for equable distributions of private and public open spaces plus communal facilities like shops, schools, clinics and places of worship. The case seems convincing; it has been demonstrated in many other countries – developed and developing.

But since 1996, the official, governmental commitment to and drive for low-cost housing has run into the sands of a sadly inapposite approach. 'There has been a major rethink on housing policy.' The Minister has told home seekers that her department will now 'test their will, their discipline, their responsibility' by requiring them to save toward their own homes (*Sunday Times*, 31 October 1999).

Given this heavily Victorian/Thatcherist reorientation, what price decent homes or humane layouts for, say, unemployed shack dwellers, evicted farm workers?

Venetian grandeur on 9th Avenue, Melville – the local ordinary made over into 'overseas' exotic.

Melville story

In my youth, Melville–Westdene was a tough working-class area; white, reactionary and inward-looking. Not a place that cosseted middle-class youngsters – future executives or professionals – were encouraged to visit. Of course we did, drawn by the rock-strewn *kopjes*: tawny hills among which to scramble for iron-age relics, to re-enact tales of the 1922 strike, then to leap into a nearby municipal swimming pool. That done, we raced our bikes, each an imaginary motor-cycle, homeward.

Now swathes of these adjoining suburbs have been gentrified; made over, I gather, by chic business and advertising folk, broadcasters, journalists, members of the liberal professions and a sprinkling of academics. There are smart restaurants, exotic delicatessens and modish take-aways; fashionable boutiques and antique stores, a jazz spot that is all the rage.

It is a cosmopolitan setting; one from which to watch an absorbing human parade and to be seen doing so. Not quite the left bank, Paris, nor London's Soho or Greenwich Village, New York, but our own. Not quite slick but far from dishevelled. Not quite integrated, but on the way.

My guided tour was on invitation from an old Melville hand, a devotee who alternately enthused and berated. He halted angrily, the car engine indignantly switched off, at buildings that despoiled his beloved suburbs. We passed slowly by houses unchanged since the neighbourhood was instituted, we paused at conspicuously altered vestiges of what had been and at sensitive additions. He spoke knowingly of owners old and new; of the 'TLC, tender loving care' they had vested in their homes.

For his wife, as for him, that is no cliché; witness their own delightfully meandering home and enchanted garden shows.

Top to bottom: more of the same unabashed, borrowed embellishment.

The area was once a characteristic highveld settlement: unelaborated individual houses fronting the roadways were set uniformly back by narrow strip gardens. More extensive vegetable, fruit, herb and other planting occurred at the rear, where the meagre servants' rooms were stowed. Roofs were rarely other than corrugated iron sheeting that also shaded open porches or wrap-around *stoeps*. All was unprepossessing, nothing architecturally demanding. Few of these buildings can have been touched by professional designers.

That has changed, radically. This is now middle-class territory; much of it decidedly prepossessing, brash and as such is attentively attractive.

While elsewhere I would probably shy off, here I am intrigued by the *chutzpah* of householders who turn a Melville cottage into a mock-Venetian *palazzo*, one of those self-assured manors on the Grand Canal – now transported to 9th Avenue, Melville. This is high nerve. Why, one wonders, the aristocratic model, why specifically the north Italian renaissance? Why . . . ? It is, plainly, not creative architectural design, nor a convincing operatic set, but in orderly suburbia, *c'est magnifique*.

Then there are the mandatory boundary walls, the spikes, protective electrical wiring and the like. These are among the burdens property owners bear as indirect emotional and monetary taxation against escalating un- and under-employment: against the crime of poverty. The walls are often inventively decorated with greenery, bright paintwork and on occasion, engaging murals. In the teeth of widespread fear, scope has been found for private ingenuity. It has been extended to make local street-scape a live phenomenon, a rarity on our otherwise dreary suburban roads – an example, 6th Avenue, Melville.

There is, though, a concern: the tendency to annexe public property for private display. Here, that takes the form of the seemingly unquestioned right of homeowners to incorporate pavement space for private purposes. Usually to plant it. Passers-by, patently, have rights of protection from the motor traffic into which they are thereby thrust. Blind people especially, merit unimpeded passage.

My guide referred to the items of local enhancement which he showed me as 'charmed-up TLC'. Although emblems of what the economist Galbraith termed 'private affluence', they do not directly contribute to what he, conversely, portrayed as 'public squalor'. On the contrary, they help marginally to ease the effects of his second, all too apposite, description. And the untouched older exteriors which we saw may serve an analogous purpose: they have acquired charm by being left as undisturbed remnants.

I turn now to the buildings – mostly, but not solely, apartment blocks and commercial premises – that triggered my colleague's switched-off motor engine. As always, these structures are . . . how to phrase it inoffensively . . . unneighbourly, cheap and nasty? They are the obverse side of his Melville story.

We examined three particularly troubling instances. The first, a decidedly non-domestic bakery, is at the corner of Main and Ayr Roads, immediately adjacent to an established group of homes. Sired by a William Blakean 'satanic mill' out of Dickens' Coketown, it pollutes its homely surrounds visually and aurally. Dark face-brick walls, with WC-type window openings, overshadow a towering flour silo which, in its turn, eclipses the neighbouring houses. An incessant roar of industrial fans, the grating gear changes of large delivery vans, the choked gasps induced by their exhausts, permeate residents' daily activities. That an alien facility of this nature, for this purpose, has been permitted here is astonishing.

Then there is a commercial block on the eastern side of Main Road: a desperately multi-coloured hangover from a past vogue at the local university department of architecture. It stands, *primus inter pares*, among other mediocrities; principally because an overwrought colour scheme fails to conceal its patent poverty of architectural imagination. No amount of flaunted paintwork will draw attention from the banal form, the miserable proportions, the vapid, meaningless façade dressing of this rowdy, attention-seeking object.

Finally, we visited a peculiarly disagreeable set of apartment blocks on Ayr Road. Bereft of design, these nonentities are neither more nor less messy than similar examples across the two suburbs and the city. They seem though, in their dedicated gimmickry, especially indifferent to the care so manifest in the surrounding houses. The efforts which occupants of the latter have made to uplift their environs have been cynically dismissed, rejected. Hold tight, listen to the plaintive cry of sullen philistinism: 'Ugly? Well, maybe, but it works!'

Public open space designed for public use – we can do it, but how rarely we do. Why?

On thin ice in Troyeville

A touch of caring grace or cut-price nastiness? Which will prevail? The commonplace view that the public sector cannot deliver is usually taken for granted. What irks most is that swathes of local officials seem repeatedly to offer credence to this dreary orthodoxy. They have done it again, now at a grubby park in Troyeville, Johannesburg, where a promising community project has been dumped. I was told by an impassioned resident that 'the council has reneged... has not fulfilled its end of the bargain'. Whether or not that is so, what one finds is a mess, a sullen denial of potential.

There are, of course, other factors: unemployment, poverty, homelessness and the accompanying low civic morale. My informant claims that Bloemenhof Park, the size of a suburban block, is now a social sink – an outdoor shebeen, a centre for drug-trafficking, for pimps and their sadly impoverished charges. All this was evident when I visited the site.

That, surely, is not what was envisaged when, in the mid-1990s, the local residents' association enlisted help from artists and architects in the area. They wished to create a neighbourhood amenity, especially for their children. Though dispiritingly incomplete, that vision calls for attention.

The steeply inclined park, bounded by Pretoria, Clarence, Dawe and Beelaerts streets, is edged by the now pedestrian area that was Wilhelmina Street. A stunning, archetypically dense city-scape is on view from that paved space: across Bezuidenhout Valley to the sculptural athletics stadium at Ellis Park and the Ponte tower plus its neighbours on the southern slopes of Yeoville ridge. The onward march of those giants is threatening; one thinks immediately of the lone house on a New York city block in Arthur Miller's stage instructions for the opening scene in *Death of a salesman*. Is that the future for this small overshadowed public space?

Top to bottom: the casual, unforced artefacts of homely pleasure – public place, public art, public delight.

My initial responses were decidedly mixed. First, rising excitement about the medley of ingeniously sculpted objects which I encountered on entry. Then astonishment, angry resentment about the slovenly dereliction of the place; particularly the desultory landscaping. The latter presents a sorry contrast to the green, richly planted park in the northern suburbs where, but two days earlier, I had walked with my small grandson. How is it that the comfortable are further comforted by publicly maintained grass berms, mature trees, profuse shrubbery – the wealth of foliage that complements their already abundant private gardens? Why is it that this serene public privilege is denied the far, far less privileged, those who hunger for greenery?

Bloemenhof Park offers no answers. It does though provide a home for the crafted objects that lift this unkempt site.

I was given a list of nine contributing architects/artists: three were instrumental in promoting the project, the rest designed and executed the items currently in place. There is the customary range of park fixtures – benches, seats for couples, litter bins, lamp standards and grates for *braai* (cook-outs). Each of these is designed with relaxed flair, each is an imaginative departure from the prototypical, the jaded municipal furniture to which, regrettably, most of us have become inured. Each, especially the sculpted benches and barbeque stands, is an inventive, wryly amusing re-reading of that everyday lumpishness. Particularly in this neglected setting, each is welcoming, companionable and above all else, often used.

There are two other similarly creative installations: a colourful mosaic-paved central area of bright ceramic tiles that resonates with, but does not imitate, Antoni Gaudi's famous Parc Guell, Barcelona and then a unique skating arena for skateboard and roller blade enthusiasts.

The latter, designed by Sarah Calburn and Rodney Place, is the centrepiece of the park. It is an oval-shaped excavated bowl, some 19 metres long and 15 wide, of gunite concrete finished with a hardened cement screed. That is supplemented by a tilted steel fence and at ground level, by elliptical tracks which form approach and exit ramps to and from the sunken skating rink. Both of these offer additional routes for speedy trick skating and airy leaps.

When not in use, the hollowed rink is a sculptural art object. When, as occurs weekly, sometimes daily, it becomes overrun by intent, noisy, ever-mobile teenagers, the effect is electrifying.

The concave surface of the bowl has been appropriated, softened by planned and impromptu graffiti. A closely focused, fragmented Coca-Cola sign on the fence picks up the inescapable three-storey rooftop advert across the valley. The rink 'belongs' to its youthful users; that is evident from the engrossed manner in which they navigate it, from the expressive graffiti they have left on its surface. It also slots into the neighbourhood; not least because of that transferred imagery – the visual echos of the massive advertisement and of the cavernous athletics stadium below the coarse Ponte tower.

Like their fellow designers, Calburn and Place have dragged art into the public domain. They have ripped their lovingly crafted products from the insulated privacy of privilege – the smart galleries, basement storerooms, private villas and all too often heavily insured, publicly inaccessible bank vaults. In that sense, the unfinished landscaping at Bloemenhof park has betrayed the artists and their sponsors, the residents of Troyeville. With the young skaters, they ride precariously on the ever-so thin ice of bureaucratic inaction.

A full forty years after John Kenneth Galbraith published his memorably perceptive *The Affluent Society*, we South Africans remain gripped in the disheartening dualism which he characterised as 'private affluence' and 'public squalor'.

This was forcibly brought home to me when, at Calburn's urging, I tried to visit the glass, copper and stainless steel sculptural piece that she and Rodney Place installed at Alexander Forbes Place, 61 Katherine Street, Sandton. Here, engulfed in a super-plush building on a richly landscaped site, uniformed security guards barred my entry. As an uninvited member of the public, without specific prearranged business at this lush venue, my request to view the sculpture was, somewhat impolitely, refused.

I cannot readily imagine a situation in which even the most demoralised of the folk who habitually occupy the derelict Bloemenhof park would act in a similarly restrictive, off-hand manner.

The Electricity Workshop, Newtown, Johannesburg – sensitive refurbishment, re-animated spaces, the lasting gifts of caring design.

The present in the past
— architecture and memory

Join me in a seemingly bizarre journey: from the world-renowned Milanese architect Aldo Rossi to an abandoned electricity power station in Newtown, Johannesburg. That's quite a leap! Rossi is probably the most influential – and erudite – European design theorist of the past four decades; so to jump from his exalted base in northern Italy to our Ferreirasdorp is an act of rare fantasy. Some might suspect it is a jump from the profound to the trite. That, though, is hardly the case.

Rossi argues that 'the relation of architecture to its location . . . lies in its being the seat of a succession of ancient and recent events, its memory'. He claims that: 'The city itself is the collective memory of its people . . . it is the locus of the collective memory'. For him, this abstract quality, memory, is the binding constituent of urban history 'the guiding thread of the entire complex urban structure'.

There are, of course, many problems with this formulation. Not least, is Rossi's notion of collective memory: an undifferentiated, disembodied group recollection that is unaffected by the differing, the often antagonistic, the frequently contested social interests of past and present. And whereas he treats the memory he ascribes to architectural place as assertive, as active, he depicts human memories – peoples' recollected lived experiences – as being passive, receptive. Buildings act, people react! Despite these and his other troubling contentions, the stress which Rossi places on architecture as assimilated memory has been a forceful one.

What, then, are designers to do when confronted by older buildings; when they are called on to adapt these supposed depositories of past memories and present recollections? How may such sensitive candidates for conversion be designed for purposes wholly other than those for which they were initially planned? The now almost completed interior of what is known as the Electricity Work-

Top to bottom: scenes from an engineered, industrial past – welcome to rural visitors eager for experience, though necessarily vicarious.

251

shop in Newtown, just off the corner of Bezuidenhout and President streets, is an illustrative case in point.

The name, Electricity Workshop, is a misnomer. Intended as the centre for supplying electrical power to the street lighting and tramway networks across 1920s Johannesburg, the building was a vast machine hall. It housed eight coal-based gas combustion engines for driving the huge dynamos which generated electrical energy. That was fed by overhead cables to the street lighting and tram carriage systems.

Coal was brought to the large engines, almost the size of steam-locomotives, *via* a railway line which passed into and out of the great double-volume hall. Having dumped their fuel loads, the trains were turned, on an internal turn-table, through 180 degrees in order to exit the hall. All this stood powerfully, massively on an extensive, single storey catacomb-like basement of concrete-encased pipes, gas and other chambers and access walkways.

The building – vigorous and of serious purpose – comprised heavy concrete walls, a central row of rugged concrete piers and a pair of symmetrically disposed corrugated iron roofs. The latter rested on delicate traceries of handsomely machined steel trusses, which also supported a large steel gantry. It was and is a grand, a quite splendidly proportioned, a majestic industrial basilica; a fitting companion to the even more magisterial interiors of the Turbine Hall complex to the immediate northeast .

The Electricity Workshop stands as a homage to the design, the manufacturing and the construction skills of the Scottish engineering tradition from which it sprang. It stands also as a tribute to the organisational prowess of those who packed and shipped the precisely fitted components from far-away northern Europe to our southern highveld.

In the event, this imposing assemblage was used for something less than a year! Apparently the chief design engineer and his colleagues omitted to take into account the high tar content of South African coal. Within the first three months, the combustion engines had begun to choke up. Soon, after desperate efforts to repair the damage, the huge, intricate process proved to be unworkable. Alternative sources and supplies of electrical power to drive the trams and light the streets were sought and used.

The project collapsed. The senior designer took his life; others endured bankruptcy, public humiliation, professional ridicule. Gutted of its machinery, the building was initially used as a workshop for maintaining railway locomotives. Later, it became an *ad hoc* storage space; an indoor parking area and final indignity, a hold for the city's Christmas decorations.

Nick Sack, who designed the now converted building, was commissioned a number of years ago by what was then the Johannesburg City Council. That was part of the continuing, the continually faltering, stop-go development of the Newtown Cultural Precinct. The Council proposed to house five separate organisations in the huge hall. Over the years, four have been accommodated elsewhere, leaving the Associated Scientific and Technical Societies as the sole intended occupants of the 4 000 square metre floor area.

The AS&TS, an umbrella body comprising groups committed to promoting science and technology, propose 'a centre with hands-on interactive displays designed to appeal to young people but also interesting to adults'. This 'Exploratorium', which is expected to draw 'over 500 000 visitors' annually, will include 'an IMAX cinema, a shop, restaurant and snack facilities'. It is an ambitious, excitingly open-ended project; one not without recognisable engineering resonances of the early purposes for which the structure was intended.

Sack and his co-designers have sought to acknowledge the origins of the building in a variety of ways. They have retained and emphasised its constructional and structural integrity: that forceful line of muscular inverted Y-shaped columns strung along the north-south axis of the plan; that filigree of elegant, fastidious roof trusses; the central gantry-joist of hefty bolted steel; the two parallel sets of continuous roof lanterns; those brawny perimeter walls with their seemingly slender piers; the stately colonnades of arched windows and spandrels that march confidently across the façades.

The interior has been immeasurably enhanced by the decision to remove the ground-level floor slab, to open the former basement level to the entire building. The engine hall now comprises an enfolding, a dynamic volume that sweeps uninterrupted through three storeys, beyond the truss space to the ridges of the roof lights. It is an athletic, a noble enclosure; the direct continuity of which is underscored by a restrained use of colour, mostly white lime-wash with occasional splashes of blue, russet and similarly vibrant hues.

This fine space is occupied by four sets of reinforced concrete platforms plus the stairs, ramps, lift shafts, walkways and galleries that lead to or off them. Each thirteen metre square platform consists of coffered, so-called waffle slabs that span between four crisp, reinforced edge beams which are supported at each corner on a substantial, comfortingly solid circular column.

These powerful beam and slab, trabeated, structures provide additional levels of floor space. They are located in the same positions as were the two sets of gas combustion engines. They represent, as the architect stressed, 'the memory' of those distinctive operational features of the then new building.

There are also the finely crafted, the handsomely detailed new metal balustrades to the stairs, ramps, galleries and platforms. Tough and durable, they echo the engineered strength of the building and the machined functions it was expected to perform. They call attention to the directional elements to which they are fixed: to ramps that soar through the space, open stairways that penetrate the volume vertically, to the stretches of upper-level gallery and the firm, four-square platforms.

Where the landing balustrades are semi-circular, they are, the architect told me, yet another evocation of the past. They are reminders of the curved, sheet-metal guardrails behind which, in my childhood, the uniformed tram drivers used to stand, gripping their gleaming brass driving handles and stamping a foot to clang the pleasingly raucous tram bells.

Even in its present state, without the exhibits of the clumsily named Exploratorium, the converted electricity workshop is a memorable building. Whether or not many of those 500 000 visitors each year will recognise and participate in the 'memories' which the designers have opted for is another matter. Indeed, I wonder how many of our fellow citizens share my perhaps mawkish recollections of the city's long-gone tramways or of its tough-minded, abandoned engineering structures?

The massive muscularity of the Electricity Workshop made manifest.

Contemporary educational cloisters at the Wits Technikon, Doornfontein, Johannesburg – unfettered urbanity.

Educating desire

Architecture is in a mess, a state of creative torpor. Modish whim has usurped principled design, practitioners are entangled in debilitating struggles to win and retain commissions, fees are slashed, payment at agreed times is rare. The construction industry remains fragmented, dated, inefficient, often ineffectual. Above all, the public seems indifferent. Who among us cares a damn about architecture? And, given the entrenched narcissism of contemporary design, who can blame us?

So it is a delight to stumble onto something of worth, even if but a solitary item – a sturdily detailed stairway, an exactly positioned window, a well-turned corner. Most anything can excite an expectant imagination. An entire building is almost too much to bear, especially when it is flanked by pleasing neighbours. I've recently had such an experience – alongside, astonishingly, that overbearing monster of tertiary education, the Wits Technikon's John Orr Building on its Doornfontein site.

There, strung out in an east-west line on an as yet unconvincing campus layout, I was shown a newly completed clinic, a set of lecture theatres, an administrative office block and a central stores building. The office unit is bland, closed-off, without noticeable merit or especially shuddering demerit. One is not surprised to learn that, by his admission, this design task did not engage my host's, the architect's imaginative attention.

The clinic to the west and the eastern stores block, the Magazine, are compactly massed, precisely detailed, phlegmatically utilitarian. The appeal deriving from them is, though, lessened by the apparently unmanageable urge with which many architects seem drawn to faddish stick-on games. In this instance, it is hefty masonry columns and walls that support spindly, projecting eaves braces; a visual gimmick without structural justification or constructional content.

Top to bottom: more of that relaxed, practised finesse at the 'Jo'burg Tech'.

Though related to its neighbours by materials and mode of construction, the Lecture Theatre Complex is of a different order. It is a daring, innovative, exciting design. It has the makings of architecture – structurally, spatially and socially.

Located next to an embankment, the building is on two levels; one of which opens onto an upper roadway to the north and the other to a sunken southern garden. The lower floor contains eight lecture theatres plus a bank of toilets; all of which are directly accessible from what, on the plans, is described as a 'circulation area'. This semi-enclosed space leads to an open outer volume and a curved, free-form pathway to the John Orr block. The upper floor replicates that layout. Here, though, two lecture rooms are joined to form an auditorium while two others are combined to provide a study area. And here too the circulation space leads, *via* an elegantly elevated access bridge, to the main seven-storey block. A lift and generous stairway connects the two levels.

This bald description conveys nothing of the thrill I felt on seeing the building. While the plan form reminded me of Konstantin Melnikov's ruggedly cubist Rusakov Club in Moscow (1927–28) – one of the few built exemplars of the uniquely far-seeing Russian constructivist movement – I was also made all too aware that this is pre-eminently a local design. Those *khotla*-like circulation areas could hardly have been envisaged for conditions other than our highveld climate.

The complex is particularly gripping spatially and structurally. Whereas that interest applies most markedly to the soaring space under the hovering shell-shaped roof, it also characterises the six metre height at the lower level. In its own way, each of these expressive volumes flows outward to embrace and be embraced by the garden area beyond. Each is also allowed to 'leak' through slit-like openings on the north and west. Each is related closely to the other by their shared overall form and the elements that penetrate both: a commanding double-volume void, the free-standing stairway and the tense structural support that passes through the two spaces.

Jointly, these two casually depicted, mis-named 'circulation areas' form the social heart of the building, perhaps of the entire campus. Covered but not closed off, they provide a potentially gregarious core; a meeting place for informal encounters and organised occasions – for happenings, debates, concerts, theatrical performances, for accommodating the all-important social desire to see others and be seen by them. Some of these events have, I am told, occurred; particularly personal meetings and casual gatherings of small groups. More structured occasions probably take time to develop, they might best be left to grow as students and staff make these splendid spaces their own.

That, however, is far from certain. The promise of this implicitly convivial kernel of the building, will not, I suspect, be realised before the necessities of successful public open spaces are made available. These include fountains, pools, shade, refreshments and most essential, ample seating – often on the ledges and edges of buildings. That adjoining garden, the landscaping of which was being completed during my visits, provides little scope for such congenial amenities. There are, to be sure, saplings, lawns and flowerbeds, but the area is far too sanitised, too static. It has none of the anticipated animation afforded by seats, water, a discreet food and drink kiosk; all of which could be installed readily, inexpensively.

William Morris, a nineteenth-century designer, poet, novelist and social philosopher, viewed architecture as a means of 'educating desire' – people's desires for full, for fulfilling social lives. Like the handsome Baxter Theatre at the University of Cape Town or that serene pool with its out-of-the-way seating recesses on the forecourt to the school of architecture at Wits University, this appealing building could help to affirm his humane ideal.

The lecture complex was completed recently, early in 1997. The timing is appropriate. Privileged private schools apart, educational institutions across the country – and across the customary age groupings – are increasingly short on funding. Restrained, forthright, cost-conscious design is, surely, what architects could contribute, what they ought to be best equipped to offer. This clean-cut, boldly innovative, unpretentious building suggests that some are doing just that.

Futures in the past – President Paul Kruger's home on Church Street, Pretoria – tactfully attuned to the social life of its times, a timely challenge to contemporary design.

Glittering futures, utopias realised?

In the years immediately preceding and still in those now firmly entered into the new, the twenty-first century, we remain under sustained siege. In this cusp of a fresh millennium, the media pundits are hard at work. Some shroud us in itemised summaries of the years past, others envelop us in titillating premonitions of times to come. The latter are, as ever, either anxiously sour or confidently ebullient. Our futures are, evidently, to be either barren or ecstatic. It is, clearly, a time for anticipatory musings; not least about where, in our towns and cities, we might be heading.

Unsurprisingly, urban South Africa is still scarred by the ugly, abused society which shaped it. People continue to crowd into unlovely cities that are often indifferent to social use. Now though, as we are reminded repeatedly, our society is in transition – emerging, new

To most of us that sounds and is promising: 'I have a sort of faith . . . no one bidden to be any man's *servant*, every one scorning to be any man's *master*; people will then . . . bring forth decorative, noble, *popular* art. That art will make our streets as beautiful as the woods, as elevating as the mountain sides: it will be a pleasure and a rest, and not a weight upon the spirits to come from the open country into a town' (William Morris, late-nineteenth-century designer and practitioner of utopian desire).

An impractical goal, a vaporous fantasy? Possibly, indeed emphatically so for hard headed, here-and-now, feet-on-the-ground, tough-minded realists. For others, a map of the future that fails to indicate, however inexactly, a port of hope is not worth having. Even in that dislodged snatch, Morris offers just such a pointer, a challenge as well as a vision: how to fuse social being, fulfilling work and the arts of urban life?

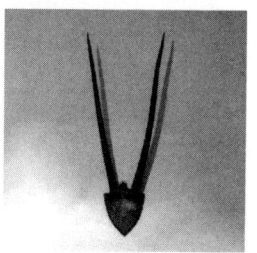

Top to bottom: three inviting details – design at its modest, pared down, essential best.

Patently, for realist and dreamer alike, there will be no ready whisking away of what now weighs so heavily, no easy walk to Utopia, RSA. Of course many, if not most utopias are disarmingly dystopian. They depict static worlds; worlds without conflicting interests, free of social change, of movement. That does not seem a likely stop-over along the South African path. What, then, might we expect as we scramble our way toward decent living environments? Probably a patchwork of the too, too familiar with occasional clearings of urban dignity.

Take those *dorpe*, the small and even largish towns scattered across the sub-continent. To enter them from open country is usually to pass through dispiriting 'locations' of poverty, dust, squalor, rotting garbage heaps. If not this, there is worse: makeshift camps, shacks of cast-off zinc sheeting, plywood, plastic, even cardboard – urban degradation. Then past the laager-like rings of servant-tended suburbs into centres where those otherwise confined to the edges are permitted to toil; where they are free to spend their dismal earnings – often, still, at segregated, hole-in-the-wall shop counters.

Is that the glory of Swellendam, the charm of Pilgrim's Rest, the delight of so many graceful main street Grand Hotels, the *ubuntu* calm of organic mud-block and thatch hamlets? Certainly not. But even those deservedly cherished places offer but passing 'pleasure and rest'. They too have been disfigured by the emotional burdens of *baasskap* (roughly translated, mastership).

To talk here of glittering utopian futures is, I suspect, to by-pass people's immediate hopes. These might best be conveyed by that supplement to William Morris's faith 'every man's house will be fair and decent, soothing to his mind and helpful to his work'. That, surely, is a sufficiently gargantuan task, a probably realisable utopia.

Pass now to our major towns, our cities. Here, unarguably, we have made it. Well, almost. We've struck utopia: the international, the electronic, the interest-yielding flatulence of central Bangkok, Sydney, Warsaw, Lagos, London, Denver ... of downtown somewhere, anywhere, everywhere. We are dwarfed by acres of glaring mirror-glass, muscular concrete, satin-smooth aluminium, by burnished bricks in the sky. That – and the rest of the façade-making industry: the facile office blocks, hospitals, hotels, conference centres, apartment buildings ... parking garages. All are wrapped in their towering indifference to us, the citizenry.

Everywhere is filled with clones of downtown nowhere. Everywhere they stand apart, aloof, awesome but, of course, profitable – particularly for those shut off in cosy social amnesia.

Others, especially among the hard-to-forget majority, may well be less enraptured. The walled *laagers* of suburban comfort elude them. They find that the realities of their imagined El Dorados – Hillbrow in Johannesburg, the Warwick Triangle, Durban – are filled with sad street children, rack-rent landlords, sleazy buildings, broken-down services, orchestrated crime, casual brutality. These phenomena, they soon learn, are also commonplace in the congested distress of distant townships, of shack camps, of site and service settlements.

The burgeoning urban degradation seems inescapable. It is the price which, apparently, all must pay for those swaggering city towers, those mock-historic office parks, those walled-off housing complexes set among golf courses and ornamental lakes.

To speculate, on these sites of despair, about grand physical fabrics for ideal futures is, I suggest, to offend real aspirations. To call again on the megastructures of so-called visionary architecture, such as Sant'Elia's fascistic Futurist City (1914), Le Corbusier's hierarchical Radiant City (1931), Ron Herron's sci-fi Plug-in City (1964), is to treat Huxley's *Brave new world* as a beckoning text rather than what it surely is, a cautionary tale.

Here too William Morris offers an humane alternative. One that springs from a prospect of labour which is not grossly alienated. It arises from a view of work as art, as a collaborative activity embracing all the things women and men shape – their social institutions as well as their physical settings.

Morris invoked a unity of the reasonable and beautiful: 'nothing of beauty and splendour that man's mind and hand may compass shall be wanting from our public buildings, so in no private dwelling will there be signs of . . . pomp or insolence'. That is a future for which, as he urged, one might 'cross rivers of fire'.

And those instances of urban dignity which I mentioned earlier, where might they be found? Often in the unpretentious vernacular buildings of our towns and cities: as in Newtown, Johannesburg; in historic places like Graaff-Reinet; in relics of late colonial sensitivity to place, climate and social structure – on the Berea, Durban, and at Paul Kruger's sometime home on Church Street, Pretoria.

Regrettably for us all, dignity no longer walks the streets of District Six, the *lapas* of forcibly removed Ndebele settlements, the *stoeps* of old Sophiatown; or, in memory, many other loved elsewheres. It is, though, still to be found in a few public buildings and urban spaces: such as at the convivial Woodmead School north of Johannesburg; among the serene, smiling Hindu temples of KwaZulu-Natal; at an open-air, and socially open, pavement café off agitated von Brandis Street in central Johannesburg; at a Bloemfontein church set back from the roadway for an inviting garden; in an hospitable complex of low-cost housing at Belhar on the Cape Flats. These and others exist . . . to be searched out, patiently, assiduously.

The social affirmations of everyday living are fortunately, more pervasive and robust. They occur wherever people bring vibrancy to public life: at local, informal markets; at taxi and bus stops; at impromptu street corner gatherings; in the cadenced dances and chants of open-air, robed, prayer meetings; on grassed suburban pavements; in parks . . . whenever men and women override the day-to-day injuries done to their citizenship.

Look not, Morris might be heard to counsel present-day utopians, to hi-tech visionaries, to millenarian soothsayers. The roads to desired futures lie at our feet. Each day we, each of us, is a potential shaper of utopias.

Further readings

The newspaper articles from which this collection has been drawn constituted a new venture for me; one which I undertook joyfully on my return to South Africa in 1990. They departed from my mainly academic writings prior to that date and, to a lesser extent, the relative few on which I have engaged since coming home. I had by then become a mite weary of adhering, for four and more decades, to the learned paraphernalia surrounding scholarly discourse: cautious, exhaustively demonstrated interpretations and conclusions, extensive massing of evidence, careful attention to contrary views ... and fastidious referencing. This fresh, less inhibited but nonetheless wary, mode offered a release from much of the weight of scholarly writing.

Readers will, I trust, appreciate the consequences of this new-found freedom. Like me, they will be at ease with this more open form of reportage. They will, in particular, pardon the absence, from this collection, of closely recorded textual references. Here, in the main, my citations focus on common, literary sources rather than on less widely available works of architectural erudition. However, a handful of suggested readings may well prove to be of use for those who wish to interrogate the argumentative views recorded in these opinionated pages. In this context, I suggest this, for me formative, somewhat unorthodox, often age-battered, selection from my book shelves: I recall each as having shaped my ideas.

Ardener, Shirley (ed.): *Women and Space: Ground Rules and Social Maps,* London: Croom Helm, 1981.

Attoe, Wayne: *Architecture and Critical Imagination,* Chichester: John Wiley, 1978.

Davis, Mike: *City of Quartz: Excavating the Future in Los Angeles,* London: Verso, 1990.

Dean, Andrea Oppenheimer: *Bruno Zevi on Modern Architecture,* New York: Rizolli, 1983.

Fathy, Hassan: *Architecture for the Poor: An Experiment in Rural Egypt,* Chicago: University of Chicago Press, 1973.

Foster, Hal (ed.): *Postmodern Culture,* Pluto Press, 1985.

Giedion, Sigfried: *Architecture, You and Me,* London: Oxford University Press, 1958.

Ghirardo, Diane: *Architecture After Modernism,* London: Thames & Hudson, 1996.

Frampton, Kenneth: *Modern Architecture: A Critical History,* London: Thames & Hudson, 1980.

Mace, Rodney: *Trafalgar Square: Emblem of Empire,* London: Lawrence and Wishart, 1976.

Martienssen, R D: *The Idea of Space in Greek Architecture: With Special Reference to the Doric Temple and Its Setting,* Johannesburg: Witwatesrand University Press, 1956.

Mumford, Lewis: *The City in History: Its Origins, Its Transformations and Its Prospects,* London: Secker & Warburg, 1961.

Relph, E: *Place and Placelessness,* London: Pion Press, 1976.

Sommer, Robert: *Tight Spaces: Hard Architecture and How to Humanize It,* New York: Prentice-Hall, 1974.

Tafuri, Manfredo and Dal Co, Francesco: *Modern Architecture 1 and 2,* London: Faber & Faber, 1976.

White, Jerry: *Rothschild Buildings: Life in an East End Tenement Block 1887-1920,* London: Routledge & Kegan Paul, 1980.